FINDING FRE

All rights reserved. No part of this publication may be reproduced, stored in a retrieval system, or transmitted in any form or by any means, electronic, electrostatic, recording, magnetic tape, mechanical, photocopying or otherwise, without prior permission in writing from the publisher.

The publisher makes no representation, express or implied, with regard to the accuracy of the information contained in this publication and cannot accept any responsibility in law for any errors or omissions.

The right of Paul Brett to be identified as the author of this work has been asserted by them in accordance with sections 77 and 78 of the Copyright,
Designs and Patents Act 1988. No part of this book may be reproduced in any form without permission from the publisher except for the quotation of brief passages in reviews.

A catalogue record for this book is available from the British Library.

This edition © This Day In Music Books 2021.
Text ©This Day In Music Books 2021

ISBN: 978-1-8383798-8-9

Front and back cover concept by Liz Sánchez and Neil Cossar

Interior page layout and design by Gary Bishop

Printed in the UK by Sound Performance

This Day In Music Books Bishopswood Road, Prestatyn, LL199PL

www.thisdayinmusicbooks.com

Email: editor@thisdayinmusic.com

Exclusive Distributors: Music Sales Limited 14/15 Berners St London W1T 3JL

FINDING FRETLESS
A true story of history, mystery and intrigue

An unexpected question, an enquiring mind, a relentless search and amazing discoveries.

Take a journey back to the 1960s, the heyday of exciting new music in California and the British Invasion that stirred it all up. The dawn of innovation, experimentation and creativity in the fledging development of electrified instruments.

Follow the revelations and discoveries, as we investigate one distinctive prototype guitar that led to a veritable gold mine of associations with the origins of the most iconic instrument of the 21st Century, the electric guitar.

Read previously untold memories of some of the most influential creators in the development of the electric guitar, including Barth, Beauchamp, Rickenbacker, Fender, and the Dopyera brothers.

Meet the innovators, the risk takers, and a forgotten founding father of the electric guitar. The electrifying instrument played by legendary artists who over the decades have made the electric guitar a global phenomenon.

Be blown away by the discovery of the missing Beatles guitar, the prototype Bartell fretless guitar from a small-town Californian company and its incredible associations with John Lennon, George Harrison, Jimi Hendrix, Frank Zappa, leading to the BBC's *Antiques Roadshow* and beyond…

Discover the guitar's associations with Charles Manson's infamous murderous cult, a million-dollar lawsuit, fire, frying pans, drunken fist-fights, corporate shenanigans, Elvis Presley, The Wrecking Crew, and much more.

FINDING FRETLESS - THE FOREWORDS

In the mid-1970s, 1980s and start of the 1990s, London was home to more than 100 commercial studios that were booked open-ended to record music. Towards the latter part of the '80s, I was working with Heaven 17 and Tina Turner, the former writing and recording their songs with a Fairlight, one of the first samplers that could synchronise with an analogue multitrack tape machine (not forgetting the earlier Mellotron, which used tape samples of strings in semitones, as heard on 'Strawberry Fields Forever').

Since the rock'n'roll revolution and the rise of the solo singer, a team of musicians would make their living playing recording sessions. In those days you were pleaded with to work all night and start the craziness all over again the next day. Session or recording musicians, as we were called, would consist of an A-team that were always the first call to the record date. The Wrecking Crew in America did a similar job.

The creative outcome of these records was to make the song spin up the charts, with the musicians basically a rhythm section of four or five very adaptable musicians who were at the height of group creativity. Their cognitive flow was always in the moment and had an organic toolbox that could traverse and solve any musical problem whilst being very conversant with recording techniques. For my part I would take five guitars, all sounding different because of the musical demands made on me, and be able to double-track solos, remembering them note for note and stopping and starting songs or film music anywhere in the score, carrying on with the same intensity - a difficult human action that requires a skillset that has to be spot on, as the tape machine is not easily deceived. So, your sound, your time, your creativity and your group skills were always tested to the full. And if you're under 50, you might not have been aware of the music industry at its peak.

Let's move on to 1985. One of my favourite sessions would be to record film scores for George Harrison's company, HandMade Films, working with composer Mike Moran, engineer Richard Dodd (who also recorded The Travelling Wilburys), and a rhythm section of Barry Morgan on drums and Paul Westwood on bass guitar. All of which are worth looking up for their multitude of hit records. We also played on *The Life of Brian* (1979) and *Time Bandits* (1981) soundtracks.

Enter the Bartell fretless.

In mid-1985 there came a call to record the music to HandMade Films' *Water*, recorded over two weeks, with some tunes composed on the spot as quite a few things changed in the picture, so we had to make the score fit. The shoot was on a tight timeline, so the music was even tighter. You could say we went the extra mile. Sometimes we would play music that you would think sounded like a Beatles track, and particularly George Harrison and Eric Clapton.

On the second week, Richard Dodd casually mentioned that George had loaned a fretless guitar to John Lennon, who had been playing it for a while. Hearing what I was playing, George thought I might have more use for it. And when a Beatle, especially George Harrison offers you a guitar, you just say yes! Very quickly, I seem to remember. The next day, it turned up and we had fun playing all sorts of music with it.

So, time moves on and in my collection of guitars I have this Bartell fretless, that has been in my guitar rack since 1985. It was well kept, played spasmodically and looked after, having a pride of place which gained attention more as an anomaly. And although it was a well-made guitar, people who tried it found it hard not to fall desperately sharp or flat. It's not an easy instrument, but fun! It just has that sound that only this guitar has, which is so original.

Time passed, dear George died, and the guitar and I looked at each other every day. Then in 2019 I was doing a shoot for StarCards, a charity for Great Ormond Street Hospital started by my friend Paul Brett. He was looking at the guitar and was taken by it, so I told him the story… which seemed more surreal as it unfolded. He was very impressed by the guitar and its lineage. About 10 days later he announced that the BBC's *Antiques Roadshow* was calling at Battle Abbey in East Sussex that July, which happened to be near us.

I was in two minds. It meant sticking my head above the parapet. However, I called the Roadshow production office and the PA said the programme bookings were high. I felt slightly relieved, but two minutes later, the producer got very excited about myself and Paul bringing the guitar down the next day.

Suddenly, we were there and it was busy, with a worm-like queue of lampshades and furniture. We noticed a sudden swarm of guys with earpieces crowding around us. We were transported to an executive area. After a short while, we were asked to attend the set, which was elaborate for a live outside recording. Luckily, I took my amp and did some woodshedding (practising) beforehand, reacquainting myself with a fretless guitar. I played a thing which resembled 'Come Together'. Jon Baddeley, the antiques specialist from Bonhams, was very interested in the lineage, pictures and news articles, and of course the guitar itself.

It spread like wildfire, and the following weekend it was another BBC programme, *The One Show*. And then there was Channel 4's *Gogglebox* and a question about the guitar on ITV's Ant and Dec's *Saturday Night Takeaway*.

Since then, lots of information has come to light. My favourite story of those is that of how the guitar was delivered to George's house in Los Angeles in Blue Jay Way. There he was, waiting for his friends to arrive. He thought it was them. Now I understand how the song 'Blue Jay Way' came about. And we all miss George, of course. He was a very underrated guitar player.

Dr Ray Russell
Hailsham, East Sussex, UK

Ray Russell at home with George's 'mad' guitar

Richard Bennett in 2008. Credit Mike Humeniuk

My name is Richard and I'm a Bartell owner. There, I said it.

It was smack dab in the middle of the 1960s. I'd already been playing guitar for several years, taking lessons from Forrest Skaggs as well as doing some teaching for him at his music store in Phoenix, Arizona. I happened to be in the shop one afternoon when a salesman came by hoping to interest Skaggs in stocking a few guitars for resale. Skaggs didn't think much of them, but one instrument really caught my eye, a shiny, red sunburst job with two pick-ups, four knobs, a three-way toggle-switch and a large red naugahyde pad on the back. Smitten, I made my own deal with the salesman and, much to the displeasure of Mr Skaggs, became the proud owner of a Bartell.

I was still too young to drive when I began playing the country beer joints around Phoenix, and I did so with that Bartell in hand. I remember Sunday mornings, having played the previous two nights, diligently cleaning the guitar with lemon-scented polish, hoping to rid it of cigarette smoke. It was a short-lived affair, my infatuation with the red sunburst quickly dimming when I purchased a Telecaster. The Bartell was banished to its case, where she laid for a long winter's rest.

However, it wasn't my final encounter with a Bartell. A former student of Skaggs', Al Casey, had gone on to become one of Hollywood's busiest session musicians, a member of the so-called Wrecking Crew. It was through Forrest Skaggs that I'd met Al and his wife Maxine, and they both took me under their wing. The Caseys had recently opened a music store in Hollywood. Being a small shop, they couldn't get the name franchises, like Fender, Gibson, Martin, etc. and relied on independent brands like Mosrite, Hagstrom (from Sweden), Giannini (from Brazil), Ovation and Bartell, as well as taking in used instruments for resale.

I was living on the West Coast between '66 and '67 and encountered a very strange bird at the Casey's music store, a Bartell similar to mine but one that had a very smooth, polished fingerboard and no frets. There was a hell of a buzz around the store then, as it was going to be delivered as a gift to George Harrison, who had rented a home in the Hollywood Hills on Blue Jay Way. I can't quite recall every detail of the event, but somehow remember it was Maxine Casey who made the delivery, as Al was constantly busy doing record dates. Wow - a Bartell to a Beatle!

Not too many months ago I received a note from Paul Brett. He'd heard that I'd owned a Bartell and was wondering if I still had the instrument as he was researching this book you're holding now. I was pleased to tell him that I indeed had the guitar and promised to send him a picture. When I opened the case, I realised that red sunburst guitar hadn't seen the light of day in all these decades since the 1960s. It brought back so many wonderful memories as I gave her a good polish, a fresh set of strings and a pat on her naugahyde back.

That Bartell… She still shines like a morning star and rings like a bell.

Richard Bennett
Nashville, Tennessee, USA

CONTENTS

INTRODUCTION	3
FOREWORDS - RAY RUSSELL/RICHARD BENNETT	4 - 7
PICK A CARD	11
RAY RUSSELL	13
ONE MORE TIME	17
WHAT IS A FRETLESS GUITAR?	19
THE BARTELL COMPANY	22
TED EUGENE PECKELS	23
PAUL MARTIN BARTH	37
THE DOPYERA BROTHERS	56
DEANS CUSTOM FURNITURE	62
BARTELL EMPLOYEES, FRIENDS & CO-WORKERS	66 - 99
FRETTING OVER THE NUMBERS	100 - 103
THE DISCOVERED FRETLESS MODELS	104 - 155
THE BARTELL FRETLESS PROTOTYPE	104
RICHARD BENNETT	104
AL CASEY	107
GEORGE HARRISON	109
JOHN LENNON	114
TOP GEAR MUSIC	119
WATER	120
ANTIQUES ROADSHOW	120
ANTIQUES ROADSHOW ON AIR	126
THE BEATLES' WHITE ALBUM	129
THE AUCTION	131
THE AUCTION APPROACHES	132
AUCTION DAY	136
DAVE PECKELS	146
GREG SEGAL	151

FRETLESS - MISSING IN ACTION	156 - 179
MIKE DEASY	156
FRANK ZAPPA FRETLESS ACOUSTIC	163
FRANK ZAPPA - ACOUSTIC BLACK WIDOW	165
BOB CORONATO	166
JIMI HENDRIX - BARTELL FRETLESS	168
ACOUSTIC CONTROL CORPORATION	170
JIMI HENDRIX - BLACK WIDOW	171
MORT MARKER - THE GUITAR MAN	173
BARTELL FRETLESS BASS	176
FAMOUS BARTELL / BARTH / ACOUSTIC PLAYERS	180 - 189
JOHN FRUSCIANTE	180
JOHN PAUL JONES	181
WALTER BECKER`	181
CHUCK BERRY - ACOUSTIC BLACK WIDOW	184
LARRY CORYELL - ACOUSTIC BLACK WIDOW	185
SHERIFF JOHN & THE WAGONMASTERS	187
RORY GALLAGHER - BARTH GUITAR	187
CC DEVILLE	189
THE BARTELL REUNION	190
DISCOGRAPHY	191
ACKNOWLEDGEMENTS	193
ABOUT THE AUTHOR	194

PICK A CARD

Hailsham, East Sussex, England, 2016

"Hi Ray, would you sign a playing card for a charity auction?"

I didn't expect that a chance meeting with one of the UK's finest guitarists, asking him to support my charity StarCards - which involves celebrity-signed playing cards to raise funds for London's Great Ormond Street Hospital - would ever lead me to tapping away on a keyboard, writing a book about rediscovered vintage guitars, a look back in history at the origins of the electric guitar, links to some of the biggest legends in music history, or a global search for missing fretless guitars.

I was introduced to veteran Ray Russell by my good friend and master guitarist, Phil Hilborne, who had been StarCards' 'official' supporter for a number of years, and in this social media age we were soon Facebook 'friends'.

Ray with Paul's StarCards

Phil Hilborne (above) and Paul Brett with Phil

That was it, nothing remarkable, we gradually became aware of each other and I thoroughly enjoyed a few gigs that Ray performed at. It was a pleasure to join him at London's iconic 606 club in Chelsea with Phil to celebrate Ray's 70th birthday, also featuring Mo Foster and other brilliant musicians, namely Mark Mondesir and Ralph Salmins on drums, Geoff Castle on keyboards, Chris Biscoe on saxophone, George Baldwin on Chapman stick, and Phil himself as a guest guitarist.

Then on 5 May 2019, Ray casually posted on Facebook,

'Today I'm playing the guitar that dear George Harrison gave me, memories. I've been trying to trace the maker but no joy so far, do any of my US friends know him?'

I remember thinking, 'What the …! George Harrison gave Ray a guitar? How cool is that!' Looking at the picture Ray posted, it was obviously vintage and had the name Bartell of California on the headstock.

I hit Google, and thought, 'Wow, this is interesting!'

Ray at 606 with Fusion

RAY RUSSELL

Born 4 April 1947, Ray is a highly-respected professional guitarist, renowned as a record producer, teacher and prolific composer. He has created groundbreaking jazz-rock works such as 1968's *Turn Circle* and 1969's *Dragon Hill*. As a composer and guitarist Russell launched himself on a fertile '60s London music scene as a ubiquitous session musician, along with fellow guitarists John McLaughlin and Jimmy Page. He became a member of the band Mouse in 1973, that outfit releasing a progressive rock album entitled *Lady Killer* for the Sovereign record label.

Though he may not have ultimately attained the same guitar hero status in the United States as his two UK contemporaries, Russell has remained a respected figure throughout the world, each new visionary release met with wild anticipation by the cognoscenti.

Royal Television Society award-winning Ray has spent decades composing TV soundtracks and shaping his expressive guitar sound to the whims of stars such as John Barry, Phil Spector, The Ronettes, Van Morrison, Art Garfunkel, Dionne Warwick, Bryan Ferry, Jack Bruce, Cat Stevens, Phil Collins, Alex Harvey, Mark Isham, Georgie Fame, Cliff Richard, and Frankie Miller.

You will have heard Ray play on David Bowie's 'Space Oddity', Tina Turner's 'Private Dancer', and numerous other tracks with artists as diverse as Freddie Mercury, Gil Evans and Andy Williams.

Ray is also a prolific composer, having composed thousands of production library tracks for Universal Music, FirstCom and Made Up Music. His TV compositions have included those for *A Touch of Frost, Bergerac, Plain Jane, A Bit of a Do, Rich Tea and Sympathy, The Inspector Alleyn Mysteries, Dangerfield* and *Grafters*, among many other British and American television programmes.

In recent years Russell has studied fastidiously, finally graduating as a Doctor of Philosophy, with his subject matter the Fluid Architecture of Music in the World of Recording, from Leeds' Beckett University.

Ray married his lovely wife, former model Sally, on 5 September 1985. Sally studied at the Guildhall School of Music and Drama, graduating in 1982. She is an artist in her own right and a passionate animal rights campaigner, and a trustee at War Paws, a charity dedicated to alleviating the pain and suffering of animals in hostile environments and areas of civil conflict.

It's great fun and a privilege listening to all the wonderful stories this seasoned session musician tells.

Ray recalled, "One of my early gigs was with Cat Stevens, in May 1967. We did a tour of Sweden where Cat was headlining, and The Jimi Hendrix Experience were the support band."

On 19 May 1967, The Jimi Hendrix Experience performed two sold-out concerts at the Konserthallen, Liseberg and Liseberg Nojespark in Gothenberg, Sweden, a show also featuring Cat Stevens and local band Mats & Brita, introduced by DJ Clem Dalton.

Sally and Missy

The tour then moved to the Bongo in Malmo on 23 May, and Gröna Lund in Stockholm on 24 May.

Ray Russell: "I remember one time, somewhere in Sweden, I was lying in my bed trying to get to sleep, and Jimi was knocking on my window, obviously on the ground floor. He'd got locked out. I let him in through the window, we had a cup of tea and chatted about music for 10 minutes, and then he went to bed."

As it turned out, Ray and Jimi would in future years have more in common than once being on tour together, their associations with Bartell Fretless Guitars proving strong.

Jimi Hendrix backstage at the opening night of the Walker Brothers' UK tour. From left: Jimi Hendrix, Cat Stevens, Gary Leeds, Engelbert Humperdinck. Credit Alamy stock photo

Geoff Whitehorn, Ray Russell and Phil Hilborne. Credit Phil Hilborne

In 2008, Ray's colleagues, drummer Ralph Salmins and sound engineer Rik Walton, created a library of recordings by the name of Made Up Music, distributed via its website and sending portable hard drives to music editors. The company also sells music by Mo Foster, Steve Donnelly, and Simon Eyre.

I first remember seeing Ray perform with Gary Moore on 8 August 2009 at a festival called Vibes from the Vines in Horam, East Sussex. The band consisted of Gary Moore, Ray Russell, Mo Foster, Ralph Salmins, Jim Watson, and Rupert Cobb. What a gig that was!

Ken Scott & Ray Russell

I was there primarily as a huge fan of Gary Moore, but also in my fundraising capacity. I arranged to meet Gary and get a photo of him with the signed 'StarCard' he'd already signed for me. It looked great all framed and was going to be a cool item of Gary memorabilia to auction. When I met him after the gig, Gary thought a pro photographer from *Guitarist* magazine was going to be taking the shots. When I told him it was just me, he said 'Piss off!' Fortunately, he was smiling at the time though, and I still got my shot.

Gary Moore with his StarCard

ONE MORE TIME

In 2020, Ray was one of a number of veteran musicians featured in a film directed by Alan Boyd and Christine Cowin for Little Sparta Productions, capturing the legacy of the British recording scene from the late 1950s to the early 1980s, as seen through the eyes of session players who both defined and were defined by that era, and who played on some of the most well-known and well-loved songs still enjoyed today.

Tracing their history - borne out of the ashes of the Second World War when instruments were home-made and rationed, through to the changing world of technology in the early 1980s – *One More Time* aimed to bring musicians together for studio sessions in London, recording new versions of some of the best-known songs with artists like Tom Jones, Lulu, Donovan and PP Arnold. The film looked to offer a rare insight into how music was made at a time when musicians faced gruelling schedules, racing around London's renowned studios recording thousands of tracks in a golden era of British recording. Think The Wrecking Crew on steroids!

The players featured were Mo Foster, Ray Russell, Brian Bennett, Herbie Flowers, Clem Cattini, Vic Flick, Bob Henrit, Dave Richmond, Alan Hawkshaw, Dougie Wright, and Graham Preskett, those classic songs showcased including:

- 'Alfie' - Cilla Black
- 'James Bond Theme' - The John Barry Seven
- 'Space Oddity' - David Bowie
- 'You Really Got Me' - The Kinks
- 'This Boy' - The Beatles
- 'Je T'aime (Moi Non Plus)' – Jane Birkin & Serge Gainsbourg
- 'Walk on the Wild Side' - Lou Reed
- 'Your Song' - Elton John
- 'Green, Green Grass of Home' - Tom Jones
- 'The Champ' - The Mohawks
- 'Hurdy Gurdy Man' - Donovan
- 'Telstar' - The Tornados
- 'So You Win Again' - Hot Chocolate
- 'Shakin' All Over' - Johnny Kidd & The Pirates
- 'Bye Bye Baby' - Bay City Rollers
- 'The Ballad of Bonnie & Clyde' - Georgie Fame
- 'I Close My Eyes and Count to Ten' - Dusty Springfield
- '5-4-3-2-1' - Manfred Mann
- 'Private Dancer' - Tina Turner
- 'One More Night' - Phil Collins
- 'Diamonds are Forever' - Shirley Bassey
- 'The Sun Ain't Gonna Shine Anymore' - The Walker Brothers
- 'Dandy in the Underworld' - T-Rex
- 'Baker Street' - Gerry Rafferty
- 'Rock on' - David Essex
- 'The Pink Panther Theme' - Henry Mancini
- 'Hi-Ho Silver Lining' - Jeff Beck
- 'Pray' – Jay-Z

FINDING FRETLESS

Mo Foster with a One More Time poster and with the team in the studio.

Credit Alan Boyd

WHAT IS A FRETLESS GUITAR?

This is the story of a special guitar and the company that produced it. And the Bartell is fretless, but what does that mean? A fretless guitar is a rare breed, an oddball with a chequered history. A guitar normally has frets on the fingerboard which guide the guitarist to a well-established musical pattern to produce notes and chords. By pressing down on a string, on the fingerboard against the fret, the string vibrates between the fret and the bridge to produce a specific note. Frets are strips of metal, generally an alloy of nickel and brass, embedded along a guitar's fretboard, known as the neck.

However, on a fretless guitar the string vibrates from the bridge directly to the finger position and not the fret, similar to a violin. Therefore, there are infinite, miniscule musical differences and subtle warm tone variations that create a very distinctive and unique sound. They can be very challenging to master. Playing a fretless guitar involves learning exactly where notes lie on a fretboard. This means taking into account all the natural microtones that get cut out of the picture when frets are added to a neck. You need to develop a very good ear for intonation and pitch.

While fretless instruments allow for more fluidity, they also allow for users to make bigger mistakes that are more noticeable. But they are also very rewarding, with the great advantage in the range of sound you can produce. It also improves your skills when you pick up a fretted guitar again. Painted (or notched) 'frets' allow users to employ the marking as a guide while they learn unfretted techniques.

© Fusion Guitars

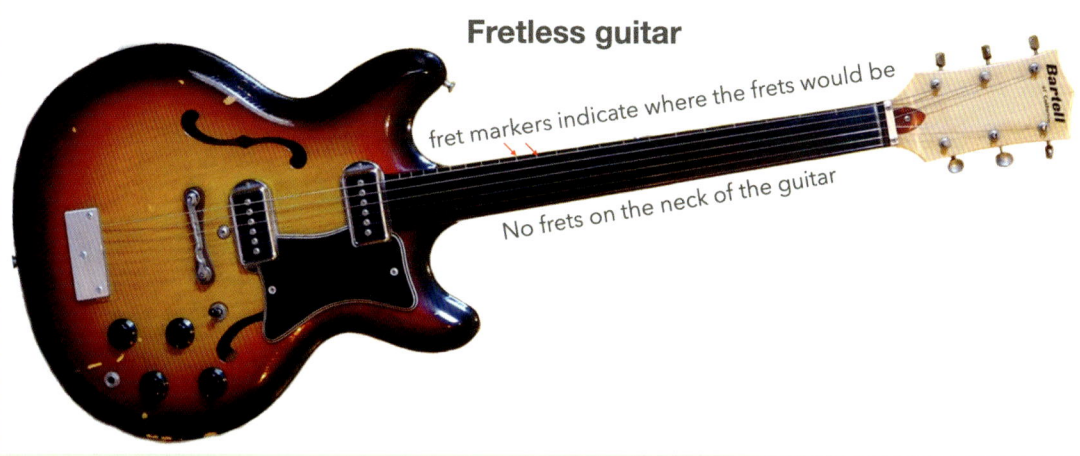

FINDING FRETLESS

Respected guitarist, composer and academic Dr Richard Perks is a UK-based lecturer in Music Performance at the University of Kent, and a lecturer in Popular Music at the Institute of Contemporary Music Performance.

In his article, 'Fretless Architecture: Towards the Development of Original Techniques and Musical Notation Specific to the Fretless Electric Guitar' (*Music and Practice, New Perspectives on Technique and Practice, Vol. 4,* April 2019), he describes the most common types of fretless vibrato, and suggests the following musical notations.

Pivot vibrato - "this method is akin to that customarily used by Classical strings players and is produced by tilting the fingertip back and forth whilst maintaining pressure at a fixed position on the fingerboard. The result is a regular, smooth, and shallow fluctuation in pitch both above and below the fingered note."

Horizontal vibrato - "executed by performing a mini-sliding action, moving equidistantly back and forth along the string-length either side of the desired pitch whilst maintaining pressure on the fingerboard. This creates a 'wider sounding vibrato – typically a quarter-tone up and down – and is particularly effective on wound strings."

Note that this type of vibrato is not possible on a fretted guitar without a slide or whammy bar.

Richard explains, "Unlike conventional guitar, a fretless instrument can produce slow, even slides in a truly portamento fashion [...] sounding far more smooth"

Slide effects

A slide technique on a fretted guitar using a finger cylinder, or bottleneck can have similar sound to a fretless guitar. However, unusual bending, a subtle vibrato difference and a smoother, slower slide can be achieved on a fretless guitar. With a slide barrel, all six strings contact the fretboard in the same place along the neck, whereas on a fretless all four fingers can slide independently.

Microtones

Microtonal music is music that does not use the standard 12-tone equal temperament of 'normal' Western music. Fretless is perfect for exploring microtones, reminiscent of Eastern European and Middle Eastern stringed instruments. It's worth looking up US composer Harry Partch for his research in this area.

For the lowdown on anything fretless I highly recommend referring to unfretted.com, where Jeff Berg has all the information you need on everything related to the subject. His very informative and comprehensive website is the go-to place for the history, hardware and setup, luthiers and artists, and much more. He has also published *Fretless Guitar - The Definitive Guide*, a great read by a knowledgeable author.

DIY fretless modification

Guitarists sometimes experiment by removing frets from their guitars, filing the gaps with an epoxy filler, wood putty, veneers or plastic, which need to be sanded down to a smooth finish, a very drastic measure with varying results.

Alternatively, some guitar luthiers and manufacturers make professional bespoke models, like these very nice Vigier Excalibur fretless guitars.

Photo credit: Vigier Guitars

THE BARTELL COMPANY

The Bartell company was established in 1964 by owner and company president Ted Eugene Peckels and director/head of design Paul Martin Barth, who previously worked for Rickenbacker, Magnatone, and National as a designer and engineer.

The Bartell name blends the beginning and end of Paul Barth and Ted Peckels' surnames.

Bartell produced guitars and amplifiers from 1964 to 1968. Ted's store, the House of Note, was a popular place for every musician in the Riverside, San Bernardino area of California to hang out, which may be a clue to their relationships with some very high-profile musicians.

The sunny city of Riverside, home to the University of California, is surrounded by a mountain range which gets a winter dusting of snow, its climate generally hot and dry with relatively wet winters. It's located approximately 55 miles east of downtown Los Angeles, just under 50 miles from the Pacific Ocean, and close to Orange County. During the summer months the fragrant smell of orange blossom fills the air.

Located at the House of Note at 6202 Magnolia (at the intersection of Magnolia and Jurupa) in Riverside was the store owned by Peckels in the Magnolia Centre, closed around 1969 or 1970. The building is no longer there.

There was a small 1,500 square foot commercial unit on Arlington Avenue where the production and assembly took place, while woodworking took place at another facility.

Barth and Peckels began manufacturing Bartell guitars, working on Strat-style double cutaways with a Mosrite-inspired headstock, with 'German Carve' bevelled ridges (again, similar to the body of a Mosrite) and two single-coil pickups.

Peckels estimated that around 2,000 instruments were produced based on the innovated designs of master craftsman Paul Barth. The Bartell company also rebranded their products for Hohner, St. George, Lancer and Acoustic corporation, selling across the USA, Bartell-branded guitars' sales distribution limited to southern California and Arizona.

Bartell of California appears on labels inside Hohner fretless basses, St George guitars, Natural Music Guild, and Contessa amplifiers.

TED EUGENE PECKELS

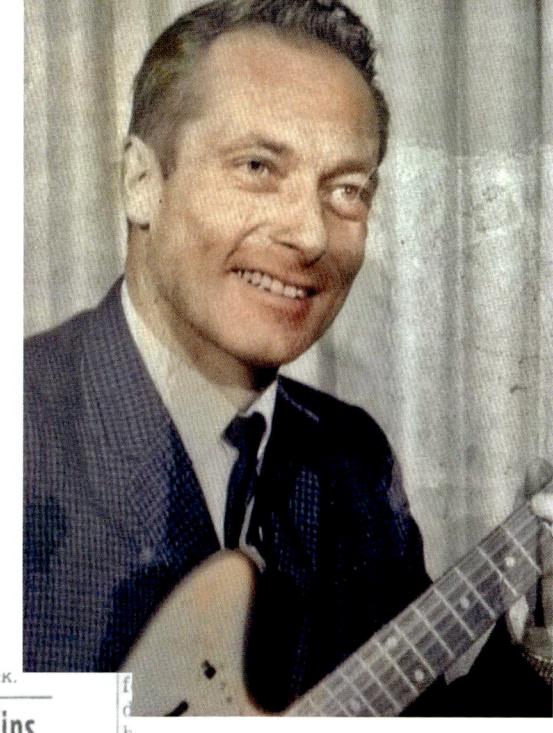

Bartell founder and owner, Ted Eugene Peckels was born in 1925 in Colton, San Bernardino County, California. His home city was named after David Douty Colton, Brigadier General of the California State Militia prior to the Civil War, originally the home of the Serrano, Guachama and San Gorgonio Indians. The city evolved via New Mexico pioneers and British settler George Cooley, who owned a 200-acre estate along the Santa Ana River.

Ted lived in Colton for 18 years before moving to Riverside, where he remained for the next 48 years. Serving in the US Army Air Corps from 28 August 1944, he saw World War II service as an aerial gunner with the Pyote Birds unit of the Red Raiders.

Photo Credit: The Peckels Family

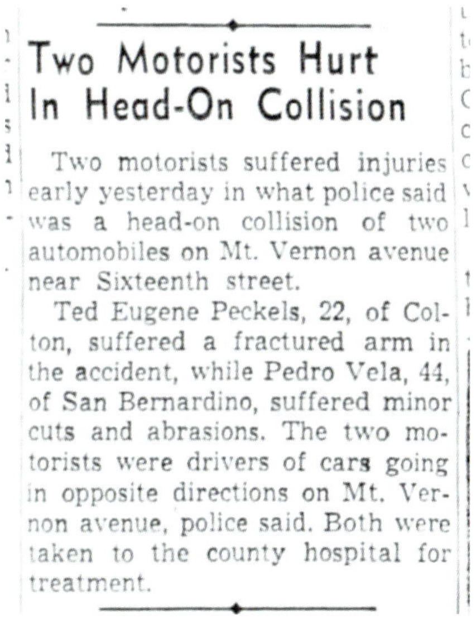

Two Motorists Hurt In Head-On Collision

Two motorists suffered injuries early yesterday in what police said was a head-on collision of two automobiles on Mt. Vernon avenue near Sixteenth street.

Ted Eugene Peckels, 22, of Colton, suffered a fractured arm in the accident, while Pedro Vela, 44, of San Bernardino, suffered minor cuts and abrasions. The two motorists were drivers of cars going in opposite directions on Mt. Vernon avenue, police said. Both were taken to the county hospital for treatment.

Whilst driving in the late summer of 1946, Ted aged 22 was involved in a road traffic accident, suffering a fractured arm.

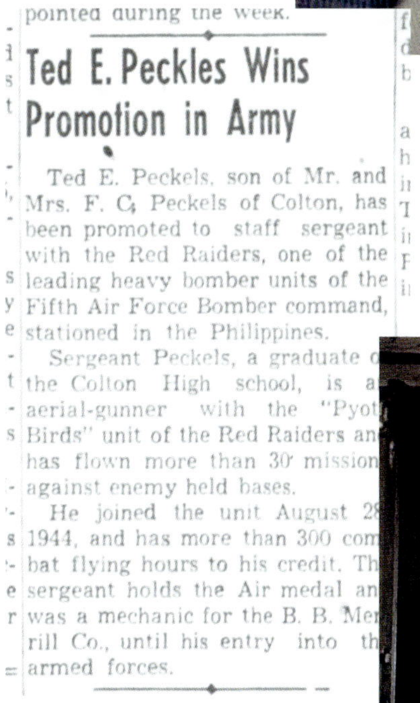

pointed during the week.

Ted E. Peckles Wins Promotion in Army

Ted E. Peckels, son of Mr. and Mrs. F. C. Peckels of Colton, has been promoted to staff sergeant with the Red Raiders, one of the leading heavy bomber units of the Fifth Air Force Bomber command, stationed in the Philippines.

Sergeant Peckels, a graduate of the Colton High school, is an aerial-gunner with the "Pyote Birds" unit of the Red Raiders and has flown more than 30 missions against enemy held bases.

He joined the unit August 28, 1944, and has more than 300 combat flying hours to his credit. The sergeant holds the Air medal and was a mechanic for the B. B. Merrill Co., until his entry into the armed forces.

On the 27th June 1945 Ted's promotion to Staff Sergeant was reported. Newspaper cuttings: The San Bernardino County Sun.

Ted Peckels married his sweetheart Donna Lou Imig at 7pm on 16 December 1950, at the Little Church of the West in Las Vegas. At the time he was employed at Hayman's House & Appliance Company, with Donna a graduate of San Bernardino High School working in Pasadena for the Southern California Telephone Co.

Ted was also a keen petrolhead, interested in land speed racing, with his treasured Mazda RX7 built by his good friend Jim Hennegan, racing on high desert dry lakes in San Bernardino County, California. They were both enthusiastic members of the Eliminators Car Club.

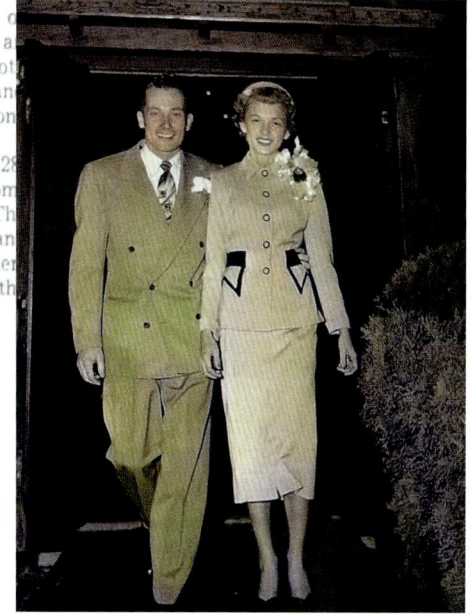

Ted Peckels and his wife Donna

FINDING FRETLESS

They would race regularly at El Mirage on the high desert dry lakes in San Bernardino County and once a year head out to the Bonneville flats.

El Mirage Lake is a dry lakebed in the northwestern Victor Valley of the central Mojave Desert, San Bernardino County. The Bonneville Salt Flats are a densely packed salt pan in Tooele County in northwestern Utah.

Ted racing at El Mirage Lake, and his Mazda Rx7, No.212

In April 2021 I spoke to Jim Hennegan, who told me:

"I met Ted about 1988. I went into a store to buy an amplifier, I was a part-time musician in my late 20s and recently moved to Riverside, California. Over the course of the next three months we found out we had a lot of common interests, and one of the big ones was land speed racing.

"In his early days when Ted got back from the war, he raced an early single-seat Ford flat-head V8. They got pretty fast in that thing! He also told me that they were trying to put together a car using a P38 belly-tank as the body that was totally home-built.

"When he got into business, he stopped racing. It was in the late 1980s and early 1990s that we got together and started racing again. I helped Ted build two cars. I was basically the mechanic and he was the driver.

"We were racing Mazda RX7's, we had two - one was candy red, that was his personal car, which was pretty fast, but we built another one.

"We were members of the Eliminators Club, doing land speed racing. SCTA was the organisation. We called our race team Allegro Racing, a musical term meaning fast. We did that for quite a few years. In fact, he held a couple of records out at El Mirage. Once a year we would race out at Bonneville.

"Over the course of the years we got the Red RX7 (No. 212) doing 157mph over the dry lakes, so in the class we were in we held that record for about a year.

"Near the end when we were building a yellow RX7, we could get those very fast because of the rotary engine in them. We were competing in a class of small V8s and we were doing very well at that. The yellow one we were streamlining - we chopped the top down. It was putting us up in another class, but we never got that one running.

"When Ted died, his wife Donna sold the Coopers Action Music site. There were three or four other businesses on the lot that Ted owned. There was also a double garage behind Coopers that was our race shop. We had the car at one side and all the tools at the other. Right after he died, somebody broke in there. The tools, engines and all that kind of stuff went. Then Donna sold the whole thing to Mike's Music."

Jim Hennegan continued, "It was in Riverside around 1988, during Ted's time running Coopers Action Music that I knew him. Ted and I became very close friends, I considered him like my father. When I was a young teenager and my father wasn't much in my life, Ted picked me up and gave me the direction that I have today. He really influenced my life.

"I was invited to some of the family functions. Christmas was always at Ted's place, and all the family came over. I would play Santa Claus. I would come in and pass out toys and then go change into my regular clothes. I remember one kid about 12 years old, he comes up to me and says, 'You're Santa Claus!' I said, 'No, I'm not!' He tapped my watch and says, 'Next time, lose the watch!'

Did you ever go to the Bartell factory?

"No, it had shut down before I knew Ted in the late 1980s.

"What Ted did that was really unique to the Bartell, they took a mathematician to set their fret machine that he used to have at his Coopers Action Music store. They had the intonation of the guitar mathematically figured out. If you had a Bartell Guitar and you listened to it, they sounded a lot better than other guitars.

"The most amazing thing about Ted, he would call me up and say, 'Hey, I need to go down to Orange County,' and we'd show up at the G&L factory and he is talking to those guys man to man, talking about instruments. The guy who worked with Leo Fender doing his amplifiers, Tom Mitchell, plus Don Randell and Leo Fender, they all knew each other."

(Fender's final company, G&L Musical Instruments, is on Fender Avenue)

"I was impressed with Leo Fender and Mitchell. Mitchell was a guy who made speakers. He was very interesting and into Porsche 911s. We would go over to his barn and tinker with his cars. I had a couple of his Mitchell speakers. They were great, he messed around a lot trying to get a better sound out of them by having the back cavity shaped and stuff like that. The amount of engineering that went into some of this early '60s and '70s stuff when these guys were messing with it was out of this world. Leo was looking for the perfect sound and he made amplifiers that everybody loved, because when they start cracking up they still have this perfect sound."

Jim Hennegan continued, "Leo was a very frustrated guitarist, but he was a very good electronics guy. The Telecaster for example was fantastic, but if you look at what he did, he was looking to build a guitar that could be cheaply repaired. That's the kind of engineering that Ted and all of them were into, they were always trying to perfect something.

"What I found amazing about Ted, he would walk up to these major music industry heavyweights and just start talking to them. He would introduce me, they were like idols of mine. We would just be sitting down and having lunch with them. He never thought they or him were important people, they were just friends he did business with and they would be joking and laughing about the old days."

Did Ted ever speak to you about how Bartell came to an end?

"It was a mix between economy and family, he had to make these financial decisions. When Bartell closed, Ted started selling cars, and then he bought Coopers music store, and he was able to support his family off that.

"Some major bands used to come to Coopers, like Great White and Faster Pussycats, because Ted had either taught one of them or given them some stuff for their first gigs, something like that. Ted would lend them maybe amplifiers, and they would bring them back after the gig. A handshake was good credit for Ted, he was good like that.

"When Guitar Center moved into San Bernardino and were selling guitars at such a cheap price, Ted couldn't make a profit on a Fender guitar after that, so he went into cheaper lines to try and stay in business. That really hurt the music sales industry. The business was struggling at the end of Ted's life.

"In his later years Ted was playing pedal steel guitar. We would sit around at night-time at his house, he had a room set up where I would play his box jazz guitar, a Vega, and a pedal steel. We would play for hours. It was a lot of fun.

"At Ted's funeral in 1998 I was honoured to sit with the family. I eventually moved out of Southern California around 2012."

During the 1950s, Peckels had a number of music studios where he taught young students to play. Rather than wait for students to come to him, Peckels employed a salesman who went door to door, recruiting them.

"He had a guy named Stan Dumont," remembers Ted's son Dave. "My Dad said he was the best salesman he ever met. He was an older man and was just a real good talker and would go door to door. That was when people, especially moms, were home during the day.

Roy Harris (The Ris-Kays/The Truths) at the House of Note (Riverside) 1964-65

"He would give prospective students a little aptitude test, which most of the time they passed, then he would sign them up for lessons. I think it was steel guitar at first, and accordion. Then when the electric guitar became popular, they'd do that as well."

"It was a little bit of a different life back then, I think," says Gary Peckels, another of Ted's sons. "You couldn't go door to door now, trying to hustle for guitar students! But that's how he started out. He rented a room on Magnolia, his mom was the receptionist, and he had over

ENCORE

THE SELDOM-SEEN BARTELL GUITARS originated in Riverside, California, during the 1960s. Ted Peckels, Bartell's owner and founder, recalls, "It seems like we started in 1964, but it took a couple years to get a product worth selling." The company's factory-made instruments for St. George, Acoustic, and Hohner were sold nationwide, although Bartell brand guitars had a rather limited distribution system—a lone salesman who covered southern California and Arizona. While Bartell made at least 2,000 instruments, Peckels (currently owner of Cooper's Action Music in Riverside) estimates that only two dozen were doublenecks. Of that small group, most were 6/12 combos, although Ted remembers a couple of bass/6-strings and a mandolin/6-string. The retail price of our four-pickup 6/12 was probably about $500.

Bartell's chief engineer and craftsman was Paul Barth—a nephew of John Dopyera, inventor of National and Dobro guitars. Paul had worked for National, Rickenbacker, and Magnatone. Ted Peckels says, "He was one of the pioneers, you might say—he knew his guitars." Look closely and you can see the Barth touch, especially in the carved bevel around the top. Instrument courtesy Subway Guitars, Berkeley, CA; photo by Paul Haggard. —*Richard Smith*

Ted's son Mark Peckels remembers the July 1991 edition of Guitar Player magazine in an article written by Richard Smith. Ted is quoted "it seems we started in 1964, but it took a couple of years to get a product worth selling". Copyright Guitar Player magazine, 1991. Used by permission.

FINDING FRETLESS

200 students before he opened up the House of Note. That's doing it on your own!"

Occasionally local radio stations would broadcast live music out of Peckels' store. Western music, in the early days and, later, rock'n'roll.

Dave Peckels remembers KFXM broadcasting from the store and sponsoring a Battle of the Bands competition in the adjacent driveway. "I think the reason I remember it was because their mascot was a tiger and they brought the tiger down - a real tiger!"

The original KFXM (now KTIE) was a Top-40 formatted station at 590 kHz on the AM band in the Riverside and San Bernardino market area from the 1950s to the 1980s. They introduced the KFXM tiger in 1964. The newsletter, cartoon tiger was depicted standing on his hind legs, holding a stage microphone, looking suave, usually wearing glasses, clad in either a tuxedo or a sweater.

KFXM advertising salesman Al Barnett, whose hobbies included raising exotic animals, announced in 1966 that he was getting a baby Bengal tiger. Barnett's tiger cub arrived via Riverside's Flabob Airport, after being picked up in Portland, Oregon. The mascot's name was Jocko.

By late 1966, Jocko had been to a feed store in Rubidoux and to restaurants in Redlands, Ontario

Credit David Allen/Riverside Press-Enterprise

and San Bernardino. He was kind of adorable in his photos, still looking like a cub.

In a photo six months later, Jocko looked full-grown and was said to weigh nearly 260lb.

Riverside native Julie Lewis used to catch glimpses of the tiger in its cage behind a Victorian home on Main Street downtown — Barnett's home, perhaps — as she went to and from Central Junior High in the early 1970s.

"It was in the back of somebody's house," she recalls. "It was in a big cage. He would walk back and forth."

"Ted was a true gentleman, always willing to help younger musicians."

In the late 1960s the store also included separate stores selling eight-track tapes and handcrafted leather and suede goods.

The only known release on House of Note Records was released in December 1962, featuring Chauncey Romero's band, with Ted Peckels sitting in on bass on the Hustlers' first single, 'Hangin' Five' b/w 'Barefooted Venture', cut at Paul Buff's PAL studio. An alternate version exists on tape.

Most copies were sold through the stores, both of which had a small record section carrying lots of releases by bands that frequented the stores.

And Ted had a great reputation with local musicians.

Steve Anderson: "Sometime in '68, my band Shades of Time had a falling out with our manager, who owned a bunch of the equipment. We had a crisis and had a gig the next night at The Cheetah, a big deal venue at Santa Monica pier. We talked with Ted. He loaned us three Ampeg stacks to do our show. No problems, no credit cards, no parents' signatures, just, 'Here you go, guys'. It was a major favour from a quality guy. I've never forgotten that."

"Peckels was an excellent guitar and steel player, steeped in country and western music. He was so humble, but could play steel or standard guitar great"

Hal Davis: "I think the Shades' biggest claims to fame were sharing the bill with the Standells at the Anaheim Convention Center Auto Show and opening, along with The Light, who were a great band, and for Buffalo Springfield at the Purple Haze in January '68."

Ted was a respected music retailer, owning the House of Note music store in Riverside from 1960, located at 6202 Magnolia Avenue.

Lier's Music and the House of Note played a big part in the history of the Inland Empire music scene, with pretty much every musician from that era passing through the doors of either one or both of these establishments.

The House of Note at the original Riverside location, first opened by Ted Peckels around 1960. Mention Ted Peckels to any musician from the Riverside area and they will

Shades Of Time

remember him not only as a storeowner, but also as a teacher and a mentor figure.

Dave Peckels: "He enjoyed talking to musicians and helping them out. Finally, my parents had to change their home phone number, because he'd get calls in the middle of the night, guys breaking a guitar string and wanting my dad to go down and open up the store and bring them a string. He did that for a while but got a little tired of it. I think my mom probably got a little tired of that too!"

Ted was always willing to lend a hand, even allowing touring musicians to stay overnight at his house if they had no place to go. On more than one occasion people took advantage of his trusting nature. "Before the Beach Boys were big they played down at either the Fox or the De Anza Theatre's, and needed some PA equipment," recounts Gary Peckels. "So my Dad loaned it to them and they left town with it. He never got it back!"

A Bartell 12 string

THE FENDER RELATIONSHIP

The only stores that had the Fender franchise, which during those times were true franchises, were House of Note and Lier's in the Inland Empire.

Fender was probably the most popular brand they sold at the stores back then, and consequently House of Note had a special relationship with the company.

"I actually used to go down to Leo Fender's factory and pick up the guitars in Fullerton, and bring them back to Riverside for the store," remembers Roly Sanders. "I used to go in the factory and watch 'em work on the guitars, shave down the necks and all that, so those are pretty awesome memories."

"It was the big deal," confirms Roly Sanders. "Once a month, Ted or Chauncey (Romero) would drive into Fullerton and do their thing. They would talk to Leo Fender and those people down there, they'd have lunch and come back with all these wonderful instruments and amplifiers and all.

"At that time Fender Instruments were what you called a fair trade or a franchise item, and their prices were fixed. In those days a Fender Stratocaster was $289, so your deal was you didn't sell it for a dollar below that, because their deal was that you'd been selected as the franchise Fender person in this area and that's what the guitar or amp is sold for.

"We saw early on that that was an egg we needed to break, so we would sell things at the franchise price but would say, 'We could probably throw in the case here for this guitar'- which is probably $70 or whatever a hard-shell case was - and so those things would kind of go out the door and just not be written on the ticket, or thrown in. Everything was sold at the Fender franchise price, but I know that the House of Note bought enough stuff; I think they did enough volume to be treated right."

Meanwhile, inspired by his dealings with Leo Fender, Ted Peckels formed the Bartell Company with partner Paul Barth, making guitars and amplifiers between 1964-69, including a fretless electric bass guitar and a double-neck electric guitar.

Red Bartell Spyder F-155

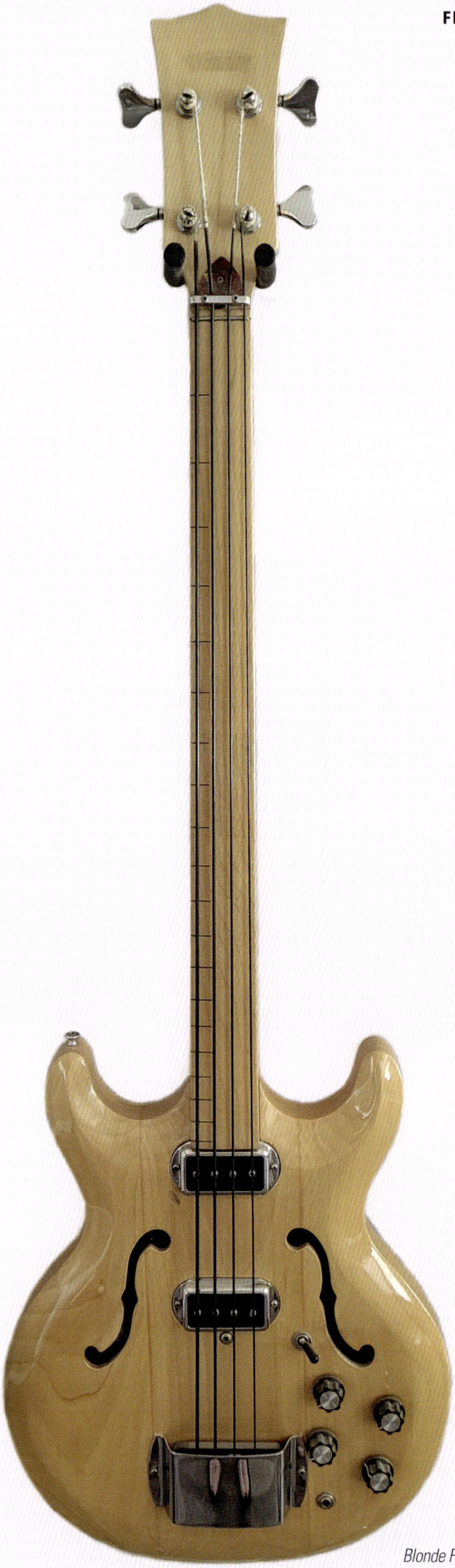

FINDING FRETLESS

Local musician Bob Nye remembered: "I smashed my 73 Coupe DeVille into a station wagon pulling out of the shop on to Magnolia Avenue. Ted had just rented me a PA system for a show. Ted was always a little tipsy from having drinks at the bar next door. We got some amazing deals on equipment! My band, The Conditionz thanked him on our first album in 1985.

"The bar next door, if I remember correctly, was Freddie Hookers, now called Pepitos. Ted's shop was called Coopers Action Music, but it's Music Mike's now".

Ted's House of Note store was a place to meet, talk, trade, and jam, with bands often playing out back in the yard under the pepper trees, next to Jerl's Muffler & Brake.

"Ted was such a softy," Bob Nye continued. "My bass player and I were homeless at one point and he told us we could live in the back room at the shop. We would literally walk in, grab a guitar off the wall, and say, 'I'll pay you for this next week'.

"He would smile and wave. Most of the time we would bring the gear back after a month or so, say we didn't like it, and grab something else. I borrowed a beautiful vintage Fender Bassman amp head for about a year once. I should have bought it from him. They're worth a couple of grand today. RIP Ted Peckels."

Photo credit Bob Nye

Blonde Fretless Bass, credit Dave Peckels

32

Jerl's Muffler & Brake was situated between Center Lumber and House of Note - across the street from Crowleys.

Greg Stoever recalled: "I just couldn't let construction crews bulldoze this piece of history down when the new underpass was constructed. So my buddy and I got orange cones, construction vests and hard hats and we took this sign down, like a construction crew.

"This sign was a landmark as we cruised down Magnolia in the '60s and '70s, and Jerl's Muffler & Brake just had to live on.

"He was a great guy, and always had a smile on his face. RIP my friend. Your legacy in Riverside lives on."

Jerl Shipley, the original owner of Jerl's Muffler & Brake, was born 20 June 1937 in Dora, Missouri. He passed away on 26 December 2018 due to complications with Parkinson's disease.

Bartell had a close relationship with Acoustic Control Corporation, a manufacturer of instrument amplifiers founded by Steve Marks and his father in the late 1960s. Its original location was a shack on Sunset Boulevard, Los Angeles.

Acoustic Control Corporation went out of business in 1980, returning later in a few different forms. Today, it is a thriving company again.

Yellow Double Neck, credit Dave Peckels

> *"Ted Peckels' music stores in Riverside and Redlands helped give rise to the Inland Empire's fertile surf and garage rock scenes"*
> *- Mike Stax*

Running into financial problems, the House of Note closed in the early '70s, and in 1978 Ted bought Coopers Action Music, down the road at 6511 Magnolia, which he operated until he passed away.

Terry Wade was a regular customer and posted an image of Ted at Coopers Action Music on Facebook, with the comment, 'Remembering what an awesome person Ted Peckels was'.

Coopers Action Music - 6511 Magnolia Avenue, Riverside

This was the third location of Coopers. Ted brought the business from a Mrs Cooper. It was located on Brockton Avenue, in a small house next to the AK convenience store near the corner of Beatty Drive. Ted moved the store to Tom Mitchell's building on Magnolia Avenue, formerly Mitchell Music and Pro Sound Music, now Pepito's Bar.

Tom Mitchell didn't want to sell to Ted, so he bought Mundy's Central Pharmacy two doors down and changed the name to Coopers Action Music. When Ted died, his widow Donna sold the building to Mike Torrence, around 1999, and it became Music Mike's. When Mike retired, he sold the building to the Guitar Center Corp, calling it Music & Arts, that business planning to move to the Plaza, next to Panera, at the time of writing.

Ted Peckels died of complications from surgery in 1998 at Parkview Community Hospital Medical Center, aged 73. He was survived by his wife, Donna; a daughter, Becky Koenig, of Riverside; sons Mark, of Riverside, David, of Long Beach, and Gary, of Moreno Valley; six grandchildren; his mother, Frances Bourns, of Colton; and a sister, Jackie Walker of Oregon.

Donna Lou Peckels remained active after Ted died. She worked for more than 20 years at Provident Savings, went to the gym three to four times a week with her daughter Becky and loved her trips to the casino with her sister Peggy and niece Jan. Donna died on 19 January 2019 at home, surrounded by her loving family, aged 91. She was buried alongside Ted at Montecito Memorial Park in Colton a week later.

Donna's father, George Jacob Imig, was the son of first cousins Carl Imig, who at age 10 immigrated with his parents on 5 May 1858 from Bremen, Germany to New York on the ship, Caroline; and Anna Imig, who crossed the Atlantic with her parents in about 1870.

George was born on 13 June 1892. He had a trucking company in the 1920s in Nebraska and hauled hogs out of Omaha. He moved in about 1930 to San Bernardino, California from Seward Co., Nebraska, with his wife and children.

George spoke German and taught some to his children, such as a prayer before dinner. He was said to have a witty, engaging sense of humour and a cheerful, generous personality, which he particularly displayed with children. During his life George was an entrepreneur, pet shop proprietor, and renowned breeder of champion bulldogs.

Formerly Ted Peckels' Coopers Action Music - 6511 Magnolia Avenue. Image capture Jun 2018 ©2021 Google

Donna's mother, Alice Imig, nee Hageman, an elementary school and piano teacher, was born on a farm southeast of Seward on 28 September 1896, to S. P. and Viola Wallick Hageman. She married George Imig on 20 August 1917, and they moved to San Bernardino in the mid-1920s. Alice died aged 83 on 4 August 1979 in Riverside, California. She was buried in Montecito Memorial Park, San Bernardino.

Alice and George, who celebrated their golden wedding with their children in August 1967, had six children - Mrs. Nick Weaver, Mrs. Frank Stipak, Mrs. Neil Johnson, Mrs. Ted Peckels, Mrs. James Morris and Bob Imig - plus 20 grandchildren and one great-grandchild.

George and Alice Imig celebrate their 50th wedding anniversary with their children, August 1967

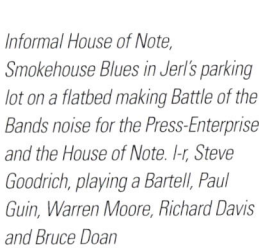

Informal House of Note, Smokehouse Blues in Jerl's parking lot on a flatbed making Battle of the Bands noise for the Press-Enterprise and the House of Note. l-r, Steve Goodrich, playing a Bartell, Paul Guin, Warren Moore, Richard Davis and Bruce Doan

PAUL MARTIN BARTH

Bartell Director, Chief Engineer and Designer.

Paul Martin Barth was born 1 November 1908 in San Mateo County, California. His father, Martin Barth and mother, Irma Dopyera, were immigrants from the Austro-Hungarian region of eastern Europe. From military records at the age of 32 we know that Paul was 6ft tall, weighed 152lbs, had blue eyes, black hair and dark skin. He also had a younger brother, Carl who worked in the industry, and a sister, Elfrieda.

From 1940 to 1952, Paul lived at 401 Rosecrans, Manhattan Beach, California.

Although he dropped out of school at 16, Paul seemed destined for a career in the music industry. With his father a wood-shop foreman for the National company and his mother the sister of renowned instrument makers the Dopyera Brothers - Ed, John and Rudy - his formative years provided a solid apprenticeship, later becoming an innovator, visionary and prolific designer of the electric guitar.

In the early 1920s he went to work with John Dopyera in his shop at 50th and Broadway in New York. And in the mid-1920s he joined the Dopyeras, living and working in the brothers' banjo shop. Paul then worked at the National factory from about 1928 to at least 1934, as an assistant to John, the factory superintendent, dealing with day to day matters of the company. Paul then moved on to make electric guitars with George Beauchamp at Rickenbacker.

Paul's uncle John Dopyera had an instrument shop in Los Angeles where he invented steel resonator guitars, forming the Dobro and National instrument manufacturing companies.

And by the 1930s, Paul was head of the design department at Rickenbacker and instrumental in designing the Capri model.

Paul Barth became a founding member of the National String Instrument Corporation, with the renowned Adolph Rickenbacher, with the first board meeting on 29 February 1928. He also participated in the development of the first purely electrically-amplified guitar, the iconic Frying Pan, alongside George Beauchamp and Harry Watson.

He is also credited with helping Leo Fender set up the original semi-automated assembly line in Santa Ana in the early '50s, when the Stratocaster was first being built. Paul built many of the woodworking jigs that were used to shape necks and bodies for the very first Jazzmaster, Jaguar, and Stratocaster guitars. He also built all the jigs

National String Instrument Corporation - catalogue back cover 1930.
Clockwise from top: Ted E. Kleinmeyer, President; George D. Beauchamp, secretary and general manager; C L Farr, director and company lawyer; Glenn E. Harger, assistant secretary; Adolph Rickenbacher, engineer; Harry Watson, factory superintendent; Jack Levy, sales representative; Paul M. Barth, vice president.

used for Bartell guitars. Paul worked with Semie Moseley (Mosrite) as well as other notable guitar designers and companies, including Magnatone and Hohner (designing and building the Black Widow for Hohner).

Paul Barth was an initial partner in the Ro-Pat-In Corporation, which later became the Electro String

The National Guitar factory circa 1929. The photo was used in the 1930 catalogue.

Instrument Corporation. Paul, along with Billy Lane, having helped with an early pre-amplifier design, had small financial interests in the company. Electro's primary focus was on the Rickenbacker brand. Not only was Paul an electro-magnetic pickup inventor and guru, he also had a great sense of style and a good eye for aesthetics, becoming chief designer for the Rickenbacker Combo 600 and 800 guitar designs of the mid-1950s.

Electro String was sold to a new owner in 1953. Paul Barth left soon after to start his own guitar company, Barth Guitars. Paul stayed with Electro until 1957. Once an ambitious, innovator and designer George Beauchamp was disillusioned with the situation at Electro and he left in October 1940 submitting a resignation letter to company President Adolf Rickenbacker. George went off to follow his passion for deep sea fishing, design lures and patenting one for manufacture.

The Electro ES-17 made by the Electro String Instrument Corporation.

Designed by Rickenbacker co-founder George Beauchamp and assisted by Paul Barth and Harry Watson. The company known then as Electro String Instrument Corporation, added the Rickenbacker name to its instruments.

In the 1950s, the Electro name was dropped and Rickenbacker became the only brand banner, but the company chose to revive the Electro logo in the early 1960s for use on 2 – 6 string solid body electrics. Many of the early examples bear the name Electro.

Paul Barth is linked to George Harrison and the Beatles in many ways. Paul made major design contributions to the Electro ES-17. You can see the DNA that feed into the Rickenbacker Jetglo owned by George.

The 11 October 1940 resignation letter of George Beauchamp from the Electro String Instrument Company

Beauchamp died aged just 42 within in a year of leaving Electro, while on a fishing trip near Los Angeles in 1941. The procession at his funeral was said to be two miles long.

He was survived by his wife, Myrtle Johnson, the pair having married in 1917. They had two children, Frances and Nolan.

Much of the legacy of the electric guitar evolution passed that fateful day with George Beauchamp, to this day largely unrecognised for his contribution to the world's favourite instrument.

Harry Watson, although a skilled craftsman, was an obnoxious character. Carl Barth remembers Watson, who learned to fight in the Royal Navy, in the National office, punching Paul Barth and breaking one of his teeth. He said, "There must have been some alcohol around. A guy would have to be off his rocker to punch my brother, who was such a mild-mannered character".

Electro ES -17

The Boys from Dixie

Watson also had a bust up with George Beauchamp when drinking heavily in Mexican border town Tijuana. They got into a fist-fight, which was unresolved overnight. The next morning Carl Barth and others were waiting at the factory for the keyholder, when Watson arrived and said, "Stick around for the show, Beauchamp's coming, and we are going to finish our fight here". Beauchamp was no measure to Watson's height and didn't turn up. But Carl did see George a few days later with his face swollen and scarred. Watson had caught up with him and gave him a beating.

A blue Barth guitar from Music Mike's, Ohio, was made by the legend himself, with a double-bound body shape reminiscent of the Rickenbacker Capri, another Beatles favourite.

Paul combines Magnatone and Rickenbacker elements, with a three-bolt neck joint, graceful cutaways, painted fretboard, and full-body white pick-guard.

In the late 1950s, after working at Rickenbacker and before moving to Magnatone, Paul Barth signed a contract with the Natural Music Guild in Santa Ana, California to distribute his guitars. Another unique Paul Barth item was an incredibly rare Natural Music Guild Magnatone lap steel and amp combo Consolectric, sold by Natural Music Guild in Santa Ana in 1953, with serial number 1036.

According to the very informative magnatoneamps.com website, in 1958 - after leaving what became a fiasco at National/Rickenbacker/RO-PAT-IN/Dobro - Paul Barth made a fresh start as a respected engineer, inventor and designer with the Magna Electronics Company. The executives hired Barth due to his extensive experience, bringing him in to develop the design for their new Spanish-style guitars. It is interesting to note that the previous incumbent designer was none other than Paul Bigsby.

1963 Rickenbacker Jetglo 425

41

Photo credit: Jaimie Muehlhausen/ Consolectric

The first Barth guitar designed for Magnatone was the Mark VI bass. Barth's designs were manufactured at Magna's Inglewood facility in Los Angeles between January and March 1959. The assembly line couldn't get the quality right and Barth eventually agreed to supply his own Barth guitars, built at his own facility, rebranding them Magnatone on the headstock. These models were known as the Mark VII, VIII, and Mark IX, although Magna would call them the Artist Series in catalogues. Barth designed the Rickenbacker Combo 600 and 800 guitars for Electro String. As iconic as the Ric Combo guitar design has become, it is amazing that Paul Barth's name is not more well known, that design the basis of what became the signature design accents of the Rickenbacker guitar. Barth was hired again on a full-time basis by Estey between 1964-1966 to utilise his design experience on the Starstream guitars, teaming up with head of Estey design, Tony Price and Larry Ludwick, who was put in charge of tooling and set-up of the jigs for the routing of the guitar components. This was all carried out at Estey's manufacturing facility at Torrance from 1964, where a consistent good quality guitar was now rolling off the production line. The guitars were fitted with Barth's single coil pickups. Towards the end of '65, Barth, Ludwick and Price made alterations to the design of the Starstream headstock, a second generation, the completely new headpiece designed for easier tuning, perfect string alignment and featuring double-sided keys for a straight string pull. The new unique design helped distinguish the Starstream from the standard Fender set-up.

"Paul Barth was one of the pioneers... he knew his guitars. Look closely and you can see the Barth touch, especially in the carved bevel around the top. Listen closely to any Bartell guitar and you'll hear that Barth magic in every note you play" - Ted Peckels

Tony Price said, "The solid body guitars were designed by Paul Barth, who was in my department. He was a real nice, quiet guy, considerably older than me, with lots of practical experience. We came up with a special head with three keys each side, and straight string pull."

The Frying Pan, with the Horseshoe pickup Paul Barth helped George Beauchamp design on a kitchen table with a sewing machine, patented by Beauchamp. Photo: Sebastian Müller

Guitar designer and luthier Paul Barth, left.

Prototypes of a semi-hollow body guitar produced at the same time bear a strong resemblance to the guitars Barth was producing with the Bartell company in California at the time. Ditto the pickups, which seemed to suggest Barth probably made the prototypes.

In 1967, after Tony Price had left the company, Paul Barth was enticed by Estey president Jack McClintock to up-sticks from California for a short relocation to Harmony, Pennsylvania to get production established. Never one to be idle, Barth quickly opened a small guitar shop of his own, locally. However, life in Harmony for Barth and his wife Kay was not to be, and it seems they had returned to the West coast by 1970.

Andy Crescenzo worked with Paul Barth at Estey's Magnatone plant in Harmony, PA.

"Paul opened a small storefront on main street, Zelienople, a mile from Harmony, where he spun pick-ups on all these spinners in the back room. In the front were all kinds of do-dads, strings, pick-ups, etc.

"I would go in after school and work with him. Although we knew he was someone, we really had no grasp of his stature at the time. I worked with him many days, many times into the night, when I would hitchhike home.

"We made pick-ups together, oodles of 'em, all kinds, but mostly single-coil, and many cool exp. models. He gave me a super Guild pickup with monster poles on it for Christmas that he made of white ceramic, the only one of its kind! He talked about Rickenbacker a little, but I was gonzo for Fender. Said he could make Fender pickups better than Fender.

"He was a very kind old man, good to us small-town guitar-hungry kids. Then, one day, just as quickly as he appeared, he was gone. We never found out where.

"Brings tears to my eyes to think that so many years ago I worked very closely with such a legend. He liked me and I will never forget him. I am just now finding out how famous Paul was/is in today's music world." (source - bartell.vintageusaguitars.com)

"God Bless Paul Barth, a true innovator" - Andy Crescenzo

During the 1960s and early 1970s, Paul ran his business from a small repair shop on Magnolia Avenue in Riverside, California. Paul and his wife lived over the shop, selling used and vintage instruments, mostly on consignment.

Former employee Wes Lambert recalled, "I do remember one of the early model 'frying pan' lap steels on display near the cash register. Paul was always willing to teach those who were interested how to properly maintain their instruments."

In the words of author Robb Lawrence, "Paul was an unsung hero who ushered in the advent of resophonic and electric guitars".

On 13 August 1959, The Palos Verdes Peninsula News reported the wedding of Paul and Frances' only child, revealing, "Mrs Michael Coulson Sagar married Saturday at St Francis' Episcopal Church, Palos Verdes Estates. Wedding vows were exchanged in a two o'clock ceremony ... by Miss Sharon Allison Barth, daughter of Mr and Mrs Paul Martin Barth of Palos Verdes Estates, and Michael Coulson Sagar, son of Mr and Mrs Carroll Sagar of Los Angeles. The service was conducted by Rev. Robert Allen Tourigney, the bride given in marriage by her father. Her wedding gown was of floor-length silk organza with bustle back, and she wore a fingertip-length scalloped veil. Her bouquet was white orchids and lilies of the valley.

"Attending the bride as maid of honour was Miss Norma Hoeneman, bridesmaids being Miss Marvalee Ahlen and Miss Jeanne Kinney. All three were attired in street length dresses of blue organza with full puff sleeves, blue picture hats and carried bouquets of purple orchids. The bridegroom was attended by Thomas Morey as best man. Ushers were William Kentle and John Baker. The reception was held at La Venta Inn in Palos Verdes Estates. La Venta was the first structure built on the Palos Verdes peninsula, its gardens designed by the Olmstead brothers."

Paul Barth - Family Relationships

29 September 1930	Paul M. Barth, 21, and Frances S. Parker, 25, are engaged, Santa Ana
2 October 1930	Paul Barth marries Frances Stanley Parker.
13 August 1959	Sharon Barth marries Michael Coulson Sagar
Circa 1960	Paul and Francis divorce Paul later remarries Kay
4 October 1973	Paul Barth dies, Magnolia Drive, Riverside, California
15 January 1992	Frances Barth dies, Orange County, California

Paul Barth – timeline

1920s – working with his uncle, John Dopyera, at 50th and Broadway, New York

1928 to 1934 – rises from Assistant Factory Superintendent to Vice President at the National String Instrument Company with John Dopyera, Adolph Rickenbacher and George Beauchamp

1931 – also with the Ro-Pat-In Corporation, renamed in 1933 the Electro-Patent Instrument Company, in Los Angeles

Mid-1930s – heads the design department at National, which becomes Rickenbacker

16 October 1940 – undergoes military service training at Hermosa Beach, California

Early 1950s – sets up jigs at Fender for the Stratocaster, Jaguar and Jazzmaster

1953 - contracted to the Natural Music Guild in Santa Ana, California

1957 – leaves the Electro String company to set up the Barth Musical Instrument Company on 169th St, Gardena, California

1958 to 1961 – joins Magnatone in Harmony, Pennsylvania

1964 to 1968 – forms Bartell Guitars with Ted Peckels in Riverside, California

1964 to 1966 – rejoins Etsy/Magnatone in Harmony while running a shop in nearby Zelienople, Pennsylvania, with the company designing the Starstream series

1969 to 1973 - sets up the Barth guitar shop on Magnolia Avenue in Riverside, California

Paul Barth Addresses

1920s - living in New York working with the Dopyera family

1940 to 1952 – with wife Frances lived at 401 Rosecrans, Manhattan Beach, California

1952 to 1962 - living at 3956 Hawthorne Avenue, Riverside, California

1962 to 1967 – living at 25033 Pennsylvania Avenue, Riverside, California

1967 to 1969 – with second wife Kay at 3253 Wickham Drive, Riverside, California

1969 to 1973 – with Kay above the Barth guitar shop on Magnolia Avenue, California

Virginia Carmona Vorster: "I was Paul and Kay's neighbour for several years before they moved to live above the shop in Magnolia. We lived at Wickham Drive in Riverside. They were only there a few years.

"Paul and Kay were some of the most genuine, caring and generous people I've ever known. I was very close to Kay, who was like a second mother to me. I was 12 to 14 when we were neighbours. She and I would sit together at the kitchen table while Paul was in the shop - having converted the garage into a shop - and talk about everything and anything.

"They were among the few people in the neighbourhood who had a pool, and Kay was always telling me that I could throw a pool party for my friends anytime I wanted to at their home - that's what I mean by generous. She was the second mom that you could tell things to that you wouldn't tell your own mom.

"When they moved to live above the shop, Kay had a little ceramics business. I would ride my bike to the shop and paint ceramics, for which she refused to take any money for.

"I remember hearing about Paul's sudden passing, and I was so upset, more so because I knew how much Kay loved him and I know she had to have been devastated. I had no idea that Paul was such a legend in the field. To me, they were just my kind and loving neighbours that I was fortunate to have lived next door to."

1967 - 69 Paul and Kay BARTH lived at 3256 Wickham Dr Riverside, CA 92503 - Google Maps - Image capture Mar 2019 ©2021 Google

Barth Musical Instrument Company - 1850 B West 169th St Gardena California The Location of Paul's work-shop in the late 50's early 60's - Google Maps - Image capture Dec 2020 ©2021 Google

47

Former site of Paul Barth's Guitar shop on 10685 Magnolia Avenue - as it was by 2020 - Google Maps Image capture Mar 2019 ©2021 Google

The latest picture taken by Bob Nye shows the stairs on the left where Paul suffered a fatal heart attack in 1973. Sadly, Don Underwood also suffered a heart attack going up those stairs, as Paul Barth did.

Kevin P Lynch, talking about the Barth home and shop on Magnolia Avenue in 1970, said, "I used to clean for them. They lived upstairs. Kay had a big bulldog that died in my arms while she drove to the vet. She was a master wood finisher on guitars. I remember all the sanding and guitars hanging from the ceiling."

During his time at Rickenbacker, Paul had patents registered for both a roller vibrato and detachable horseshoe pickup.

Steve Soest remembered, "Paul Barth brought about the zero fret and the neck/body 'tab' that extends under the rhythm pickup".

Paul Barth's fingerprints and influence are all over the iconic guitars we still know today.

- Electro String
- National
- Rickenbacker
- Fender
- Bartell
- Barth
- Acoustic Corp
- Hohner
- Magnatone
- Mosrite
- Natural Music Guild

Paul Barth was part of or influenced all of these famous guitar manufacturers. His name will deservedly forever remain in the history books of the guitar.

A quiet, gentle, unassuming, dedicated legend who should not be forgotten.

Paul Barth died aged 64 of a fatal heart attack while climbing the stairs from his shop to his home above on 4 October 1973 in Riverside, California.

He was laid to rest with his parents - mother Irma Barth nee Dopyera (1889-1977) and father Martin Barth (1887 - 1979) - at the Forest Lawn Memorial Park, Cypress, Orange County, California.

Through all my hours of research I tried every avenue to reach out to the family of Paul Barth. I had so much to tell them, and so many questions to ask. I had practically given up on sending my last email, in hope more than expectation.

Photo credits - Frances Cope

And then on 12 February 2021, Kristen Purll replied, "Thank you so much for contacting us, we are thrilled that you are enquiring about Paul Barth. We were so excited to hear that Grandad's guitars may have been involved in such a great story. My mother, Sharon Barth Sagar, turns 84 next month. Her father, Paul Barth, was my Grandad, and I spent some time in Riverside visiting him and his second wife, Kay. My mother has many memories of her father growing up, but not so much about the business - most kids don't know a lot about what their parents did back then!"

I was blown away that Paul's descendants were so interested in my research, sending Kristen my draft manuscript and news of a pending publishing deal. She replied, "Wonderful news! 'Wow' is all I can say. This is an amazing book!"

Photo Credit - Karen Binkley

SHARON SAGAR AND KRISTEN PURLL INTERVIEW, LAGUNA BEACH, CALIFORNIA, MARCH 2021

On 20 March 2021, I managed to track down Paul Barth's daughter, Sharon Sagar, and granddaughter, Kristen Purll, to ask for their memories of this innovative guitar maker.

What do you know about your family history, and the early days?

Kristen: "My great-grandparents came to this country with their families as immigrants from Hungary and Czechoslovakia. They were absolutely wonderful, living somewhere like Placentia, California, in a mobile home."

Sharon: "My grandfather, Martin Barth, saw a girl called Irma Dopyera on the street car and liked what he saw, so he followed her home, knocked on the door and said, 'I'd like to meet your daughter'. They said, 'Go away'. But after three months of this every day, they said, 'Come on in!'"

Photo of Paul and Kay Barth with kind permission of Sharon Sagar

Kristen: "Martin and Irma were one of the longest married couples in Orange County, it was in the papers, 63 years, I believe. He treated her like a queen to the last minute. One time there was a puddle in front of her and Grandpa had to lift her up and carry her over it. In 1941 after Pearl Harbor, Grandpa packed up his tools and went to help rebuild Pearl Harbor. They loved America and had a great life here."

Sharon: "Martin worked in the factory at times, helped do things. My grandmother's brothers are the Dopyera brothers, and her sister Valeria is a fine artist with work in the Smithsonian - she did Vallona star pottery and became a famous artist."

Kristen: "What about Paul's brother, Uncle Carl?"

Sharon: "He worked for Douglas Aircraft, he was an engineer."

What do you remember about your parents, Sharon?

Sharon: "My Dad, Paul Barth got married in 1930 to Frances Stanley Parker, my Mom. I was born in 1937. When I was in college, I started in 1955, my Mom and Dad went through the loss of the Barth guitar company and were having a lot of other problems, but they didn't phone me. In my era, no one made phone calls, I never received a phone call from my parents unless it was a tragedy, which luckily we didn't have. After I guess 30 years of marriage Frances and Paul separated, probably around 1960."

Kristen: "Mom, did you live with Paul on Rosecrans?"

Sharon: "Yes, at 401 Rosecrans, Manhattan Beach, California. This was during the '40s when I was a young girl, then I left home. Later, Paul and a lady working at the company called Kay, who liked my Dad long as I can remember, got together and eventually married. Kay was a very kind and sweet person."

Kristen: "Kay was from Kentucky, and idolised my Grandad. She said he was the kindest, most gentle man she'd ever met. After he passed away, Kay moved to Laughlin, Arizona, then to Ione, California, near Sacramento, where she passed away. She really died of a broken heart."

Your family have an incredible history. How much were you aware of that growing up and now?

Sharon: "In the beginning Paul started as a silversmith. He made forms that he would pound silver into a mould, for items like a pickup. Paul helped his uncles, the Dopyera brothers. They made the resonators, the Dobro, that's how Paul got into guitars in the first place. Dad loved making guitars."

Kristen: "Tell Paul how Dad didn't care about the money."

Sharon: "He didn't care if they made money! In fact, I worked in Electro String one summer and I discovered that the guitars were costing more than they were selling for! When you added up the parts, the materials, not even including labour, they would lose money! But he loved making guitars, that's all he wanted to do in his life."

Your Dad was very inventive, creative, originally working with George Beauchamp when they invented the horseshoe pickup. George patented it and Paul took no credit for it?

Sharon: "George, he was way more sharp, business-wise!"

So your Dad was the creator, but never seemed interested in taking the glory for something, happy for other people to do that?

Kristen: "It's a family trait, mother is the same!"

Sharon: "I remember being there at the factory when Les Paul came in and wanted my Dad to make like a double-neck guitar, but he actually wanted a triple-neck guitar."

Les Paul wanted a triple-neck! What factory was this at?

Sharon: "There was a factory next to Rickenbacker. Paul was friends with Eddie Rickenbacker, who lived with his cousin. He had a machine shop, so they started making these guitars next to the machine shop, where they could use the tools to do the pickups."

Did he ever make Les Paul that triple-neck?

Sharon: "No, he ended up getting it from Fender and not from my Dad."

Sharon: "Steven, my son was telling me that when they were making guitars at Bartell, he was there at the weekends. He went with my Dad and his friend, Ted Peckels, to Fender, where they had many friends and got stuff for the factory, they'd send him to play while they talked for hours."

I heard that Paul helped Leo Fender set up the original jigs that were used to shape necks and bodies for the very first Jazzmaster, Jaguar, and Stratocaster guitars.

Kristen: "Wow, that's awesome!"

Again, this shows Paul was instrumental in many designs and inventions, while not taking credit for anything. What do you remember about the Barth guitar shop on Magnolia Drive?

Kristen: "Part of the shop had been turned into an arts and craft shop. It was the '70s, so with Kay we would make all sorts of candles - purple and pink or yellow and orange surrounded by beach sand. She also had miniature animal shapes in ceramics. We used to paint those and Kay would sell them around town. We'd bead necklaces and lots of fun stuff. We always had a great time."

Did you visit Paul and Kay often?

Sharon: "My son was older when Paul and Kay would take my kids and my dog Billy for weekends and holidays. Kay was a wonderful grandmother to Kristen and Steven."

Kristen: "Billy was a mix, something like a Scottie with a Basset hound body, he lived until 17!"

Sharon: "Dad let my son make little surfboards instead of guitars in the shop. He wasn't really into guitars at that age."

Kristen: "Grandad didn't have a mean bone in his body. He was always the nicest, sweetest, quiet guy."

I hear that from everybody. There was a lot of love for Paul and Ted Peckels in the music community, all the musicians hanging out in their shops. Ted had a reputation for letting guys borrow stuff, not paying. I've not heard anyone say anything bad about either of them. They were loved by everyone.

Kristen: "Mom has a couple of guitars from Paul."

Sharon: "I have a story about the guitars Dad left. With some there were either no pickups or something. They were taking up room! My boyfriend and I took all the ones that didn't sell to the dump!"

Kristen: "Imagine all that value!"

So you got rid of them. Oh dear! Did you have any idea about the background to the story of Bartell Guitars, Paul Barth, Ted Peckels and their association with The Beatles, Jimi Hendrix and Frank Zappa, or were you blissfully unaware?

Kristen: "We were completely unaware!"

Sharon: "I felt very wounded by a book that came out on the Rickenbacker guitar, someone brought into the business when I was probably in high school. I can't remember his name, he never came there, I never met him and I was there a lot. He had a German guy who was a manager, who really knew nothing about guitars, I do remember that. Then someone wrote a book on Rickenbacker and only mentioned my Dad once, as the 'person who wound the coil', I mean it was absurd, this person had nothing to do with the business whatsoever except putting money in."

I would be pleased to help put the records straight about Paul's significant contribution to the development of the electric guitar. The story of the Dopyera brothers, Rickenbacker, Electro, National and Dobro is very well documented, but Paul is often missing, his legacy unappreciated.

Sharon: "It's not well documented, but it is documented."

Incidentally, Paul Barth's family and descendants have a rich history of music and art. Sharon Sagar is an artist and designer, making beautiful mosaics; Michael Sagar was a jazz trumpeter and a surfer until he was 80; Steven Sagar lives in Maui, where he surfs and still plays electric guitar and makes ceramics; Kristen Purll makes hand-painted t-shirts; Kristen's husband Simon Purll is an art director and photographer; and Samantha Purll is also an artist.

Sharon and Kristen Purll (Paul Barth's granddaughter)

FINDING FRETLESS

PAUL BARTH'S RICKENBACKER ELECTRO 'FRYING PAN'

PAUL BARTH'S RICKENBACKER NS MODEL

PAUL BARTH'S NATIONAL TRIOLIAN DOBRO BANJO TENOR GUITAR, 1929

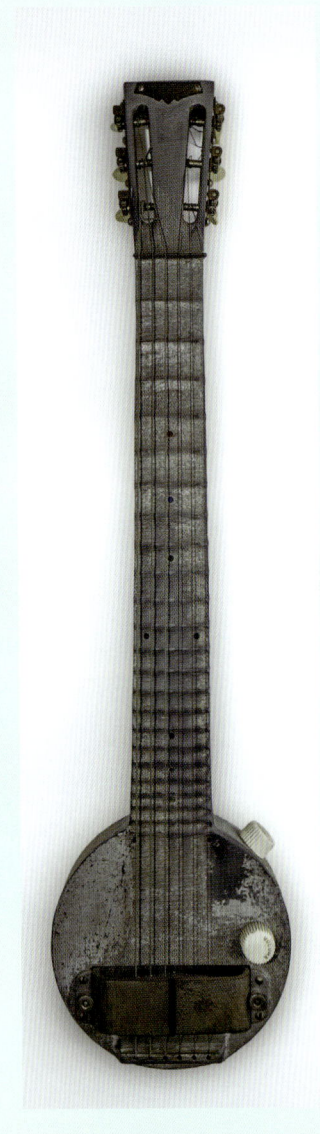

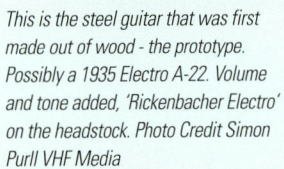

This is the steel guitar that was first made out of wood - the prototype. Possibly a 1935 Electro A-22. Volume and tone added, 'Rickenbacher Electro' on the headstock. Photo Credit Simon Purll VHF Media

STEVEN SAGAR INTERVIEW, HAWAII, APRIL 2021

What do you remember about your Grandad, Paul Barth?

"When I was a kid, I'd tell people my Grandad invented the electric guitar and him and his partner invented the pickup! They were like, 'Nah,' and I was like, 'No, he really did!'. I think he had a couple of patents, but didn't take much glory for his inventions."

You were of course very young when you knew your Grandad.

"I was born in '61, and he died in 1973, I knew him up until I was about 11. I do remember tooling around in his shop, but I was just a kid wanting to be at the beach and skate! Kay was doing little slip-mould castings and then firing them. She was amazing, just the sweetest soul, just like him. Paul was super-kind. Lots of cool guys came in and he would have every killer guitar known to man on the wall. He would sell guitars and be doing the prototype stuff on the side. He would lathe it out for the pickups, using the bandsaw and all that. So I asked, 'Hey, would you make me a surfboard?' He knocked one up on the bandsaw and then gave me some sandpaper to keep me busy for a couple of hours.

"Someone came in with plans for a killer double-necker. They had these plans over the counter. I don't know who he made it for. He was really into getting the best out of a guitar for the best players. Paul could play, but it wasn't his thing. He just liked fiddling around seeing how far he could take it, and the tube amps, he was into that too. He was a really good golfer, playing places like Wilshire Country Club. He was such a calm guy, perfect for golfing. His first wife was good too, Frances, I called her Mimi. I think he was a little savant-ish, he had a very creative mind."

Your Grandad knew Leo Fender, Adolph Rickenbacher and the Dopyera brothers.

"Yeah, his uncles - the Dopyeras - were doing the resonators to make guitars louder. We would cruise in the car and go to the Fender factory. He knew all the guys there and he'd talk for hours there while I ran round the parking lot, looking round the warehouse and seeing all those guitar bodies, necks and stuff. We'd go to Fender and Gibson, all those shops, it was awesome!
Les Paul, used to come 'round the house all the time for dinner in the old days, Kay would be, 'Oh, Les Paul's coming over?' Grandpa was, 'Whatever, he's a business partner'. Paul couldn't care less about the frame or anything, he was just doing what he loved to do, which is pretty cool."

"Les Paul would come to dinner all the time!""

I heard Paul helped Leo Fender set up the jigs for the early Fender models?

"Absolutely, he was like, 'Why would you make it 10 times when I could make you a jig and you could make a hundred in 10 minutes?'"

I have seen amazing photographs of the guitars Paul left your Mum, Sharon.

"Yeah, there is a Rickenbacker Electro there, the one with the horseshoe pickup and a couple of others. My Mum has a Dopyera four-string resonator, I used to play it all the time. I kick myself as I play now, but I wasn't interested then."

FINDING FRETLESS

THE DOPYERA BROTHERS

Paul Barth's Slovak uncles on his mother's side - the Dopyera brothers - changed the world with their musical instrument inventions.

Today, the name Dobro is synonymous with the resophonic or resonator guitar. Dobro means goodness in most Slavic languages, its five letters found in Dopyera Brothers.

Designed to produce more volume and tone before the invention of the electric guitar, the Dobro resonator was invented by these amazing siblings, the family emigrating from Dolná Krupá, near Trnava, to California in 1908.

Jozef Dopyera was a gifted musician and craftsman who not only played fiddle, but made them. He was a father of five sons and five daughters, his children inheriting his musicality and handicraft skills. The eldest son, John, was born in 1893 in Stráe, and inherited the larger part of his father's technical skills, guided by his father to make his first fiddle as a boy in Dolna, Krupá.

By 1927 John Dopyera now an inventor, and musician George Beauchamp formed the National String Instrument Corporation, with plans to produce more volume from guitars to compete against louder orchestral instruments, to be loud enough to play a melody over brass and other wind instruments. Dopyera built an ampli-phonic resonator for Beauchamp, which was patented in December 1929. John was assisted by his nephews Paul and Carl Barth, spinning the very first aluminium diaphragms on wooden bucks. They first experimented with their novel ampli-phonic design in a large walnut console instrument. Soon after, the first German silver Hawaiian guitar was built by John and Rudolph Dopyera.

John Dopyera with his 1938 resophonic violin.
Photo Elderly Instruments

In mid-1929, Dopyera left National to start the Dobro Manufacturing Company along with brothers Rudy and Ed, and Vic Smith. The Dobro design, with a single outward-facing resonator cone, was developed in competition with patented inward-facing tricone and biscuit designs produced by the National String Instrument Corporation.

Dobro and National, in competition with each other, made a wide variety of metal and wood-bodied single-cone guitars, although National continued to persevere with the tricone for a time. Both companies were provided components from National director Adolph Rickenbacher.

Hedging his bets, John Dopyera remained a major shareholder in National. In their 1930 catalogue, National listed eight key associates, including Rickenbacher, Beauchamp, Harry Watson, Paul Barth, and Jack Levy.

John Dopyera with a Dobro model 175 Delux Special (1932-34)

Timeline

1908 The Dopyeras emigrate from Dolná Krupá near Trnava, Slovakia, to California

1927 John Dopyera and George Beauchamp form the National String Instrument Corporation in Los Angeles, California

1929 John Dopyera leaves National to form the Dobro Manufacturing Company

1931 The first electrically amplified stringed instruments are marketed commercially by George Beauchamp and Paul Barth

1932 Commercial production begins under the Ro-Pat-In Corporation (Electro-Patent-Instrument Company) in Los Angeles - a partnership of Beauchamp, Adolph Rickenbacher, and Paul Barth.

1932 The Dopyera brothers gain control of both National and Dobro, merging to form the National-Dobro Company

1934 The Ro-Pat-In Corporation is renamed the Rickenbacker Electro Stringed Instrument Company

1935 The successful Frying Pan steel guitar leads to the Electro-Spanish Model B and Electro-Spanish Ken Roberts, the first full 25"-scale electric guitar in production

1940s National-Dobro becomes Valco, which after World War II ceased production of the Dobro brand, the Dopyera brothers continuing to manufacture resonator guitars under various other brand names

1964 The Dopyera brothers revive the Dobro brand name

1966 The Dobro name is sold to American luthier Semie Moseley, with authentic Dobros branded with Mosrite Dobro metal logos, most made at Mosrite's factory in Bakersfield, California

1967 The Original Musical Instrument Company (OMI) is formed by Rudy and Emile Dopyera in Gardena, California with a new brand name, Dopyera Originals, becoming Hound Dog then reverting to Dobro

1970 The Dopyeras' OMI reacquire the Dobro name

1993 The Gibson Guitar Corporation acquire OMI, including the Dobro name, becoming Gibson's Original Acoustic Instruments division

2000 Dobro production is moved to Nashville, Tennessee, manufactured by Gibson subsidiary Epiphone.

The Dopyera Brothers L. to R: Ed (Emil), John, & Rudy. Courtesy of Elderly Instruments www.elderly.com

John Dopyera (1893-1988), born Ján Dopjera, was a Slovak-American inventor and entrepreneur, and a maker of stringed instruments. His inventions included the resonator guitar and important contributions in the early development of the electric guitar. After John retired to settle in Escondido, California, he ran the Fiddle & Fret Shop, where he lived in the back of the store. He died in Grants Pass, Josephine County, Oregon on 3 January 1988, aged 94, with his ashes scattered in the southern Cascade Mountains of Oregon.

The Rancho Revellers were popular West Coast radio and vaudeville artists in the early 1930s, based on a Californian airfield in front of aviatrix Edna Mae Cooper's biplane. Rudy Dopyera, holding his hat, looks into the camera as part of a promotional photo-shoot capturing the excitement of early flight and cowboys with resophonic wonders, including a rarely seen Dobro bass.

John Dopyera and his wife Elizabeth Candee had a son, John Edward Dopyera Jr., born 16 August 1929 in Los Angeles. The family, including brother Joseph and sister Anna, moved to Grants Pass, Oregon when John Jr. was in elementary school. He excelled in his studies until his junior year at Grants Pass High School, when he decided to leave school to work in logging and lumber mills. He then enlisted in the USAF, serving as a meteorological technician, honourably discharged as a staff sergeant in 1952. With the GI Bill, he first attended San Jose State and then transferred to Reed College in Portland, Oregon, where he earned a B.A. with dual majors in psychology and sociology.

During 1990, John began to travel to Slovakia to support the development of the Dobrofest music festival, honouring his father's invention of the resonator guitar. The Dopyeras travelled to Slovakia five times between 1990 to 2001.

In 2006, John and one of his sisters accepted an award from the International Bluegrass Association on behalf of their father's contributions to traditional acoustic music.

John, who retired as a research social psychologist, died at home on 12 November 2014. He was survived by his wife, Margaret Lay-Dopyera, of Ithaca, New York; two daughters, Barbara (Douglas) Dopyera Daley of Fayetteville, New York, and Suzanne (Bruce) Kuntz, also of Ithaca.

The Rancho Revellers with a rare Dobro bass

Four generations of the Dopyera family. From left - John, Rudolf, Robert, Emil. Ronald Lazar Sr., & Ronald Lazar Jr. Courtesy of Elderly Instruments

There is also a museum in Trnava called the Dobro Hall of Fame.

After the death of John Dopyera Jr., the family sought a museum to display instruments and artefacts from the brothers' wonderful collection. There was a temporary display in Syracuse in 1998 and again at the Erie Art Museum in 2000. After that, the collection was offered for sale by Elderly Instruments. A buyer was not forthcoming, leading the family to sell the instruments individually via the Christie's auction company on 27 November 2012. The only item retained by the family was the resonator violin. The proceeds of the sale went, as per John's wishes, to his grandchildren.

Photo Credit Adrian Tribe

Today, Resonator guitars remain incredibly popular with guitarists, most notably Mark Knopfler, seen here with his Dopyera-inspired 1937 National '0' Resonator, serial number B1844

Mark, like a love-struck Romeo, bought the guitar from Steve Phillips for £120 in 1978. Mark said, "This has been my pal ever since". Mark and Steve have performed together as the Duolian String Pickers.

The most famous tracks the guitar is used on include Dire Straits' 'Romeo and Juliet' and 'Telegraph Road'. Mark's famous guitar also features on the front cover of Dire Straits' *Brothers in Arms* album.

Dobro Resonator guitar model 175 Deluxe Special, circa 1932-34, sold at auction for $8,750

A collection of wonderful Dopyera instruments

Mark Knopfler's collection also includes several other National '0' resonators, a Tricone, and a Duolian. He bought his second National (the first was a Tricone from the late 1920s) after spotting an advert in *Exchange and Mart*, buying it from a member of an orchestra based in Wales.

George Harrison was a fan of the Resonator. He also had several National and Dobro resonators in his collection

The legendary former Beatle would take his collection of ukuleles to luthier, player and historian Mark Makin for servicing and repairs. Mark is the author of *Palm Trees, Senoritas, and Rocket Ships*, an illustrated history of National, Dobro, Supro, Valco and OMI guitars, and kindly shared his images of these ukuleles from George Harrison's collection.

© Deborah Feingold. Used by permission.

Credit Mark Makin

61

DEANS CUSTOM FURNITURE

On 13 July 2020 I finally managed to contact Jenny Dean, who eight years earlier - on 22 July 2012 - said about Bartell Guitars, "My father-in-law made these guitars at Deans Custom Furniture in Riverside, California. My husband helped, and he still owns the one he made."

Her father-in-law, Leonard Dean owned the company, and sons Leonard and Bernard also worked at the store, leading me to arrange a call with Leonard Dean, Jr., 67 at the time, living in Texas but born and raised in Riverside, California, with memories of Bartell Guitars from his early teens in the mid-'60s. His father, Leonard Dean, Sr., sadly died during the time this book was written.

The business, Deans Customer Furniture, was located at 6187 Columbus Avenue, Riverside.

How did Ted Peckels and Leonard Dean, Sr. know each other?

"There was a patio store called House of Gardens, which was over the street from Ted's House of Note. It was owned by Joe Allan. Joe has a cabinet shop in the back, where they refinished furniture. My father worked for Joe Allen but eventually wanted to start his own business. Joe didn't want to let Leonard go and wasn't too pleased about it. But Dad left to start the Deans Custom Furniture company."

What did Deans do?

"Deans made, repaired and refinished antiques. Much of their work was in the Palm Springs area, due to lots of flooding and fires, people needed things fixed."

How did Leonard and Ted Peckels get together?

"Somehow Leonard and Ted got together probably as all the local business owners in the area knew each other. Joe Allen, Ted and Dad all had something to offer each other commercially.

"Ted asked Leonard to make him a guitar. Dad got it done, a complete one-off guitar. Dad invited Ted over to the house and laid it on the bed. When Ted came in, his eyes literally bugged out of his head! Ted was like, 'OK, when can we start making them?'

"I liked Ted. When he was running Coopers Music, he would come around and was always working on a hollow body, putting on a little veneer. He was always welcome, he would do his own little thing, that's just the way he was."

What parts of Bartell Guitars did Deans make?

"In the '50s, before my Dad took over the shop, it was the Bournes laboratory. They made bomb guidance equipment for the war, and it had some small rooms. Two rooms were dedicated to putting guitars together, and we had a fret machine to put the grooves in the necks. Actually, I still have some of those saw blades. Deans pretty much made the guitars there.

"On Friday, everyone went home early because Leonard would shape the guitar necks. He did it on Friday night because when the necks were blanks, they were just a square piece of wood. The truss rods were put in and they were laminated on the top with mahogany, walnut or whatever they would use. They were hand-gauged and put in a jig. If the grain was running the wrong way, that neck could explode, with a lot of the wood everywhere. That little rod would go right through you - it would go through a block wall. It was very dangerous.

"He would do that Friday night and on Saturday morning we would go on the motorcycle to the shop and we would have to clean up all those big beautiful maple shavings.

"We would press all the semi-hollow guitars with the f-holes. Those were all made out of alder. We would take those and put maybe 20 of them together at a time in a press that we made with a hydraulic jack, pressing all the skins and shaping them all. It was a very productive shop.

"On the fretless with the maple neck, there was a rosewood cap and bakelite fingerboard. That was put on to give it strength on the front, because when you take the meat out of the back of the neck, it wants to draw.

My Dad had a '63 'little window' Chevy pickup truck. They had to go to LA to get guitar parts, pickups, tuning keys … They had to get a lot of stuff. But it was the time of the Watts riots. The rioters threw a brick and put a dent in his Chevy and hit his window. He would never go there again.

(The anti-police mistreatment and anti-discrimination Watts riots, sometimes referred to as the Watts Rebellion or Watts Uprising, took place between 11 and 16 August 1965 in the Watts neighbourhood and surrounding areas of Los Angeles, after 21-year-old African-American Marquette Frye was pulled over for drunk driving.)

"We had a professional car-spray booth that we had racks in that we would spray the guitars on. They were just hanging on a wire. But also, a lot of the sunburst ones and the double-necks, the specialty ones, he would take them home and he made a kind of jig that was on the ground and you turned it like a barbecue. It would turn the body that was on a fake neck, so he could spray it evenly. He did some of them in our garage in Town and Country in Riverside over the weekends."

What Happened to Deans?

"Dad retired and got remarried, and my two brothers ran the shop for a while but then rented out the business, and then it got destroyed."

How was it destroyed?

"When the shop was rented out to a company, up in the attic there were at least 100 guitar bodies, double-necks, single-necks. There were 400 to 500 guitar necks. Everything caught on fire, and up everything went. It was the biggest fire in Riverside!"

Why did Bartell fold up?

"Well, I don't think they were selling many of the Bartell guitars. They were making parts for the guitars but not selling them. But I did hear of a big order that went wrong."

Leonard Dean's Perfect Bartell XK150

Details of the demise of Bartell as a company late in 1968 are sketchy, but Richard Weinfurtner, who worked with Ted Peckels later in his life in the mid 90's advised me, "One story I recall Ted telling me about Bartell was the botched deal that put them out of business. They got a large order to build guitars for Hohner. So they spent a bunch of money tooling up and buying woods and hardware parts, and so on, and then Hohner cancelled the order."

Did you know Paul Barth?

"I remember Paul Barth. He was a very, very talented man. Paul and Kay, his second wife, lived in the neighbourhood right across from me. He lived in the Hidden Valley homes in La Sierra, before he had the shop with the two stories. That was a very small shop, not big enough to make guitars in it."

Tell me about your own Bartell guitar.

"My Bartell XK150 hasn't been struck in over 50 years! I never did get the knack of playing guitar. It looks like a Mahogany laminate on a beautiful flawless maple neck.

"My Dad said it was a one of a kind, but maybe it was the first one. On the back of the metal plate there was supposed to be a number. There isn't a serial number, some of the plates weren't stamped."

There doesn't seem to be anything logical to the Bartell serial numbers.

"I remember at one time there was a box of those plates, maybe like we had 5,000 or 1,000 of those in, I remember how heavy those would be, but they sat outside and got all rusty and were too bad to use.

"I remember the double-neck guitars, back in the day they were like $600. You could buy a car for that kind of money!"

"We wanted to learn how to play, Ted had a guy, Gary Eye, who taught guitar. We would go to lessons, Gary knew how to play and was in a band. He would give Ted's boys lessons too. I could not play, and Gary told me, 'You ain't ever gonna play shit!'

"One day, Tom Mitchell and St George came in. He had super-long hair, he was a tall lanky guy. They were bringing me exotic pieces of wood and I was making Flying Vs for them. We would cut up the exotic wood, laminate it, glue it, shape it, inlay it, and so on.

"I remember Ted Peckels coming in when they had to make a second guitar for Hendrix because the first one was stolen. I think over in Europe somewhere. Ted knew how to wheel and deal, he knew the right people in the music industry."

I passed on the information from Leonard Dean, Jr. to Dave Peckels, who said, "I haven't talked to Leonard or his brother in over 40 years. I remember both of the Dean brothers. When we were little kids, I was in a band with them and one of my brothers. We never played any gigs, but once a week we would play together at the House of Note, instructed by one of the teachers.

"I remember Deans supplied the rough bodies and necks. As far as I know, every Bartell neck and body came from Dean. His shop was very close to the Bartell factory. I would say early production may have been done there. I was not aware that Dean actually made some finished guitars. I guess at some point Bartell took over the assembly, painting, and so on, because as a kid I used to sand down the bodies before they were painted.

"Tom Mitchell was one of the painters, and later my Dad got pretty good at painting too.

"I don't know if he invented the technique, but he liked to spray the guitar bodies through different lace fabrics. He used to go shopping with my Mom for different types of lace. I'm sure the shopkeepers thought it was a little strange that this man was so interested in lace! But It would give the guitars a really cool, custom look. I used to own one of those lace guitars, but I left it down at Bartell once, because one of the pick-ups was acting up, and it got stolen.

"The last time I was there, in 1977 or 1978, I saw that they still had all the jigs used to build the guitars. That was before CAD machines. At some point later that building burned down and I assume all of those jigs burned too."

I believe the fire at Deans was sometime in the mid to late 1980s.

On the business deal that went wrong, Dave Peckels added, "The deal that put Bartell in a real bind was with Hohner. I don't know any of the details, but apparently Hohner wanted to buy into the company. My Dad wasn't too keen on having a partner, so he told them, 'No'. They said, 'OK, we're not buying from you anymore'.

"Later he told my brother that not bringing Hohner in as a partner was the biggest mistake of his life."

This is all backed up by an article from summer 2006 on Ted Peckels and the House of Note in Issue 24 of *Ugly*

Things magazine, researched and written by Mike Stax, who wrote,

"Peckels began to run into financial difficulties with his Bartell company. The demise of Bartell, and subsequently the House of Note, began when Peckels' relationship with his biggest customer, Hohner, turned sour.

"Hohner was probably 90 per cent of Bartell's business, Dave Peckels explained. "They made primarily fretless basses for them [notably the Black Widow]. Hohner wanted to buy into the business, but my Dad was independent; he didn't want to be partners. They went around and round that for a while and finally the last time, he said no. Hohner said, 'OK, we're not buying guitars from you anymore'. All of a sudden they lost their biggest customer, and that was the beginning of the end right there."

As Chauncey Romero remembers it, "One night, Ted came in to see me and offer me a job. He wanted me to manage the Riverside store so he could give all his time to the manufacture of the guitar line. I said yes and managed the store until it closed. So I was gigging at night and managing the store, working five days a week."

Then things went sour with Hohner ...

"Ted said he made one of the biggest mistakes of his life. Hohner wanted him to put out a line of guitars with their name on it.

"The manufacturing was going great and Ted geared up with new equipment and employees, and ordered tons of parts. The mistake was he had accepted a loan from Hohner. It was large; I do not remember the figure. The bad part was Ted had not covered himself on the loan and it could be called due and payable at any time ... or something to that effect.

"He had geared up for the Hohner orders as well as his Bartell line. Hohner ordered great for a year or so, then cancelled orders and called the loan due. This buried Ted, forcing him into bankruptcy.

"I will never forget the phone call at the store. He said Hohner would be coming in and taking over the factory."

"The store had been going great, but the factory failed, so the store went down with it. So the old storyline still applies: never put all of your eggs in one basket.

"An older gentleman hung out at Teds' Riverside House of Note. Stan Dumont was a freelance music student recruiter. He had known Ted for many years and warned us about Horst Mucha and Hohner. He said beforehand that he did not trust them and that large companies like them were known to take over small businesses with ruthless tactics.

"In the 1990s Dave worked for a company that was trying to sell a karaoke machine to Hohner. He met up with one of Ted's former Hohner contacts, by the name of Horst Mucha at the Music Messe trade show in Frankfurt. Dave said, 'He told me he was very sorry about how everything worked out.'"

Horst Mucha was a Hohner apprentice in Trossingen, before he started in the export sales department at Hohner. He arrived in America in 1960 via appointments in Portugal and South America. In 1956, Horst became managing director of the Brazilian Hohner agency, and another assignment in Argentina followed. During the 1960s, Horst ran the Hohner subsidiary in the USA. From 1982 he became president of the American subsidiary and in 1996 he became a member of the management board before standing down in 2007.

FINDING FRETLESS
BARTELL EMPLOYEES, FRIENDS AND CO-WORKERS

Chris Ellington - worked for Ted at Bartell's in the 1960s with Paul Barth, Ray Masey and Tom Mitchell.

"Ted had a truck that was a Packard with the back cut out, made into a truck. That was fun to drive. Ted always made me feel important and valued my opinion, even though I was just a kid.

"I remember the fretless guitar Hendrix had, and I think we made a bass for John Paul Jones of Led Zeppelin. The fretless guitar never took off. It was too hard to play chords!

I had an Electro ES-17 at one time, purchased from The House of Note in the '60s."

When I spoke to Chris, he agreed that probably only three or four fretless guitars were made, and he remembers playing several of them.

A few years after his time at Bartell of California, Chris moved to the Bay Area, Marin County, purchasing a small houseboat. There he met Peter Kaukonen, brother of Jorma from Jefferson Airplane. He was a nice guy, really smart but way out there. They traded guitars, and Chris swapped his Gibson ES 295 for Peter's SG standard.

Jim Mesi (Left) with Chris Ellington

Later, Chris moved to the hills of Mill Valley. As it worked out, Peter lived across the street, Van Morrison lived a few houses down, and so did Craig Chaquico of Jefferson Airplane's successors, Jefferson Starship. And they spent time at Peter's house. playing guitar.

"Peter's acoustic talent was phenomenal. My roommate David played with Eddie Money. The whole neighbourhood was very musical. "

Chris had an interesting introduction to life working at the Bananas at Large music store in San Rafael, California. When he applied for the job, the owner liked the fact that he had worked at Mitchell Music and Leir Music in Riverside. But they didn't need anyone at the time.

Sammy Hagar backstage with Chris Ellington's Burns Bison

Chris said, "I got a call in a week and one of their guys tried to rob a bank and got caught! So I got the job! This was the store all the professional musicians came to, and The Grateful Dead's office was across the street. I met a lot of cool people there.

"I helped get equipment together for Huey Lewis and the News, and Tommy and the Two Tones when they signed their first contract. I knew Huey from an earlier band, Clover, and John McFee from The Doobie Brothers."

However, Chris regrets selling the Mitchell custom amp that Tom Mitchell made for him.

"It was white with Cain and Loth speaker cover, Marshall type 4, 12" speakers with a Mesa Boogie-style 100 watt top."

Chris was friends with Allen Rapport, owner of Prune Music in Mill Valley, the birthplace of Mesa Boogie amps.

"Lee Michael was also a part-owner and a nice guy. He had a 24-track studio in the back. One day Michael Bloomfield came in and looked terrible, really bad. Turns out the stories were true - he didn't sleep when working on a project. I saw him a few weeks later, we spent some time together, and he was a totally different person, happy, smiling and looking great. "

While at Prune, Chris met John Cipollina of Quicksilver Messenger Service.

"He showed me how he finger-picked and gave some other great advice. John was one of the nicest persons I met in the music business."

Moving back to Riverside, California, Chris rented a studio from Tom Mitchell and Ted Trujillo and went into business.

"I managed the band Teddy and the Razors, with Ted Trujillo on guitar, and after that I worked with a band called Alkana.

Michael Bloomfield was found dead in his car in San Francisco on 15 February 1981. He died from an accidental heroin overdose. He played in The Paul Butterfield Blues Band and The Electric Flag. He also played for Bob Dylan on his *Highway 61 Revisited* album.

Rolling Stone magazine placed him at No.22 in their 2003 Greatest Guitarists of all-time list.

Chris got married and settled in Portland, Oregon. There he met and made friends with Jim Mesi.

"He turned me on to Burns of London. I contacted the company and became their West Coast rep. I knew Sammy Hagar and asked if I could give him two Burns guitars in turn for him to play one on tour. He did, and we got a lot of business.

Chris Ellington proved a valuable source of information and great contacts as I dug deeper into the story of Bartell's and was quite a collector of guitars too.

Joe Bonamassa said his 1957 Rickenbacker Combo 400 is 'one of the rarest and perhaps most unusual' in his collection.

"This three-quarter guitar sports the horseshoe pickup, most commonly found on lap steels. 1950s Rickenbackers epitomise the quality and innovation that make vintage guitars so desirable."

Tom R Mitchell

"I think Tom painted guitars for my Dad, and probably did a lot of other stuff too. He was a very creative guy. Later he produced amps and speaker cabinets under the Mitchell name." - Dave Peckels

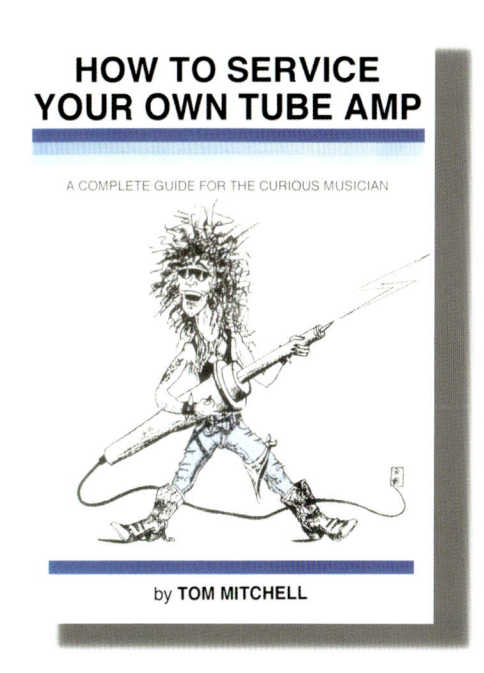

After building his first amplifier cabinets in a shed behind his mother's house, Tom borrowed enough money in 1971 to start the Mitchell Speaker Company from Mitchell's music store, located at 2906 Rubidoux Boulevard, Riverside, California, running the business into the 1980s. Chris Ellington worked there in around 1975.

Among Mitchell's amplifier clients were John Lennon, Sammy Hagar, REO Speedwagon, Dokken, Aerosmith, and The Doobie Brothers.

Chris Ellington and Ted Trujillo both confirmed that the fretless guitar was Tom Mitchell's idea. They said Ted Peckels didn't think it would work but went along with it.

I had a conversation with Tom Mitchell on 6 May 2020, first asking how he ended up working at Bartell's.

"I worked there because I was a guitar player, in Ted's music store, and we started doing guitars."

Was that the House of Note, in Riverside, California?

"Yeah."

What year did you start working there?

"I can't tell you, but it was a long time, for about six or seven years. I did most of the spraying, I did the texture, I did the spraying of the guitars, and the colours and things like that. I was the man who did that and also started the string through the base, through the inside of the guitars."

Tom Mitchell sitting on the bench at the Bartell factory, the guy to his right is Roy Tontini and bottom right is Ed Florio, holding up the bottle.

Did you know Ted Peckels and Paul Barth well?

"Yeah, I worked with Paul side by side, we were stringing guitars, I helped create the fretless bass and some of the other guitars."

Paul had a very interesting history, with his family and connections with Rickenbacker, Electro String, and

the design work he did in the formative years of the electric guitar.

"Yeah, we did a lot of stuff together."

What was Paul like as a chap, as a gentleman?

"He was very contentious about his work. He would want to make sure everything was just right on."

I hear a lot of good things about him, I think he was a fairly quiet person, dedicated to innovation and design, and like you say making sure everything was just right.

"Yeah."

How about Ted - what do you recall about him?

"Ted was a kind of freelance style, you know - take it as it is, a day at a time."

I hear he was generous with local musicians. If they came in and wanted to borrow something, he would let them borrow it.

"Oh yeah, we would have guitar players from San Bernardino come over there to Ted's shop and we helped string guitars and stuff. There was two or three main guitar players who came from over San Bernardino in there. One was real famous and I helped him, he wanted to make sure if he'd take the strings out of his guitar it would work good, and I just said, 'Boil them, boil the strings and they will come back for a while'. It worked for him!"

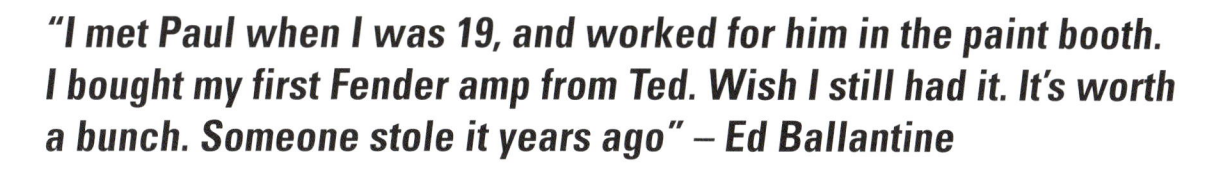

"I met Paul when I was 19, and worked for him in the paint booth. I bought my first Fender amp from Ted. Wish I still had it. It's worth a bunch. Someone stole it years ago" – Ed Ballantine

"The name of the music store that Ted Peckels owned was The House of Music in Riverside, California."

Ed has recorded, written and produced hundreds of television and radio commercials. I spoke to him on 6 July 2020, first asking about Paul Barth.

"I remember spraying a lot of those guitars. I was in the spray booth, and that stuff was pretty strong. You had to wear a ventilator.

"Paul got mad at me one day, because I over-did it. I thought I was doing a really great job as they looked so great ... until they hung them up to dry. There was so much paint on there, it started running off the guitars. Paul got mad at me, we had to redo them all!

"The booth was at the Riverside factory, outside the main building, then they would take them in to be hung.

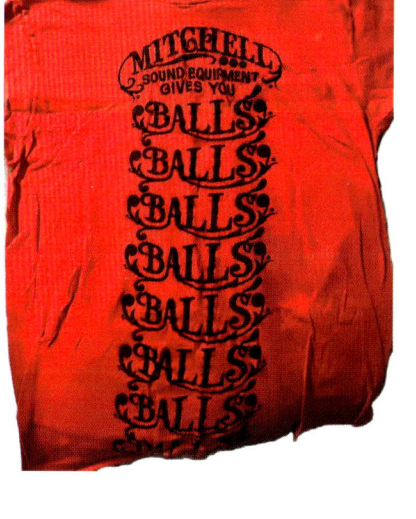

The City Limits Band: From left - Ed Ballantine on Gibson 335, Terry on drums, David on Bartell fretless bass

"Although Paul Barth got a little angry at me, he was a very nice man. At the time I had a Gibson 335. I wish I had it now. It would be worth a fortune! It had a very rare tailpiece on it. I found out later that BB King in his early days had one just like it. Paul did some work on the headstock for me, putting white binding around the headstock on a 335, which is really never done – it's only done on more expensive models like the 355s and that. It looked really cool when he put that binding on it.

"Don Underwood brought the store up from Paul. Don passed away a few years ago. He had a heart attack. He always had a bad heart. I remember we did benefits for Don. He was a good guitar player, and a dear friend I knew from school. He was one year ahead of me, we hung out and used to have jam sessions and stuff over at his house.

"Don went to Florida, he loved it there as he could walk up and down the beach. One time, Don was out in California and called me from the airplane he was on heading back to Florida, complaining of chest pains. I said, 'Don, I want you to tell the stewardess you are having chest pains. Make sure they have an ambulance waiting for you when you touch down'.

"They wanted to do a heart transplant with him, but he refused that. He came back to California and died right here in Riverside. He had given his nephew a guitar lesson and went out to Mount Rubidoux to walk up, and it was a little too much for him. That's where he succumbed. We did a lot of recording together, with a lot of well-known people.

"A lot of young musicians got screwed by people in the music business. I was looking on the internet and there was a song I wrote and played on called 'Graveyard Giggles'. I never realised that it got released, I didn't get credit for anything, not for writing it or playing the guitar on it! Well, that wasn't unusual at the time.

"Paul Barth was well on his way of becoming another Leo Fender."

"There's a photo of the vintage 355 guitar Paul Barth worked on in 1964. He bound the headstock to make it a one of a kind. In my opinion, it was one of the best Gibsons ever made. I was about 22 or 23 years old. The photo was taken at a gig I had with my band The City Limits.

"You can see BB King playing one on the internet that used a trapeze tailpiece like this one, way before he had a 355 called Lucille. That guitar today would be worth a pretty penny. I would love to know who has that guitar today. It's obviously one of a kind.

Don Underwood (1942-2013)

Born in Texas, Don adopted the stage name, Texas Donnie Quattro, and bought the Magnolia Avenue shop in Riverside from the Barth family, taking over in 1973 or early 1974 after Paul's death. While he owned it, Don lived in the apartment above the shop, just as Paul and his wife Kay had. Don's co-worker was Devon Oxford, who Don asked to 'come help with repairs and build guitars'.

Ed playing a Gibson 335 modified by Paul Barth

Don suffered his first heart attack going up those stairs, same as Paul Barth did. Those stairs are obviously not heart friendly. Don's former wife Becky said, "I visited Don in the hospital after his first heart attack in 1978. He still snuck out to smoke but quit shortly after. He became really health-conscious after that."

Don was an excellent guitarist and often gigged across the street from the Barth guitar shop at the Sundowner bar. He continued to run a successful business until around 1978, when he suffered another heart attack, retiring to live in Panama City.

"After 15 years in Florida, I was still being introduced as 'Don Underwood from California,'" he said. But Southern California was where he continued to visit family and host long-time friends and fellow musicians.

On 21 October 2013, Don passed away, visiting his sister Yvonne and nephew in California when he suffered a final fatal heart attack. Don's nephew John Williams inherited his guitars.

"He took flight from this realm on Monday after sharing a memorable guitar jam with nephew John. Halfway up the Mount Rubidoux pilgrimage, headed up toward the big white cross, he stopped to look out over the valley where we grew up, and slipped quietly away, stage right."

He was laid to rest on Wednesday 30 October at Green Acres Cemetery, Bloomington, California, the service followed by music in the park at Fairmont Park.

Boomer Castleman remembers his friend fondly, saying, "Don was one of my very best friends in California when I lived out there. What a great guitarist, musician, and inspiration he was to me. He will always be in my thoughts, for the rest of my life."

Chauncey Romero added, "So glad to have known him. He was always one of the best."

Apparently, Boomer got into a fight with Johnny Cash, when Johnny tried to 'steal' his guitar.

Yvonne Underwood Emerson said, "Don was my brother; a year and a half older. We were very close. When he bought the Barth shop, I lived several hours' drive away, on the other side of Los Angeles. I never met Paul Barth, but learned of his reputation through Don.

Don's Flying V with a Fender neck

The transparent Flying V

"Don lived above the shop and organised and managed it meticulously. He collaborated with Wayne Charvel, and interacted a lot with Fender. He performed as lead guitar continuously from his high school days (Don and the Galaxies) through decades as lead guitar (with The Desperadoes), on to Florida, where he performed in clubs and tourist show-boat bands.

"He knew what was needed to get top performance from an instrument, as well as what would improve it. Don was also an enthusiastic marathon runner."

I placed a post on the Inland Empire Music Hall of Fame Facebook page about the transparent Flying V that Don made at the Barth shop. I got a surprising reply.

Ken Warrick: "I believe I'm the original owner of that guitar!"

That's cool, what do you remember about it? When and where did you get it? Do you have any photos and do you know what happened to it?

"I purchased it around late '74 or very early '75. I used to hang at the shop all the time and purchased several guitars made by Don Underwood, as well as ones he set up, restored or modified. He said that working with Plexiglas was a real pain. He thought he would do a Strat style, but with all the curves he elected to do the V. As soon as I saw the body, I wanted it. I believe I spent around $350, with case. At the time I was starting a band in the Corona area, Hero, and once it was finished played out with it a few times but was reluctant because I didn't want to mar the Plexiglas.

"My marriage was failing and I wanted out, so on 20 August 1976 I was looking for someone who might purchase it. I got a brilliant idea and went to Anaheim Stadium to the Kiss/Ted Nugent show. I put on my best interplanetary outfit and went to the back gate with guitar in hand and said, very matter of fact, "I had a custom guitar for Paul Stanley of Kiss to look at." Once I popped open the case there was no hesitation and they let me in. I had to hang for a couple of hours before the band arrived, so I socialised. All kinds of stuff going on.

"About an hour and a half before Kiss was going on stage, Stanley and Simmons arrived and they escorted me to a hospitality trailer, where they both came after make-up, and I was able to show Paul the guitar. There was a photographer there and I know there are some pictures of Paul and me with the guitar. We talked a bit, he liked it but said he wasn't buying right now. But he gave me a number for the fella who was his guitar tech, saying he might have an opening to be an assistant and to call him the next day. Unfortunately, I didn't follow through because of a personal issue at hand.

"I later went back to Don Underwood and worked a trade for a custom SG with p90s, white with amazing custom inlay of stars and planets and a limited-edition Gibson Paisley SG case.

"Later I would buy one of his handmade Oxwood guitars (an absolute treasure) and wish I could locate it now. Great custom work in those times was hard to find, and a place like Barth was a real treat. Don's work was amazing. You didn't easily find a quality custom person in the Inland Empire. He was a wonderful guy and always interested in teaching and learning.

"My very 1st good guitar was a Bartell of California that I purchased from the House of Note, directly across the street from Mitchell's Music. Another major hang-out and source for gear and PA cabinets."

An interesting story. I'm not sure if another transparent was made for Bob Anglin, or if Bob didn't have it and Ken got it instead, but Devon Oxford shared with me a Transparent 'Strat' that they eventually made successfully.

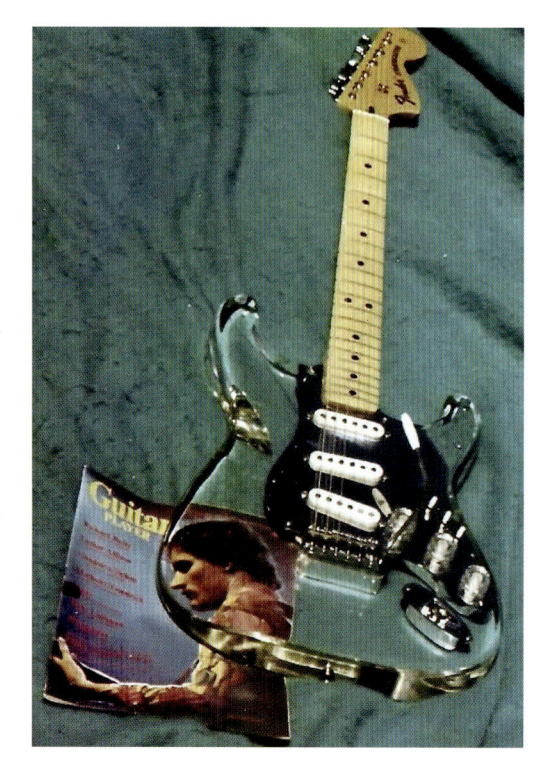

John Williams

John Williams was the nephew of Don Underwood and in awe of his talented uncle. When Don passed away, John inherited his unique 1961 Stratocaster, a Black American '61 body with '65 Coronado neck. Don left a note for John with the details. Making it even more special was the fact that Paul Barth assembled the parts and rewound the pickups personally. It has a unique seven-way switching arrangement.

John met Fred Stuart, founding Fender Custom Shop master builder, at Don's funeral. They collaborated to produce a spectacular custom Tele tribute to Don, called the Yellow Rose.

Tribute Yellow Rose Tele

Don Underwood's 1961 Stratocaster

Roger Underwood

I learned a lot about the Explorer guitar made by Barth shop luthier Devon Oxford. Roger Underwood (Don's brother) informed me that you can see it on the album cover of Joe Walsh's There Goes the Neighbourhood, just below the surfboard. Roger said, "I remember Marv. He changed his name to Devon. He was a brilliant craftsman, a brilliant guitarist and liked Southern electric rock, Lynyrd Skynyrd, Allman Brothers. There was also Fred Strobal. He was the main finisher. When I joined I think he was leaving to join the Navy or something. I lost track of Fred. There is an excellent example of Devon's finish job on what we refer to as a tangerine sunburst on the cover of There Goes The Neighbourhood, right there in the lower right corner is what looks like a vintage Explorer guitar, customised at Barth guitar by Devon and my brother."

Devon Oxford custom made Explorer

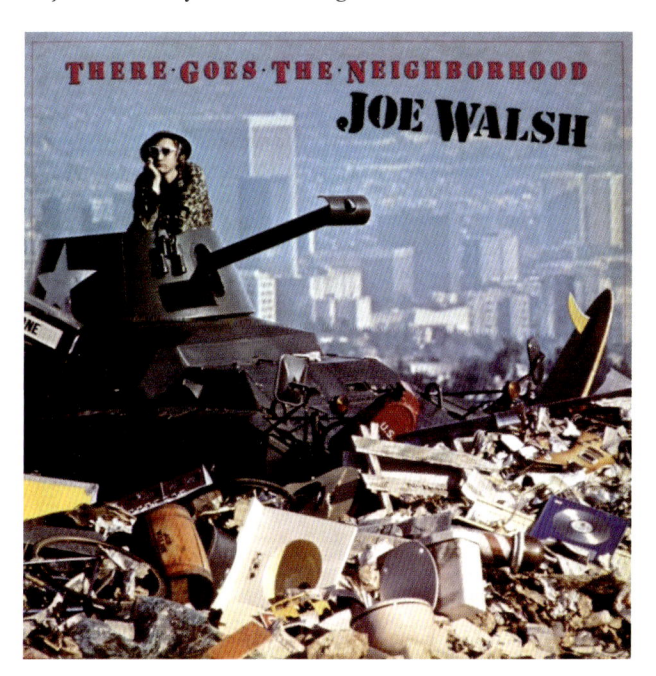

Devon confirmed he visited a guitar shop in San Diego and took measurements of a 1958 Explorer, then back at the shop built a couple of 'test' Explorers out of mahogany. When he was satisfied, he made a thin mahogany Explorer, and added a maple cap, front and back, Devon spraying it a tangerine colour. It's that model that Joe Walsh's equipment manager took from the Barth shop to Joe.

Terry Wade
Drummer of The Legendary Mustangs, said, "Ted gave me a great deal on a Ludwig White Pearl five-piece set with hardware and cymbals on a Saturday morning after my previous Ludwig kit had blown up the night before when my car was hit by a train.

"I had a gig that night, and asked Ted if I could give him a $100 deposit and pay the balance in cash on Monday when my credit union opened. He said, 'Go ahead and take it now. I know you are good for it.' He wouldn't even take a deposit.

"Ted was a magnificent human being. Needless to say, I was a House of Note customer for the duration."

Terry's Ludwig five-piece kit, with white pearl finish. "I got a lot of mileage out of that kit. I wish I could remember who bought it from me".

Chauncey Romero remembers first meeting Ted Peckels around 1961.

"I was attending college at Riverside City College when I met Ted. We were just forming The Hustlers, and Ted had opened the House of Note in Riverside. This was the first store; it was much smaller than the one we moved to at a later date. He pretty much ran the store alone. I met him when we bought our first quality guitars from him.

Terry Wade

Left to right, Bruce Tucker, Dennis Rey Lisonbee, Chip Bradley, Terry Wade, Roland Tiffany, and Ted Trujillo. Terry's Ludwig 5-piece kit with a white pearl finish. "I got a lot of mileage out of that kit. I wish I could remember who bought it from me"

They were Fender Duo-Sonics.

"Whenever I got a break or had half-days, I would hang out at Ted's. We fast became exceptional friends and he would ask me to watch the store for him when he wanted to go to lunch with music reps.

He felt Ted Peckels was as gifted as a salesman as he was a musician.

"He had that magnetism and knew his music".

Ted was a great mentor and worked with Chauncey when he suggested to Ted that he open a second House of Music store over in his hometown of Redlands.

"I had lived in Redlands all my life. They had no real guitar store, just a standard music, band rental store. That part of the Inland Empire was ripe for a second House of Note. After thinking it over, he said, 'OK. You find a place downtown and if it looks like a good location we will go!'"

In late 1962, Chauncey opened Redlands' House of Note, located on 20 North Sixth, between State and Citrus.

"Ted taught me how to drum up business and not wait for it to come to you. He would call me and say, 'OK, we're going honky tonkin' tonight'. We would pack up some of the latest amps, reverbs and guitars and go out to the western joints. He knew all the players and we would let them try out the equipment on stage. They would love the stuff. Sure enough, the word got out and they and their friends would come into the stores and purchase.

"We specialised in guitars, banjos, drums and electronic keyboards. We carried all the major brands of acoustic and electric guitars. We also had the Fender franchise at the time.

"We taught acoustic and electric guitar, lap-steel, banjo and drums. We had five regular teachers and well over a hundred students. The teaching staff composed of Norman Sanders, Greg Tomquist, John W. Sessums III, C. P. Woods, Warren Wheeler, Dean Pickard and Casey Cunningham.

"Surf music was coming into its own, and many surf bands were formed at that time. During the summer the Chamber would promote `Sidewalk Sale Days' and we would provide the bands playing on all the major corners of town.

"One of the store's favourite teachers at the time was Roly Sanders, from the successful Tornadoes. Tom Sheeley, now a well-known classical guitarist and music instructor at Northern Arizona University in Flagstaff, was also one of the student-teachers. The store closed in late 1968."

I had a further conversation, via email, with Chauncey Romero on 4 August 2020.

Do you know any details on the Bartell fretless?

"I don't know how many were produced. I don't remember Ted ever being *not* keen on the idea, as suggested by Tom Mitchell. Ted had most of the influence on the design, and Paul Barth was the engineer. The only one I remember, I believe, I sold a Bartell fretless bass to was Jimmy Farager of the Peppermint Trolley Company band, who later became Bones."

You worked for Ted and looked after The House of Note?

"There was a whole different scene happening at this time with Ted and I. Basically I was now managing his House of Note Riverside store, so he could totally concentrate on Bartell. He turned the store over to me and we had weekly meetings. He hardly ever came in the store anymore. In all the times we had the stores together, we would talk every day and meet at least twice a week to brainstorm, so we always pretty much knew where we were at."

Do you have any knowledge on the fretless models that Jimi Hendrix had?

"No knowledge about Hendrix other than Ted mentioned the deals were happening. Ted was a very humble man. Not one to brag. He did get excited, but he never dwelled on it."

What was the deal with the Acoustic Control Corporation?

"I knew Ted was working deals with them, and they got along great. We handled the line of amps and did quite well. I had the great bass amp with reverse speaker. I was also playing five nights a week at the time."

What are your memories of Paul and Ted?

"There are so many memories of Paul and Ted. They went back quite a way. With all humility, I was so blessed. The memories are endless. There is almost a small cult-like following from that time period.

"I would not know where to start. But bottom line - if it was not for Ted Peckels, I never would have got to enjoy that special place in time. He is my mentor and hero. I loved him."

He knew a lot of people, including Leo Fender.

"Ted has a very rich history with the people of Fender and Rickenbacker, and that includes Barth. He told me many early stories and took me with him many times when he would visit. Whenever we went to Fender to pick up amps and guitars, we always ended up in the president's office, or at lunch, and Ted and Tommy Walker (general manager) would hash out old times. Everyone loved Ted. What was not to love?"

Chauncey had a band called The Hustlers, which included local resident Doug Grantz and Riverside neighbour John Tavaliogne, later the county commissioner.

After the success of their first single, 'Hangin' Five', on the House of Note Records label, on 21 January 1964 they made their next single, changing their name to The Original Hustlers, probably to differentiate the group from The Hustlers with Grant Baker.

The A-side was 'Cueball', written by L. Fields and published by David Marshall Co. On the B-side was 'Barefoot' an original by The Hustlers, credited to Bedwell, Grantz, Roach, Romero, Tavaliogne, and released on the La Belle record label (L-64121).

"In that photo, Roly Sanders and I have Mosrite guitars. We were the first dealers in our area to carry the Mosrite line, because again Ted was on top of the game and knew the people well. To me, in my memories, this is when Ted got his juices going to create his own line. You can see the influence of the style in the Bartell body and head. "

In 1968, the Redlands and Riverside branches of House of Note began running advertisements in the weekly *KMENtertainer* magazine, featuring a photo of a different band each week.

The 30 November 1968 issue features Morningside, a rock and jazz group from the University of Redlands which won a battle of the bands contest in Orange County, sponsored by Chauncey Romero.

In the 9 November 1968 issue, The Fireliters Quartet featured, a jazz group from the University of Redlands.

Jumping off the counter at Redlands' House of Note are (from the left) Gerald Sanders, Chauncey Romero, Roly Sanders, and Mike Bedwell, around 1965.
Credit: Mike Stax, Ugly Things magazine

SPOTLIGHT ON BANDS

"MORNINGSIDE" from the U. of Redlands Playing Rock and Jazz

CALL PRESTON OR MIKE AT 793-2121 ext 361 OR House of Note

Preston Bailey, bass, sax, guitar; Mike Gutin, guitar, bass, organ; ...drums,

Redlands HOUSE OF NOTE
FRANCHISED *Fender* DEALER
COMPLETE LINE OF STRINGS & GUITAR ACCESSORIES
WE SELL - RENT - TEACH - SERVICE
• DRUMS • GUITARS • UKES • MANDOLINS • BANJOS
CHAUNCEY ROMERO
CALL NOW!
793-3165
20 North 6th - REDLANDS
(Located in the Center of Downtown Redlands)

"The Fireliters Quartet" a jazz group from the University of Redlands features (back row) Pat Wilson, flute and sax, Gary Locke, drums - (front row) Steve Tarter, bass, and Ron Wogen, piano. (Call Ron 792-3035)

Tom Sheely said, "When I was 11, I wandered into Chauncey's store in Redlands, the House of Note. He asked if I played guitar and I said yes. He handed me this pretty, bright-red electric guitar and basically indicated with his eyes, 'Muestra me lo' ('show me'). So I played him 'Mr. Moto' and a couple of Ventures tunes. Three years later, I started teaching there, and the rest is history - thanks Chauncey! Eres hermano verdadero!"

Jack Kaminski Richard Kaminski recalled, "My Dad Jack worked for Ted in the '50s and '60s. I remember very vaguely that Ted moved the House of Note store from some old house on Magnolia Avenue in the Wood Streets District to the location in the business district at 6202 Magnolia Avenue, near the Riverside Plaza.

"I also remember visiting Ted's house with my parents once. It was a very nice house near the School for the Deaf. That was probably about 1959 or 1960. I do remember hearing commercials on radio stations KFXM and KMEN for the House of Note. For some unknown reason I remember the ones promoting the fretless guitar."

Gary Eye began working at the Riverside store when he was 13, sweeping the floors and doing various menial tasks. By the mid-'60s though, he was teaching guitar, bass and drums. By this time the store had so many young students, it became practically a garage band factory.

"One of the concepts we did was starting to teach bass, guitar and drums, and then put the guys together to start little bands. We did Battles of the Bands there in the parking lot of the old Muffler shop next door for years. It was just a different way of teaching them and it gave them a lot more incentive to want to learn."

Richard Weingärtner worked for Ted at his second music store, Coopers Action Music, from 1995 through to 1997. **Wes Lambert** recalled, "During the late '60s and early '70s, Paul Barth had a small repair shop on Magnolia Avenue in Riverside. Paul and his wife lived upstairs, over the shop, and also sold a few used and vintage instruments - most on consignment.

"I remember one of the early-model 'Frying Pan' lap-steels on display near the cash register. Paul was always willing to teach those who were interested how to properly maintain their instruments, and I was very fortunate to have the opportunity to spend many treasured hours working for and learning from not only a true master but also a genuinely nice man."

Craig J said, "I'm still looking for my beloved red Bartell Spyder guitar, which I traded in on a Fender Tele years ago in San Diego, bought at House of Note in Riverside. I took guitar lessons from Gary Eye there. It is very nerve-racking knowing it is out there and i can't find it."

Dave Guyton added, "I miss Ted Peckels and our trips to Sires. I played in a band with Mark, Ted's son, and used to spend days at Coopers Music with them, even using the back warehouse as a practice room. Last time in there as Mike's Music, our list was still glued to a post in the room we practised in. Great times."

Dana Darwezeh said, "I got my first real guitar from Barth's. That was in 1975. I still remember how exciting it was when my Dad drove me out there and said, 'Keep it under $75!'"

Devon Oxford

In June 2020, I managed to trace Devon Oxford for an online chat. He was great and tried really hard to recall stories from 50 years ago. He had some lovely memories.

"Don Underwood and I worked together for a long time, so I have a few memories that haven't faded away yet. Time is the greatest of thieves."

Devon's palm pedal on his Peavey T60

What do you remember about Paul Barth and Ted Peckels?

"Paul was a great guy and likeable, but he could run short of patience at times. I used to spend time and buy stuff at Cooper's Music on Magnolia, so I'm sure I knew Ted. Wow... 50 years ago!

"Don took over the shop in '73 or early '74 after Paul died. I was delighted when Don asked me to come and work with him.

"There's a pic of Don and I toasting over an Explorer I had finished building, and Don and I were sort of celebrating. This explorer later went to Joe Walsh of The Eagles (and also a member of The James Gang, Barnstorm, and Ringo Starr & His All-Starr Band)."

Do you still work on guitars?

"Yes, a bit, I have a few people (and pros) that will not let anyone but me work on their guitars. The last one was Phil Brown (the one that was with Little Feat for a while). He and I are pretty fair friends. I built many custom guitars at Barth Guitar Shop over the years. The quilted maple Strat that Don played all the time was one that I built for him."

Did you ever hear any stories of the Bartell fretless guitar? George Harrison got the first one from Al Casey, a sunburst; Jimi Hendrix got a black left-handed fretless, and Frank Zappa picked up one in the early '70s.

"I would love to play and own one of those! I had heard a little, but most of it was shortly before my time. I used to have a closet full of unfinished Bartell and Mosrite bodies in the '70s. Wish I had them now! Lot of that stuff - like the fretless Bartell guitar - belongs in a museum under bullet-proof glass. We did a lot of experimenting in those days!" For example we made a Flying V with a Fender neck that you can see Don playing (on page 71) Some bespoke guitars made at the Barth guitar shop were branded Oxwood - a combination of Devon Oxford's surname and the end of Don Underwood's.

Devon added, 'I made a prototype Oxford guitar I built in 1975/76. Don kept trying to desal me out of it! I probably did 10,000 gigs with it.

Ted Trujillo, a further former member of The Legendary Mustangs, founded in 1964 and working until 2016, based in Riverside. Trujillo held music lessons at the House of Note. He also performed with Psalm 150, a Christian ministry band.

"My brother Tom and I began taking lessons in April 1963," remembers Trujillo. "If memory serves me correctly, the first lessons were in a group setting with Ted Peckels as the instructor. My next teacher was Roly Sanders, the lead guitar player with the Tornadoes. I then began studying with Ralph Rose in 1964. I continued with him until 1969."

In the summer of 1966 Trujillo became an instructor at the Riverside store, working there until at least 1969.

"Ted Peckels was a great guy, truly excited about the instruments and the kids who played them. He provided me with a great job through high school and my first year of college.

"My world pretty much revolved around the House of Note during those times. Everybody hung out there and everybody in town bought their instruments from Ted.

"I remember Ted handing me a fretless guitar and asking for my opinion. I played it at House of Note."

The Legendary Mustangs were Terry Wade, Ted Trujillo, John Tavaglione, Dennis Lisonbee, Bruce Tucker and Allen Wald.

The Legendary Mustangs. Credit Marc Piron

Matt Law is a singer-songwriter, musician, master luthier and British motorcycle owner, based in Panama City, Florida, and recalled, "My friend Don Underwood bought that shop from Mr Barth when he retired. A few years ago Don himself passed away, and left me a whole lot of Barth Guitar Shop memorabilia, including the cash box, the sign from the door, many ledgers. There is lots of cool stuff, receipts from Rickenbacker, and Magnatone. An original P-90 type pickup from Paul Barth's workbench, probably hand wound by Barth himself! There are original engineering drawings for Magnatone pickups!"

Matt gave me a call on 7 April 2021, and it was great to catch up and share our findings. I started by asking how he got to know Don.

"I met Don in Panama City after the Barth guitar shop had been closed. It really pained Don, but it was time to move on. I did his tech work for him as he got to the point where he didn't trust his eyes and hands so much. The first guitar I worked on for him was also the last guitar I worked on before he passed away, a Fender Telecaster copy that looks like a '53/'54 Telecaster. I brought it from his ex-wife. Don had built it with a friend, When Don passed away, I'm glad I had this one little box from the Barth guitar shop. Don was a bit of a pack rat to put it mildly - he couldn't throw things away!

"I have a picture of Don playing a Flying V they made with three pick-ups, a Strat whammy and a Telecaster neck. Don's shop was a veritable who's who of southern California guitar builders that all became big names in the industry - Steve Soeast, Grover Jackson, Wayne Charvel ...

"Don Underwood was a really kind soul, one of the best guitarists I've ever known."

Musician and master luthier Matt Law

What do you know of Paul Barth?

"Mr Barth was very sharp, even though he was retired for maybe the fourth time, because he could never stand still! He retired from Rickenbacker and did the Magnatone thing, then he went to Bartell and then the Barth guitar shop, so he was a hard charger and a go-getter. Don told me Mr Barth had an old tube amp built into his workbench, with a jack that he plugged into, and a switch, it was right there in the bench if he needed to test the guitar."

I don't think many people had Barth on their radar, other than those in the industry who knew about Paul. Do you think he was forgotten, and other people took the limelight?

Matt Law's British bikes

"Absolutely, he was the nuts and bolts guy, George Beauchamp was the idea guy. Paul was, 'Yeah, I can build that'. Along with Harry Watson at Rickenbacker, they built the first wooden Frying Pan. Mr Barth figured out how to do things. That's why to me so much of the early Magnatone stuff looks like Rickenbacker. You can really see the influence, because Mr Barth helped design all those solid-body Rickenbackers before Roger Rossmeisl came along.

"I think Paul Barth was every bit as important as guys like Les Paul. It comes from being in the tool and die industry and working for Mr Rickenbacher at National, and Paul was in the factory where they stamped all the cones and bodies for National from a very early age. He had a great apprenticeship!"

I was put in touch with **Jim Klepper** via Facebook page 'We Grew Up in Riverside in the '60s and '70s'. He told me, "I worked at the Bartell facility preparing bodies and necks in 1969. I was only there for about six months, before I joined the USAF. I think the facility was beginning to scale down production when I quit in the fall of 1969.

Jim Klepper

"I remember both Ted Peckels and Paul Barth, but Ted more than Paul. As I recall, Paul was around more than Ted and he often had folks (that I did not know) around him. I worked primarily on solid body bass guitars. I was a regular at Ted's House of Note music store. If I remember correctly, the manufacturing was on Jarupa Road, north of the Riverside Municipal Airport.

"Ted was a very accommodating man, the reason I went to work for Bartell. I was on one of my (usually daily) trips to the House of Note to window-shop and jabber-jaw with like-minded hanger-outers when Ted overheard me talking to a friend about losing my job. He asked if I knew anything about woodworking. He gave me a job, the rest is history.

"I remember Ed Ballentine, but did not really 'know' him. I fed him necks and bodies for paint and I got them back later for buffing, but we did not associate beyond that. The blanks were actually roughed out with basic prep at another location, then sent to us for finish work.

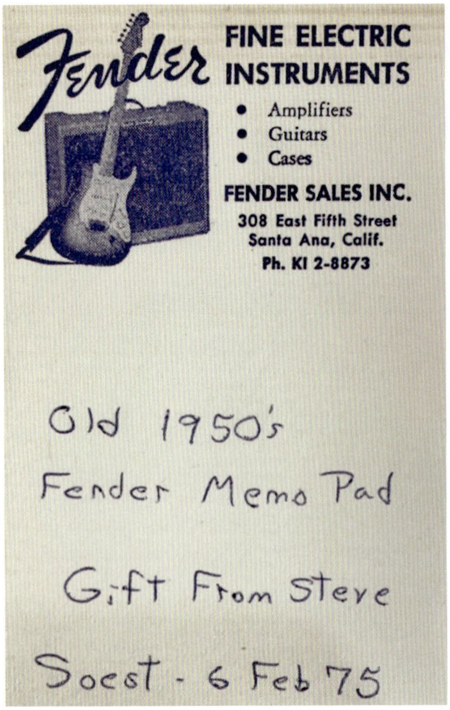

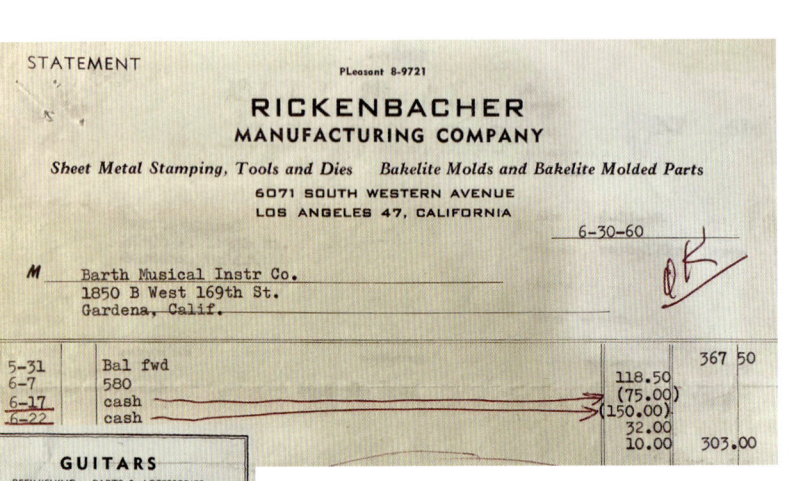

"I don't remember ever putting any branding on the headstocks at all. I remember some of us used to write some pencil notes on the body under the neck slot.

"I was in high school with Ted Trujillo and knew him from the store."

I also spoke to **Glenn Ross Campbell** on 23 July 2020, first asking how it all started for him.

"I got a bug in my ear that I wanted to take guitar lessons. My parents didn't have a lot of money although they really loved music. In the '50s my Dad moved from San Diego, when I was about seven.

"Someone told me there was this guy in walking distance from where I lived that gave guitar lessons. He was Navajo Indian, with an Irish name, Pat McGill, up in Arlington. I kept bugging my Mum about it and she said we didn't have the money for that kind of stuff, buying a guitar and all that. I finally talked her into it though, and she took me down there.

"I had a lesson on a regular guitar, but wasn't sure that's what I was looking for. Pat McGill said what kind of guitar are you looking for, I said it's kind of flat and there's something in your left hand that you slide up and down. Ah you mean, a steel slide guitar!

"He took me back and gave me a steel guitar lesson, and that was it, that's exactly what I wanted. My Mum then supported me and talked Dad into getting me a model.

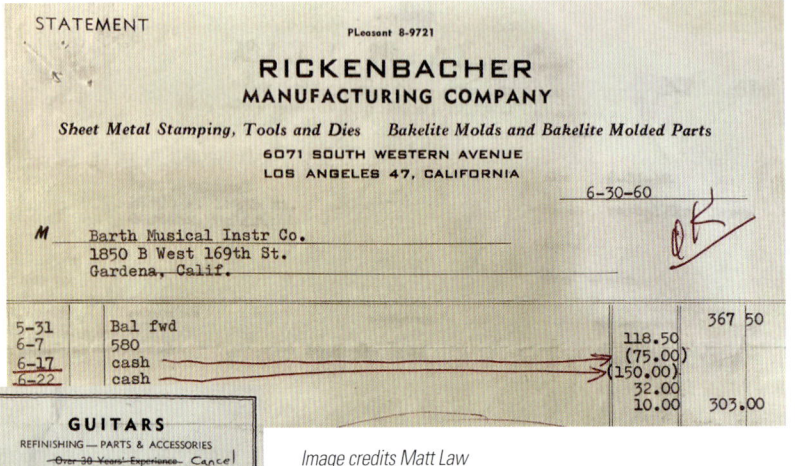

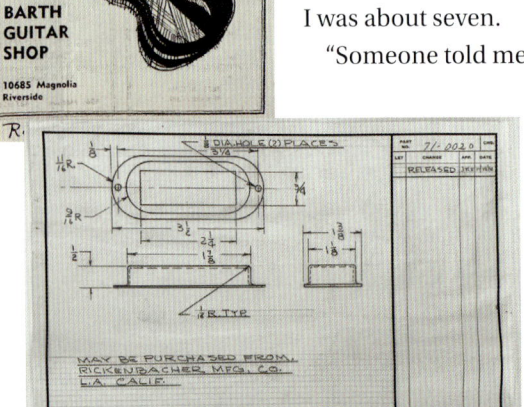

Image credits Matt Law

The Goldtones

"Pat taught me how to read music and apply it, he had a little band that was really good and I ended up in it and became one of his better students. We worked all over the place, on parades, band contests and that type of thing. We took disabled kids to Disneyland, and stuff like that.

"We moved after three years. I found another place with steel guitars all over the shop, Ted Peckels' House of Note.

I started lessons in the beginners' class. They had what they called spiders that you could connect five or six guitars that fed into a PA or amplifier. I figured out that where everyone had to set their guitar to midway volume, if I turned mine up and got louder everyone else got quieter. I made sure I got heard!

"Ted had a teacher, a guy that played music in Hawaii, lap-steel and all kind of instruments, but he went blind unfortunately. Then I join lessons with a girl who was teaching Hawaiian. It's a special complexity that I enjoyed.

"She used to hire a drummer to put on shows call Randy Seol. I formed a band with him called The Goldtones, and ventually we got a girl bass player from Ted Peckels' store. She was really good.

"We were just young teenagers. We won a big band contest at the Riverside High School two years in a row, so there was no way they were going to let us win again. We did a radio broadcast and got some good exposure from that."

Did you know Paul Barth?

"Yeah, I knew him - I had been in his place a bunch of times. I played in another band, The Urbles, with Roy Harris - he had this fuzztone distortion box that he got from New York, but man, was it expensive! He loaned it to me, it sounded fantastic, but the price was outrageous.

"I took it apart as I was pretty good at building stuff, but they had scrapped off all the code numbers on the transistors, so it couldn't be copied.

Glenn went onto bigger things with The Misunderstood

"I was down at Bartell telling them this story, and they said, 'We make distortion boxes'. It was a fraction of the price of the New York one, so I said yeah, make me one. It was called a Shatterbox, handmade by Doug Donaghue. It became part of my sound, big time.

"We were going big time over in England at the time. The Shatterbox is probably over there somewhere, as I had to trade everything in when times got bad.

"Ted Peckels took me down to the Fender company. That wasn't far from where we lived. I met Mr Fender, they were great people. He was really great, he just sorted me two white concert amps, but he never actually sold them that way.

"Then I had a lunchbox reverb which he covered the same way in white Tolex with a maroon grill cloth. They were very distinctive Fender amps. They raised a lot of interest in England when I took them over there. They had four 10's in them with white Tolex in them, which was unusual, and they were mostly brown. I really liked the look of the white ones.

"The Fender girls worked outside, dipping pickups in boiling wax which could catch fire quite easily. They had benches outside, smoking and dipping in hot wax. They had to keep it at the right temperature to sink deep into the pickup, but it could have blown up anytime. It was crazy days!

"Bartell gave me a great head start, and that Shatterbox gave me a lot of my sound!"

Glenn went on to bigger things with The Misunderstood. Incidentally, Tolex was a 1940s-era brand name that belonged not to Fender but to the General Tire and Rubber Company of Akron, Ohio.

You came to England then. What was the story there?

"British DJ John Peel … or John Ravenscroft - he was always changing his name - was working at KMEN Radio, and we met him at Tyler Mall in Riverside, where bands got up and played. We were the last ones on. He saw my steel guitar.

"He just fell in love with us, got hold of us and set up some recording. He wanted us to go to England, we were adventurous and wanted to go too. We took all our gear with us. The bass player got us some transformers from an airbase just outside of London, as the UK electrics were different.

"It wasn't exactly a grand arrival in England. John led the band to believe that they could stay with his parents in London. Arriving with all their gear by taxi, there was no-one at home to greet them.

"Mountain of equipment—amps, drums, all in cardboard boxes. We're sitting there, it starts raining on us, and we're pulling out raincoats and putting it over the equipment and getting soaked. Pretty soon the neighbours get curious, because we'd been there overnight. They came the next morning and brought us cups of tea and more blankets. We were all wrapped up like Indians on a reservation.

"We're there, literally, for a couple of days. Finally, John's parents come home. And they walked straight by us, didn't even look at us. We went banging on the door and said, 'Excuse us, but we're The Misunderstood.' And they go something like, 'Yeah, we can believe it!' The band had to wait yet another eight hours before Peel's parents got hold of their son in the States to confirm the story and let the Californians enter.

"John had arranged for his brother to have a lot of The Misunderstood flyers and bio's to take around London agents and managers before we arrived. But he never did that, not even one.

Glenn at Neil Finn's Roundhead Studios. Photo: Glenn Campbell

"When we finally got into his parents' place, the flyers were all in a box in the bedroom. That was a lot of money wasted."

The band eventually secured a deal with Fontana Records and released their first single, 'I Can Take You to the Sun' in December 1966. After a short-lived career in England, the band were forced to split.

"I eventually sold all our gear, including the white Tolex Fender amps to a little shop in London, as we were broke after being stitched up by our crooked roadie, who left us stranded in Paris.

"We got stuck on the ferry between Paris and England for three days as neither country would let us in, we were starving and had to grab food off of other people's plates.

A nine-string slide that Glenn put together

"When we finally got into England, we were stuck in cells for three days before we were released and made it back to London, where I had to sell all the gear to buy a ticket to be home."

Derek Lind Band - Glenn on the right

"If I had to list the 10 greatest performances I've seen in my life, one would be The Misunderstood at Pandora's Box, Hollywood, 1966. My God, they were a great band!" – John Peel

Dale Fortune grew up in Santa Ana, California and knew most guitar companies and people involved in the design and manufacture of instruments in the region.

Dale, a very well-respected luthier and renowned Rickenbacker expert, knew Paul Barth back in the mid-1960s, up until he passed away. He also knew 'Doc' Kauffman, Leo Fender, George Fullerton, Forrest White, and the Hall family.

Dale has quite a bit of history and information about Barth and Magnatone Guitars made and designed in the mid-1950s, while Paul was working for FC Hall, the new owner of Electro-String Rickenbacker Guitars.

"I first met 'Doc' Kauffman in the summer of 1964, when he helped me build a bass guitar for my band. In 1965 I bought a double pickup Barth Guitar from Doc, it was nice and sounded good but I didn't keep it very long. I sold it and bought a Gibson ES 330 guitar, which I still play regularly.

"When The Beatles came around, both Lennon and Harrison had the Epiphone Casino. That's what I wanted, but there were none in the music stores in the area, so I bought effectively the same guitar in that 1966 Gibson ES330. It had a scratchy volume control, so I took it to Doc Kauffman, who wanted to drill a hole in it, which I didn't want him to do, so I took it home and fixed it myself with some contact cleaner.

"In the 1950s, Paul designed the small body guitar that later became the Rickenbacker 325 Capri, used by John Lennon.

"Paul designed all the early 1953 Rickenbacker Guitars. When FC Hall bought the company, he retained Paul to stay on and build electric guitars when they made the transition from lap-steel slide guitars over to solid body electric guitars. I've also built quite a few of those as replicas."

Dale remembers the original 1953 Rickenbacker single truss rod was designed by Paul Barth in the late '50s.

"Although I met Paul Barth a few times I didn't know him very well. In the early 1970s I made trips to Paul's shop and house off Highway 91 in Riverside, and purchased various tools and parts from him as he was slowly winding down his business. What I remember most about Paul is he was a very humble person who was easy to talk to and share ideas."

Dale Fortune

From a young age Dale became fascinated with fixing, building and modifying guitars. He worked for the Electro-String Corporation in the early 1970s, along with Steve Soest, who also grew up in Santa Ana and had been working on guitars since the mid-1960s.

In the early 1970s, Dale went over to Rickenbacker and got a job starting in the woodworking department, putting bindings on. Over time he learned everything about building, by hand, Rickenbacker guitars. He was employed by Rickenbacker from 1972 to 1976.

Dale owns a Mk 1 Barth guitar with its original case, made in the 1950s. He also owned other Barth guitars in the 1960s. Some were Magnatone and some were Barth models, all the type that resembled a 325 Rickenbacker, with a longer fret scale.

"Over 30 years ago, a good friend gave me a single-pickup Magnatone Barth guitar that has all the original parts but needs restoration, because someone stripped the body finish and painted the pick-guard a maroon colour.

"Did you know that 'Pipeline' by The Chantays was played and recorded by Bob Spickard on a single-bridge pickup Barth solid body guitar?"

Magnatone Barth guitar restoration

In a 1963 photograph, you'll see Bob Spickard (middle) with his Barth guitar, and Dale with his Barth guitar. Bob Spickard's Barth guitar can be seen on display at the Surf Museum in Huntington Beach, California

The Chantays' 'Pipeline' was written by Bob Spickard and Brian Carman, the band from Santa Ana and playing surf music all over Orange County.

Robb Lawrence, a good friend of Bob from The Chantays, confirmed he used his Barth guitar on 'Pipeline'. That was the surf-rock outfit's only charting Billboard Top-40 hit, but is considered one of the staples of the genre.

By 1975, Dale had turned his garage into his own guitar shop. The following year he had to upscale his operation and move into a 1,000 square foot unit with three employees, two of whom went on to become master builders for Fender's custom shop.

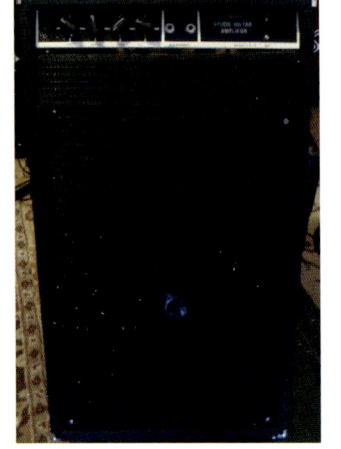

"In 1976 when Paul McCartney was on his Wings over America tour and doing a soundcheck at The Forum, his bridge triple-pickup failed on his bass. It was taken to Santa Ana to the Rick factory. They couldn't recharge the magnets on the horseshoe pickup, they were dead, so that had to be replaced with a new high-gain bridge pickup, replacing the pick-guard also as it was cracked and chipped. It was all bare wood and needed a clean-up, a light sanding and light coat of sealer on the bare wood."

In 1983, Dale moved to Aloha, a quiet location 15 miles west of Portland, Oregon where he lovingly maintains much-loved guitars for discerning clients at Fortune Guitars.

Of his Bartell amp, Dale added, "I also bought a Bartell CA-10 amp from the original owner three years ago. It has an amazing tone and sounds just like a vintage Fender Deluxe amp."

Steve Soest runs Orange County's longest-running, owner-operated independent guitar repair shop, operating for nearly 50 years, located in historic Old Town Orange, California.

His impressive rock star client list has included the Rolling Stones, Eric Clapton, Stevie Ray Vaughan, and Slash, and we spoke to each other on 17 August 2020, when I started by asking him what he remembered about Bartell guitars and Paul Barth.

"I spent a lot of time with Paul Barth at his shop on Magnolia in Riverside, California. I'm so happy that somebody is ready to recognise Paul Barth. I felt so bad when I knew him that he got no recognition for anything, especially from the Hall family at Rickenbacker. He did a lot there, and it's as if he didn't exist in their archives."

From what I understand of Paul, he was a clever guy, an inventor and innovator who would try a lot of different things. He was a quiet unassuming guy, and maybe people took advantage.

"I was never happy with the way Rickenbacker treated Paul Barth. They never gave him credit for his designs they used. Roger Rossmeisl got all the credit! I don't know what happened, but he was erased from their history."

How did you know Paul?

"I've met a few people over the years that worked for him, especially when he had his shop on Harbor Boulevard in Santa Ana, California and was working at Magnatone in Torrance.

"I knew of him because I was collecting catalogues and memorabilia and had the early national catalogue with his photo on it, when he was the vice-president of National, and I thought, that's important.

"Then at one point, I had met George Beauchamp's son, Nolan. I was working at the pawn shop and was playing a Rickenbacher Frying Pan lap-steel, some guy walks in and he's watching me, and he starts crying. He says, 'Oh, that brings back a lot of memories in my childhood. My father was the one that designed that instrument'. I said, "You're kidding me!"

So I became friendly with Nolan, and he told me stories about all the things that happened to Rickenbacker. Then Paul Barth's name came up and he said, 'Well, I don't know where Paul is'.

Did you meet Paul?

"I used to go out to all the pawn shops and I would fill up my van and buy cases, amps, pedals and guitars, and I was on Riverside one day and was driving down a little side-street from the freeway, and there's a sign, Barth Guitar Shop, so I dropped in.

"It was a freestanding building with a little staircase going upstairs to an apartment upstairs. I stopped in there, and there's some older guy, working on some frets, and I looked around and he had cool stuff, so I started talking to him and he told me he was Paul Barth. I said, "Man, I've been wanting to meet you all these years.

"I became friendly with him and would go by once a month, on my route, and talk to him whilst he worked, and sometimes guys would bring stuff in to sell to him, and he didn't want it. And he'd just go, if you want it, just go ahead', and I go, 'No Paul, I'll give you money for it,' and he'd just go, 'No, no'. He would never take any money for it. He was so nice to me.

"Paul showed me how he did fret-work and heating up necks to straighten them out. Kind of like Doc Kaufmann was. He was the same way with me, he was very nice when I was a kid. And I would just sit and watch him work for hours at a time. So I felt very special because I got to know Paul.

"I accompanied Robbie Lawrence one day, and spent several hours interviewing him. Barth told us it was the only interview he ever did. It has never been published. Robbie being the historian and photographer, he would take pictures wherever we would go".

Well, now would be a good time to dust that down and have a look at that again.

"Yeah, it would, because that's the missing link, right there."

What do you know about Paul before the Bartell setup?

"Paul worked on Harvard Boulevard in Santa Ana, down by Harvard first street, doing repairs, and built a lot of the Barth guitars there. He would get up in the morning, drive all the way to Torrance. There were no Freeways yet, and he would work at Magnatone all day, then come home, with a cocktail and a six-pack of beer waiting for him. Paul would stay up until midnight, working on guitars, go to sleep, get up at 6am and drive to Torrance again, five days a week.

"That must have been the late 1950s, and the Magnatone catalogue shows Barth instruments in it."

When Paul died in 1973, how did you hear about that?

"Robb Lawrence called me when he died. Paul had a daughter who called to tell him.

"There was a nice little set-up. The shop was downstairs, a repair shop, an office and a little showroom. He always had cool lap-steels and tweed amps and things. You'd go in there, he was very reasonable, I would always buy something from him and talk a little bit.

"There was a batch of stuff that turned up when Paul passed. A guy named Jerry Sceusa, from a cobbler down in Midway City. When I was a kid I lived in Westminster, and I would ride my bike down his shop, he re-wound a pickup for a Les Paul Junior and we got talking about things. I lost touch with him. He moved to Arizona.

"Years later, about 28 years ago, I drove out to Prescott, Arizona and I see a little ad, 'We Fix Guitars', so I drove two miles out of town into a little block building with a smokestack coming out of it. It's freezing cold, middle of winter. I walked in, this guy turned around from behind the counter, and it's Jerry Sceusa! He kind of looked like Geppetto from the *Pinocchio* story, an old guy with a moustache and white hair. A craftsman. Soon after, he got sick and moved to be with his daughter down in Tucson.

"When he passed away, a guy who had a shop on Huntingdon Beach, Orange County went down there and brought all his stuff, there were barrels of Barth Guitars, necks, bodies, and the German tremolo he used on some of the Barth guitars. I got a whole bunch of stuff from him and told the guy I would come back next week and buy all the Barth stuff. I was a big fan of his. I went back the next week and the store was closed and empty. There were probably 40 necks and 20 bodies left and some of the pick-guard material that looked like patio covering, that fibre-glass stuff he used, a kind of green colour with the little specks in it. Kluson gears, all kind of stuff. I missed out on that. That was the last Barth stuff that popped up.

"At one time there was a guy out in the Inland Empire in San Bernardino who had a shop called Woody and Lena's. They were from Nashville originally, and she was a recording session player. They were closing their store and called me out to their barn. It was full of Mosrites, Standel, Barths and Bartells!

"He said this was all my inventory from my store, did I want it? There were brand new, old stock, St George 12-strings, zipper bags in metallic red and green. I brought everything he had and there was like a couple of the Bartell double-necks, unfinished, just the bodies, the German carve with the bound body and the f-hole. I was able to put them together with the parts I got from before and sold them. Those were really cool, they were 6/12 double-necks."

Do you have any Barth/Bartell stock remaining?

"I think it's all gone now, that was at my last shop. I've been here for eight years. It's probably 25 years since I went out to Woody's place and cleared out the barn. There were Mosrite celebrity models, new and old stock, serial number 3, 4 and 5, that kind of stuff. I thought I better buy it or somebody else will!"

Did you ever see the Bartell six-string fretless model?

"No, I never saw one. Did they have some weird fingerboard, a phenolic fingerboard, with little cuts in it so you

The Danelectro Hodad model was the first ground-up design by Steve

could see where you were, fret-markers?"

Exactly right. Did you know Al Casey and his Hollywood music store?

"I met him when he retired out in Palm Desert. He bought a motel. I ran into him at a swap meet at night, it was too hot during the day. He said stay over, call me tomorrow morning, I'll take you over to my place. In each of the motel rooms, one was full of lawnmowers, one full of TVs, one was full of dishes, and he had a motel room full of guitars, so I brought 20 guitars. Next time I went out there nobody knew where he went."

"This is all fascinating to me and it's sad that it's all slipping away. I'm very happy that you want to tell the story."

The reoccurring theme of Paul Barth being largely ignored in the history books is recognised by the author of the excellent Magnatone website. A detailed history of the company highlights the impact Barth had on a number of Magnatone models and his highly-regarded influence on the ongoing development of the electric guitar.

"Barth designed the Rickenbacker Combo 600 and 800 guitars for Electro-String. As iconic as the Rick combo guitar design has become, it is amazing that Paul Barth's name is not more well known. That design is the basis of what became the signature design accents of the Rickenbacker guitar."

Doug Donaghue

Sadly, Doug Donaghue passed away in recent years, but he had great knowledge and memories of his time at Bartell and posted on the excellent Bartell guitar fansite, describing his invention, the Bartell Shatterbox.

"I can absolutely guarantee that I built that one, in my garage, because I designed it and laid out the single-sided printed circuit board that it's built on, taped up the artwork, printed the silkscreen, hand cut and screened the circuit boards, drilled them, etched them - that etching solution is nasty stuff - and soldered in all of the components and tested them.

"There were only 100 ever built and I built every last one of them with my very own two little hands.

"Inside it's a fairly simple little transistor amplifier - if I remember correctly I used a 2N2222 - that's biased near cut-off, so the tops of the signal get 'clipped' and cause a lot of odd-order harmonic distortion. I wanted to re-mix the original signal with the distorted signal inside the box, but Ted convinced me it would be better to bring the two signals out so the performer could put them through two channels of their amplifier and adjust the tone and volume of each independently."

Chris Ellington also remembered the Shatterbox, adding, "Wow, blast from the past. I do remember those. Doug was the son of Ray Massey, who worked in the amp and electronics department. They also worked on a very small distortion unit that plugs into the guitar and a cord plugs into it."

The Bartell Shatterbox was part of Glenn Ross Campbell's early arsenal, after first seeing Roy Harris use one in their short-lived band together, The Urbles.

David Sandell was the house sound engineer for Temecula Stampede. He sadly passed away towards the end of 2019, but worked with Paul Barth, Tommy Mitchell et al, at Bartell and recorded his memories.

"I remember Paul teaching me how to use the pickup winding contraption he made of a floor drill press with a lot of special jigs to make it work right. John Kinder once said he had some of the original pickups and possibly a Black Widow guitar. There were a lot of fretless basses when I worked there in 1970. Ted Peckels was a trip!"

Dave Arine was also there at the time, and added, "It's exciting to know how far our guitars made it about."

As I neared completion of the book, I was missing photos of the Bartell site and the crew that worked there. Then thankfully, **Glenn Miller** turned up with his memories and photos.

The Bartell Shatterbox, part of Glenn Ross Campbell's early arsenal, after first seeing Roy Harris. Photos Dave Friedman

"Ted Peckels was cool. I bought a guitar and was short on all the funds, so we shook and I was on the books. Myself and five or six pals all worked at Bartell, and I took many photos. There is a lot of history just with Paul Barth alone. Ted was in and out daily while running the House of Note. Paul was the boss on a daily basis, with Ray supporting him. They were very smooth, easy to talk to.

"In the shop we made amps on contract for Hohner, named Contessa, and I ran the wood shop in its last days until the place was sold. There was an electronics area headed by 'Rolaid Ray' with a team of gals doing the electric bench work. In the rear of the plant was the wood shop, headed by myself, with up to five or six workers at times. On the production line, the amp and speaker boxes were produced and then went down the line to the hot glue and covering department. From there they went to have the speaker and grill cloth installed, before the electronics department installed the amp and wiring. Finally, they were tested, boxed and readied for shipping.

"The centre of the plant was where the various guitars were built, The work crew was made up of a bunch of local music guys and all their weird pals - Tommy Mitchell, Tiny (Roy Tontini), Doug Chandler, Eric Weisbrod, Glenn Miller, Dick Chandler, Eddy Florio, Keyboard Bert, Chip Larson, Mark Pape, Tex (Phil Geribeno), Brother

Jake, Larry Cass, plus the gals up front. There was always a crew of 20 to 25, depending on how many orders we got for amps and guitars.

"As time passed, Ted sold out to a German firm that had connections to Hohner. They brought in their own employees to just produce the Hohner brand name items, and from there who knows what happened, we were all out of a job!

"From the old crew, many have passed, some went on to produce their own items, Tommy Mitchell started his own music store and went on to produce Mitchell speakers. He was an inventor and the 'Folded Horn' speaker may be credited to him.

"And it was always a fun time working there with this band of Blues, Country and Rock playing 1960s misfits - we all played. We clicked, we had great times and were a great team.

"When the place sold I got the two company cats, Boomer and Willard. OMG, what memories!

"Fast forward about 40 years and reading an old guitar mag I decided to do a search on Paul Barth. What a treasure and innovator of many of the early electric guitar tricks, fine-wire hand-wound pickups and more. Glad I was part of Bartell to its last days!"

"Paul Barth? He never bragged. Just a soft, quiet, genius type, never uptight." – Glenn Miller

Robb Lawrence

If there is just one person you need to talk to about the history of the guitar, resonators, Rickenbacker, National, Electro-String, and basically anything related to the development of the electric guitar and the main players involved, get in touch with Robb Lawrence. Better still, buy his excellent books. Robb can certainly be regarded as one of the most knowledgeable guitar historians, with a wealth of important historical contacts and industry friends, and a plethora of magazine articles and publications to his name.

I had my chance to speak to the renowned Mr Lawrence on 25 August 2020. I only regret that I didn't find Robb sooner. Our conversation went like this.

How did it all start for you?

"I started with a Kay acoustic then a Fender Duosonic guitar in the early '60s in San Diego. I graduated to a Gibson Les Paul while teaching in 1967. On my guitar safari I met Les Paul in 1972 through Bud Eastman, founder of *Guitar Player* magazine. We soon became great friends. That friendship grew when I lived with him, Wally Kamin and his son Bobby. Years later it resulted in a two-volume, boxset on his career and famous signature guitar.

"The historical aspects originally started for me by meeting inventor John Dopyera and his apprentice Dave Flood at the Fiddle & Fret shop in nearby Escondido. David is still one of my best friends. I soon started interviewing John, and eventually his brothers Rudolph and Emile. Then I met Paul and Martin Barth, and George Beauchamp's brother Jess and son Nolan to hear the rest of the story. They were the nuts and bolts behind the Resophonic and first electric guitars.

"Paul Barth, with his brother Carl were spinning the first resonators for John and George, setting the National company in motion. A few years later, after the Dopyeras left to do Dobro, Paul helped design the single resonator models and was winding pickup coils with George. I never met Carl, but I did meet his father Martin Barth, who was the National factory foreman.

"Adolph Rickenbacher became the engineer, stamping out the production metal bodies because he had the only deep-draw press for molding auto-body parts on the West Coast. I spent a couple of days with Adolph. During our interviews we visited Martin and his wife (sister of the Dopyeras). They hadn't seen each other for a long time.

FINDING FRETLESS

Doug Wires at the Bartell factory

Eric covering speakers, The Bartell Factory

Lunch time crew,

The Bartell factory parking lot

Dick Chandler and Glenn Miller.

Rolaid Ray and Glenn Miller, image credits Glenn Miller

I brought him by Steve Soest's shop to say hello and then we went around the corner to Martin's home.

"Mr Rickenbacher was great to spend time with, and quite lucid. He showed me the bakelite 'Kleen-Between'" toothbrush he kept in his dresser, lots of fascinating photographs, and even gave me some of his old catalogues.

"I also knew Don Underwood, who worked with Paul Barth."

You actually interviewed Paul?

"Yes, that was when I was doing most of my Fender and Rickenbacker interviews. I was out doing interviews all around Orange County, I would come up from San Diego on the train and stay with Steve Soest. Don Underwood invited us to come out to see Paul Barth. Steve Soest and I went to his upstairs apartment above his shop and he basically 'spilled the beans' to us. Paul had a lot to talk about. In my interview with him you can hear the ice rattling in Paul's glass. He and George had become drinking buddies at National.

"Paul marvelled at how Freddie Tavares and Leo Fender could get such beautiful tonal output from a Fender pro amp with so few parts. Paul worked on the Rickenbacker amps through the years, including those cool grey ones. Paul had a lot of respect for Freddie and Leo as a team."

What happened with Paul Barth when the Dopyera brothers left National?

"John Dopyera explained to me why. Emile, Rudolph and John left because there was a lot of mayhem going on back in the '20s. There were fist fights and target practice in the factory. Coupled with all that drinking, it got pretty rough. George and Paul became great drinking buddies, their friendship became very strong. The Dopyeras were teetotalers! They were developing the spider bridge and concave/convex resonators.

"When the Dopyera brothers left National they wanted Paul to come with them to Dobro, and Paul told Steve (Soest) and I that he couldn't kick his best friend in the teeth, so he stayed with National. The alcohol situation at National was difficult for John and Emile. Rudolph was reluctant to talk because he was still bitter about it all. I talked to Jess Beauchamp, George's brother too. He had become bitter about the whole story because some non-factual articles had come out.

"This was before I started writing for *Guitar Player* magazine. I discovered these articles upset a number of people that were involved. Paul made some statements about the later National/Dobro company that quite startled Steve and I.

"Back in 1971, it all seemed like such a fascinating novel to me. Over the years I've given four-hour slideshow lectures on all three companies. They created a revolution that I have written a trilogy about - National, Dobro and Rickenbacker - featuring my interviews, ads, catalogues, portraits and hundreds of colour transparencies of instruments I've shot since the early '70s. Paul unfortunately died shortly after I interviewed him, so I guess I am the only person who ever interviewed Paul Barth. He had a real hand in the amplified guitar more than anyone I ever met. And I have it all on tape!"

"I am the only person who interviewed Paul Barth" – Robb Lawrence

"I love the old Magnatones and the Rickenbackers that Paul designed. I thought Paul Barth was overlooked in the history books. I feel Barth's name should be included on a number of patents for his input with Beauchamp. I love the history, the fact that the electric guitar was co-designed by Paul Barth on his mother's kitchen table, with a sewing machine. It was fantastic, and at nearly the same time, Art Stimson up there in Seattle was working on an electric guitar pickup with Paul Tutmarc.

"Art left up there with their idea and came down to Dobro. Vic Smith told me about that story. Seems great things came out of the ether, with multiple similar inventions and different people. They kind of all happened out of necessity at the same time."

"I love the history, the fact that the electric guitar was co-designed by Paul Barth" – Robb Lawrence

Did you know Al Casey?

"Yes, I did. Mitch Holder was a good friend of his, *The Tonight Show* guitarist and a protege of Howard Roberts. I met Al once, but I understand his wife Maxine bought that fretless guitar up to Blue Jay Way for George Harrison.

"During 1973 I did a number of interviews with Leo Fender, George Fullerton, Freddie Tavares and Bill Carson. Because of my friendship with John Dopyera, Bob Eastman from *Guitar Player*, and Les Paul, who in turn put me in touch with Julius Bellson, Seth Lover, Walt Fuller from Gibson … it blossomed into a series of seven books. I felt it was important to gather this history before these people died.

"So I went out and interviewed the guitar players and folks behind the scenes in these factories. At the time no one used the term vintage, they were just used guitars!"

Les Paul and Robb Lawrence - Milwaukee book signing. Photo: Erol Reyal

FRETTING OVER THE NUMBERS

Bearing in mind Bartell also rebranded their products for Hohner, St George, Lancer, Contessa and the Acoustic corporation, how many fretless six-string Bartell/Acoustic guitar models were made?

Although Bartell made a wide range of models, they were innovators, experimenting with designs, styles and configurations. It is still possible today to find the popular fretless bass, or a double-neck six and 12-string combo, but the six-string fretless model was a prototype and market tester, with numbers unconfirmed but evidence suggesting only seven or eight were made and the guitar failed to reach production.

Unfortunately, Dave Peckels, son of Ted Peckels, confirmed that no known company records, inventories or ledgers exist.

There was no fretless six-string model listed in the 1969 Acoustic Control product catalogue, despite a fretless bass being included.

On 1 July 2019 I called former Acoustic employee Harvey Gerst and spoke to both him and his wife Karen to ask them how many fretless guitars there were.

Harvey relied, "There were very few of those made."

We think maybe four at the most (only learning later about a few more fretless models).

ac 500 black widow
Designed for the serious "blues" player, special weighted bridge for maximum string sustain, steel guitar dual pick-ups with individually adjustable pole pieces, separate volume and tone controls for each pick-up, three-position pick-up selector, precision gear-driven high ratio tuning keys, and padded back. Beautifully finished in hand-rubbed black laquer with triple binding. "Ebonite" fret board.

ac 600 black widow bass ac 600 fretless black widow bass
Identical specifications to AC 500 Black Widow.

ac 650 ss black widow
Identical specifications to AC 600 except short-scale bass neck.

ac 700 black widow 12-string
Identical specifications to AC 500 Black Widow.

Harvey responded, "Yes, that sounds about right."

Although Bartell made a fretless bass for Hohner, there seem to be no records or evidence that a six-string fretless guitar was ever produced and branded Hohner by the Bartell company.

Scrutinising Hohner's historical records, there is a fretless guitar that was manufactured decades later, between 1993 and 1996, detailed as a model JB FL fretless. Guitar hardware:

2 x Volume Control

Tone Control

Pickup Configuration: 3

However, the Hohner fretless bass model was identical to the Bartell fretless guitar - all of them made by Bartell. Spot the similarity. Confusing!

Photo credits, Bonhams Wessex Auction Rooms and Dave Peckels

On 6 May 2020, former Bartell employee Chris Ellington contacted me, and said, "I finally got hold of Tom Mitchell. Interesting information he had. There were about 60 fretless guitars made, most were black, and around 12 were sunburst. Two were made for Hendrix, both left-handed."

That changed the picture considerably. Was Tom correct, or was he confusing the fretless bass model with the fretless six-string guitar?

He replied, "I assumed we were talking about guitars. I was also surprised with the count. I know assumed is a word that counts here and will find out exactly what he was saying. The fretless guitar was Tom's idea (Ted Trujillo said this, and Tom confirmed this). Ted didn't think it would work but went along with it. Remember two were made for Hendrix, both left-handed. He knew The Beatles had a fretless and John had some of his Mitchell amps. Just a side-note, Tom built a toilet-seat bass back in the mid-'60s, maybe the first!"

Well, there was something to go on, and I then spoke to Tom Mitchell that same day, first pointing out that he mentioned he helped design the fretless bass, you can still find them out there and they are very popular, people having very good things to say about them, so he obviously did a good job.

"Yeah, the fretless was not a real go-getter, because it was hard to comprehend, you know, to play, to know where you are at, so they weren't real famous that way. But as far as bass playing, they were really good, being good tone quality and everything."

What I am particularly interested in is … well, let me give you the background and the story of where I'm coming from. A friend of mine, a musician since the '60s who toured with Cat Stevens, Jimi Hendrix, Tina Turner …

"I did stuff with Jimi!"

That's cool, and Ray Russell, who lives in England, was busy on the London music scene as a session player for lots of people. I have been friends with him for a few years now and he posted on Facebook that he had this six-string Bartell fretless, not the bass but the six-string. He didn't know much about it, that's when the research began, so to cut a long story short, we took it along to the *Antiques Roadshow* TV programme in the UK, it caused a lot of interest and bit of a media sensation, because they valued it at $500,000, because it was associated with The Beatles.

Ray got it because he worked on a film with George Harrison in 1985 and was playing the fretless Bartell, and George said, 'You play it better than I do, why don't you keep it'. So that's how Ray got it. Anyway, I'm writing a book and adding some history about Bartell, particularly the six-string fretless models. What can you tell me about those particular guitars? I believe there were very few of those made.

"Very few, very few."

About four or five, or less or more?

"You are talking probably 16, maybe 17 of them at the most."

Can you remember much about them? We have stories about one being given to The Beatles. And Jimi Hendrix had two, I believe, both left-handed. Is that correct?

"Yeah."

Both black?

"Oh yeah. I started the first sunburst one, because they were all black at first, then I started making some with sunburst on them."

That's great, as the one George Harrison gave to Ray is sunburst.

"Yeah, I made that."

Excellent, that's good news and very interesting to know. What can you tell me about it? I do appreciate it was a long time ago.

"A long time. They were really hard to get absolute tone quality on them, because sometimes the frets would change, and you would play them one time and the next time they would be out of tune. The best thing about them was they had a very good quality on sound, as far as when you played a note, an E or an A, you really got that note of what the string would sound like."

The one Ray has is serial number A132. Do you know anything about the convention for the serial numbers?

"Well, I put most of the serial numbers on those bass guitars. I'm the one who put them on there. A lot of times they wouldn't take very good, and you really had to go back and redo them, because they weren't good at taking a good serial number on them."

How many sunburst models for the six-string do you remember making?

"About eight."

Did they all sell, and go out to retail stores?

"They were shipped all over - we shipped them to England, the Netherlands, different places, we shipped them all over. They were shipped right out of the state."

So you think round about eight sunburst, mostly black for the rest of them? We have one, Ted Peckels' son Dave has a brown walnut-coloured one. Do you remember much about that?

"Not too much. It was a rough one to do because it was a natural colour and it was hard to get a finished colour on it, to be standard. As we went along, we had to have a close standard set for guitars, because Ted wouldn't let them go out the door unless they were right up to power."

I have a feeling as time passes and more comes to light, this list will become more complete. It will certainly not grow much at all in terms of overall numbers, but hopefully the details and life history of these rare guitars will be revealed in due course.

Tom Mitchell's memory on the number of fretless six-string guitars varies from 60 in his conversation with Chris Ellington, then talking to me it reduced to 16 or 17. Bearing in mind this was way back in 1967 and the fretless guitar was made along with the fretless bass, which had the same body type, it must be difficult to be certain on the actual numbers.

Harvey Gerst thought very few of the fretless guitars were made - maybe four.

Then we have first-hand accounts of other fretless guitars being sold by Al Casey in Hollywood at his store, which I cover in more detail on each individual guitar in the following chapters.

Then we have the Deans furniture store fire, in which hundreds of Bartell guitars, bodies and necks were lost to the fire. Were some of the fretless guitars lost at this time?

At the time of writing, the data shows the current list of known Bartell fretless guitars, with bass guitars excluded.

Rows seven and eight are highlighted, as this could be the same model Frank Zappa had, later owned by Greg Segal, but this is currently not fully proven beyond all reasonable doubt.

All of them were designed by Paul Barth, and I believe they were made by Tom Mitchell.

Tom Mitchell's Ford Model T Roadster (opposite page) and an unusual creation by Tom, a toilet-seat bass. Photos: Tom Mitchell

List of known Bartell made Fretless guitars

	Brand	Serial #	Colour	Owner 1	Owner 2	Owner 3	Current Location
1	Bartell	A132	Sunburst	**George Harrison**	**Ray Russell**	Bonhams bidder	Unknown
2	Bartell	Unknown	Black	**Jimi Hendrix**	Unknown	Unknown	Unknown
3	Bartell	Unknown	Black	**Jimi Hendrix**	Unknown	Unknown	Unknown
4	Bartell	Unknown	Sunburst	**Mike Deasy**	**The Warehouse Minsitry**	Unknown	Unknown
5	TBC	Unknown	Red	**Mort Marker**	sold at a gig in 1968	Unknown	Unknown
6	Acoustic	A163	Walnut	Unknown	**James Mayfield**	**Dave Peckels**	Riverside California
7	Acoustic	A130	Black	Unknown	Possibly Frank Zappa	**Greg Segal** from 1985	Portland Oregon
8	Acoustic	Unknown	Black	Guitar Centre	**Frank Zappa** until 1985	Probably **Greg Segal**	

THE DISCOVERED FRETLESS MODELS

Serial Number A132 - the first prototype Bartell fretless guitar

Made sometime before the end of July 1967, and branded with the Bartell company name.

"I remember my dad, Ted telling me that they had given a guitar to George Harrison. I always assumed it was probably an Acoustic rep that had given it to him." - Dave Peckels

Comparing a Bartell fretless guitar with an early but since modified Bartell Black Widow

The following chapters reveal the incredible history of this special guitar.

Richard Bennett

I am so grateful to Richard Bennett, who helped me make some big Bartell discoveries along the way.

I was lucky to meet Richard backstage at Mark Knopfler gigs a couple of times in Brighton during the 1990s. I remember chatting to him about life on the road, remembering how easy going and charming he was to talk to. When I discovered one of Richard's first guitars was a Bartell, I hoped he might have some memories of it. I had no doubt Richard would not know who I was - how many backstage conversations had he had in a 50-year career? It was a very productive first email though, and a typically friendly reply got the conversation going after all these years.

Richard is one of Mark Knopfler's preferred guitar players in the studio and consistently on the road since 1994, as well as spending 17 great years with Neil Diamond. Richard has also recorded with The Beatles' Ringo Starr, Brenda Lee, Gene Vincent, Andy Williams, Sammy Davis Jr., Peggy Lee and Johnny Mathis, and has produced in Nashville for artists such as Steve Earle, Emmylou Harris, Marty Stuart, and Iris DeMent. And one of Richard's early guitars was a Bartell.

"It was my first decent electric guitar, the very first being a Kay Vanguard with two pickups, nearly unplayable. I bought my Bartell while working at Skaggs Music Centre in Phoenix, around 1965. The Bartell rep came to the store trying to interest the owner, Forrest Skaggs, in stocking them. I happened to be in the shop and bought one

Photo credit, Bonhams

directly from the rep. I played that guitar for a couple of years and on my first little club gigs. I bought a Telecaster after that and the Bartell was retired.

"I don't think the guitar has seen the light of day in 30 years or more. Just as I remember it, a wide-ish, shallow, flat-neck profile. I gave it a polish-up, oiled the fingerboard and put a fresh set of strings on. She'll be in good shape for another 30 years, I reckon."

On 1 February 2020 I had a further email conversation with Richard Bennett.

"I have an interesting story about my friend and mentor Al Casey delivering a fretless to Harrison when they were all staying up in the Hollywood Hills in the late 1960s (1 August 1967, to be precise).

Photo credit - Nick Bennett

"I remember a fretless was delivered up to George via Al Casey, although it was actually Al's wife Maxine - who ran their music store in Hollywood - who delivered it as Al was always busy doing sessions." – Richard Bennett

"I do recall putting my hands on one of those fretless jobs at Al's store and thinking, 'This'll never fly'. No sustain and of course to a 16-year-old, pitch would've been out the window.

"I wish now I'd have paid a bit closer attention, but in many ways, it was just another day of business. Famous players and artists hung out, came and went all the time because they all knew Al and they all loved Maxine, and … it was Hollywood in the late '60s.

"I remember holding down the fort one afternoon while Maxine went next door for lunch and a guy came in and bought a Martin that was for sale. I wrote him up, took the money and off he went. When Max got back from lunch, I was so proud of myself for selling an expensive guitar. She asked who it was, and I pulled the receipt to look at the name. It was Peter Fonda! I didn't even know who he was. That kind of stuff happened all the time.

"Bobby Darin used to come in around that time. He was going through his folk period, wearing all denim and calling himself Bob. Really nice guy, and we'd sit around with acoustic guitars and play 'Wabash Cannonball' and 'Freight Train', things like that.

Photo credit: Mike Humeniuk

Richard Bennett with Mark Knopfler on his Kill to Get Crimson tour, Edinburgh 2008. Credit Mike Humeniuk

"Anyway, the fact that an instrument was going to be delivered to George Harrison was just another day at the office.

Around 1964, the first time Richard Bennett met Al Casey and Maxine. This is the back of Skaggs Music Center in Phoenix, Arizona. The Caseys had come for a weekend to visit Al's folks and his sister.

Richard (left) with Al, showing the guitar lick to a hit record Al played it on, 'The Fool' by Sanford Clark, from 1956. It was the first national hit record to be recorded in Phoenix, written and produced by Lee Hazlewood.

6 January 1980. From the left - Richard Bennett, Forrest Skaggs, Al Casey. Taken in Casey's home in Hollywood. Skaggs was in town from Phoenix to appear in Neil Diamond's re-make of The Jazz Singer movie.

Al Casey

Alvin Wayne Casey (1936–2006) was born in Long Beach, California, on 26 October 1936, and at the age of two moved with his family to Phoenix, Arizona. His father got him started early on a ukulele to match his small fingers, until he was eight years old and started guitar lessons.

Al became successful as an artist, songwriter and guitarist. He eventually moved to Los Angeles, working through the '60s, '70s and '80s as a top studio player with legends such as Elvis Presley, Duane Eddy, Dean Martin, Frank Sinatra, The Beach Boys, and Glen Campbell.

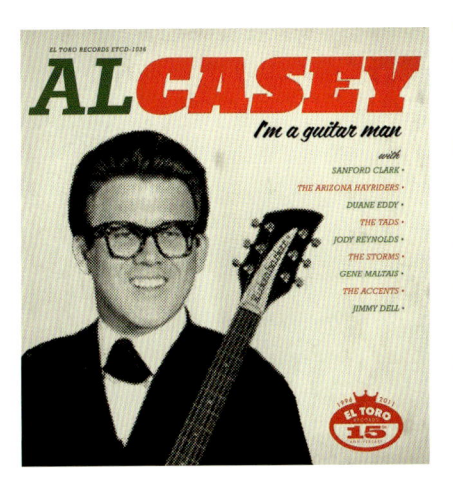

No wonder Richard Bennett held him in such high regard.

In the late 1960s, at his peak, Casey worked two to three sessions a day, and ran a music store in Hollywood called Al Casey's Music Room from 1966 until 1970.

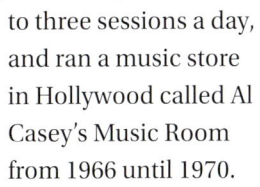

In the early 60s he worked together with first wife Corki as The Al Casey Combo, as well as a folk act known as The Raintree County Singers.

Credit - The Desert Sun

Richard Bennett & Al Casey, 1999

In 1983 Casey moved back to Phoenix, where he taught guitar lessons at Ziggie's Music and performed for occasional shows.

Al was honoured in 2005 by induction to the Rockabilly Hall of Fame and the Arizona Music and Entertainment Hall of Fame.

Richard Bennett confirmed an amusing story about Al.

"While touring as The Al Casey Combo, for a bit of humour Al had attached a mandolin neck and pickup, somehow, to a toilet seat. To that was also attached a toilet roll and paper."

In 2008, Casey was remembered along with fellow session musicians in documentary film, *The Wrecking Crew*.

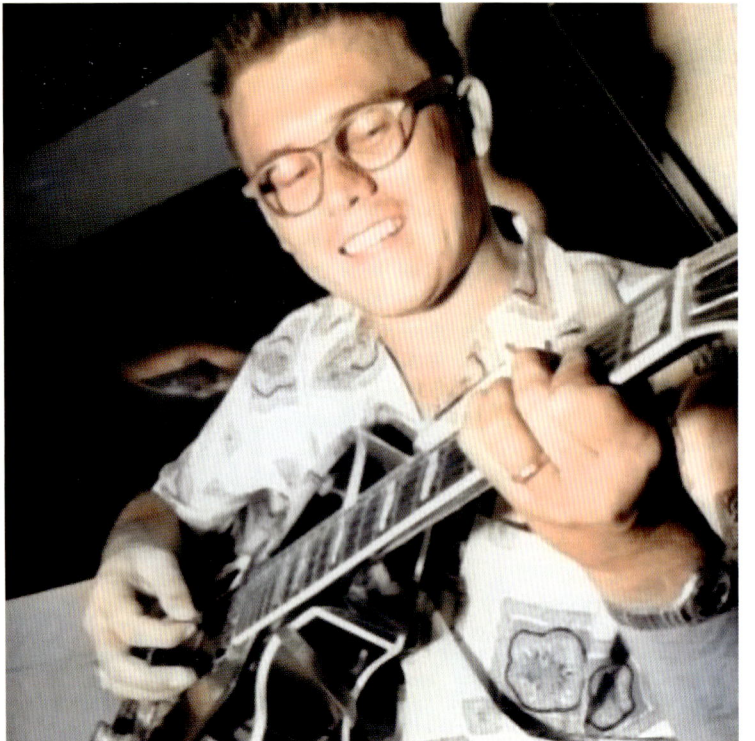

Al Casey and Mike Deasy played together on many hits with the biggest names in the music and film industry. Elvis Presley ('*68 Comeback Special*), The Monkees ('Mary, Mary'), The Association ('Never Mind My Love' and 'Windy'), Bobby Darin ('If I Were A Carpenter'), and many more. And the significance of this will be seen in the coming chapters.

The 1958 Duane Eddy hit 'Ramrod' was written by Al Casey. The Beatles used it in their early repertoire, and it turns up on a home recording from 1960, known as the 'The Braun Tape'. *Rolling Stone* reported, "The George Harrison show resumes with some fast-paced fretwork on this pacy instrumental. You want to know why Lennon let him into the band? This is why. Kid could play better than the others, as he would have had to in order to hang with this older lot. It's a Duane Eddy number, and too little has been made about his influence on Harrison's style, almost as if Eddy, with his clean image and clean-sounding licks, wasn't hip enough to associate with wannabe Teddy Boy bad-asses." It was also recorded during the 'Get Back' sessions on 24 January 1969.

Al Casey

Al continued teaching until aged 69 he passed away peacefully on 17 September 2006. A graveside service was held on Friday 22 September at Phoenix Memorial Park, 200 West Beardsley Road, Phoenix.

He was survived by his wife, Maxine Casey; sister, Sharon James; sons, Al, Jr., Mike and Lee Casey; daughters, Diana Rose, Sandra Blevens, and Colleen Maranello. The Al Casey Music Scholarship Fund was set up in his memory.

Maxine Casey died peacefully at her home in Columbus on 10 December 2011.

The Wrecking Crew

The studio musicians known as The Wrecking Crew are behind many of the most important recordings in music history, a group of all-purpose, highly-revered musicians who appeared on thousands of popular records.

Among the leading musicians who were members at various times were Tommy Tedesco, Earl Palmer, Barney Kessel, Plas Johnson,

Al Casey, Glen Campbell, James Burton, Don Peake, Leon Russell, Larry Knechtel, Jack Nitzsche, Mike Melvoin, Don Randi, Al DeLory, Billy Strange, Howard Roberts, Jerry Cole, Louie Shelton, Mike Deasy, Bill Pitman, Lyle Ritz, Chuck Berghofer, Joe Osborn, Ray Pohlman, Jim Gordon, Chuck Findley, Ollie Mitchell, Lew McCreary, Jay Migliori, Jim Horn, Steve Douglas, Allan Beutler, Roy Caton, Carol Kaye and Jackie Kelso.

Hal Blaine said the name was in ironic reference to the complaints of older musicians that these young studio performers were embracing rock and pop, and thereby going to 'wreck' the music industry.

George Harrison and the Summer of 1967

After the release of *Sgt. Pepper's Lonely Hearts Club Band* on 26 May, The Beatles' seemingly unstoppable momentum continued throughout the summer of 1967. And having signed a contract to represent the BBC and Great Britain, they took part in *Our World* on 25 June, the world's first live television satellite link-up, ultimately seen by around 400 million viewers across five continents.

John Lennon wrote the song 'All You Need Is Love' especially for the occasion, to a brief given by the BBC. It had to be a song deemed simple enough for viewers around the world to understand it.

Our World was broadcast on 25 June 1967, and between the announcement and the broadcast date, The Beatles recorded the rhythm track and basic vocals.

Among the stories involving The Beatles in the press that summer, the public learned that George Harrison received a £6 fine for breaking the speed limit in his black Mini Cooper car, while all four band members were seen hanging out with members of The Who, Eric Clapton, Procol Harum, Dusty Springfield, and The Monkees at a party at the Speakeasy in London.

Meanwhile, John Lennon and Paul McCartney attended a Rolling Stones recording session at Olympic Studios, where they contributed backing vocals, handclaps and percussion to the song 'We Love You', and in late July The Beatles took out a full-page advertisement in *The Times* newspaper, signed by 64 of the most prominent members of British society, calling for the legalisation of marijuana.

After a break in Greece, George Harrison, wife Pattie and Beatles assistant Mal Evans returned to England on Saturday 29 July to prepare for a trip to Los Angeles.

Pattie Harrison, nee Boyd, was one of the leading international models of the 1960s, and was cast by Richard Lester as a schoolgirl in the Fab Four's 1964 film *A Hard Day's Night*, on the set of which she met and befriended the group's lead guitarist. They married in January 1966.

On 1 August, George, Pattie, engineer Yannis Alexis 'Magic Alex' Mardas, and fellow close friend of the band Neil Aspinall flew from London to LA, where they were set to stay at 1567 Blue Jay Way in the Sunset Strip area of West Hollywood, with The Sunset Strip, Beverly Hills and Century City just minutes away.

George's stay was arranged by Brian Epstein, who called The Beatles' attorney Robert Fitzpatrick to enquire whether a house could be leased. Fitzpatrick persuaded the owner of the house, a fellow entertainment attorney named Ludwig Gerber, to lend his exclusive LA residence.

Gerber, a former US Army colonel and also a film producer, had managed Peggy Lee for many years.

Magic Alex was a former teenage science prodigy, moving from Greece to England in the early '60s, meeting the Rolling Stones' Brian Jones in around 1963. The group went on to commission him to design a way to link sounds to lights for their live shows.

Having befriended John Dunbar, owner of the Indica art gallery in London, the pair shared a flat on Bentinck Street, and it was there in 1966 that he first met John Lennon, who nicknamed him Magic Alex because of his impressive technological and scientific knowledge.

John often called him his 'guru', and he became part of The Beatles' extended entourage after they stopped touring. Magic Alex appeared briefly in the *Magical Mystery Tour* film, and travelled with The Beatles to India to study transcendental meditation with the Maharishi Mahesh Yogi.

Neil Aspinall had been a schoolfriend of Paul and George and became a personal assistant to The Beatles. He later went on to head The Beatles' company Apple Corps. He accompanied the band on their first trip to America, and when George Harrison became ill with a fever – with a temperature of 102 °F (39 °C) - and ordered to stay in bed, Neil stood in for him for rehearsals of *The Ed Sullivan Show*. Neil died of lung cancer in New York City in 2008.

At Gerber's house, George was waiting for Beatles publicist Derek Taylor, who apparently got lost trying to find the place. The property could only be reached from downtown Los Angeles via a complicated street route, which proved difficult to navigate on a foggy night.

George was bored and sleepy after the flight from London to LA, and wanted to stay awake until Derek arrived, so he plonked himself down, played Gerber's Hammond S-6 organ, and ended up writing a new song.

He recalled, "Derek got held up. He rang to say he'd be late. I told him on the phone that the house was in Blue Jay Way. And he said he could find it OK … he could always ask a cop. So I waited and waited. I felt really knackered with the flight, but I didn't want to go to sleep until he came.

"There was a fog, and it got later and later. To keep myself awake, just as a joke to pass the time while I waited, I wrote a song about waiting for him in Blue Jay Way. There was a little Hammond organ in the corner of this house which I hadn't noticed until then… so I messed around on it and the song came."

'Blue Jay Way', written by George, produced by 'Big George Martin' (as the LP credits would have it), and engineered by Geoff Emerick, was mostly recorded between September and October 1967 and released on the

group's *Magical Mystery Tour*, released as a double-EP in the UK (8 December) and an album in America (27 November).

It proved to be George's sole songwriting contribution to the *Magical Mystery Tour* soundtrack other than group composition 'Flying', and in the film he 'performed' the song while playing a keyboard chalked on to the ground. In one of the movie's more psychedelic sequences, his appearance is subjected to dated camera techniques involving prism refractions to create multiple images.

According to some reports, Paul Simon wrote, 'Bridge Over Troubled Water' at the same house on Blue Jay Way. The last song written for Simon and Garfunkel's fifth and final studio album, it became their biggest hit, and was recorded in California to make it easier for Art Garfunkel to get to Mexico to film the movie adaptation of *Catch-22*.

The band returned to Abbey Road on 22 August to work on material for the Magical Mystery Tour soundtrack, the title taken from a song they recorded back in May which served the same basic purpose as the title song for *Sgt. Pepper's* – an introduction for the listener to the adventure they were about to take, it's key lyric, 'Roll up, roll up …' serving the dual purpose of harkening back to the old circus barkers as well as a veiled reference to rolling a joint.

George Harrison's LA Timeline, August 1967

Beatle George In L.A. For Short Visit

LOS ANGELES (UPI)—Beatle George Harrison arrived from London Tuesday to attend a Hollywood Bowl concert featuring Indian Ravi Shankar.

Harrison and his wife, model Patti Boyd, were met by friends who whisked them off to an undisclosed hideaway.

When he left London, Harrison told newsmen he planned to be away about a week. The concert will be Friday night.

About 200 fans who waited at the airport were disappointed because Pan American World Airways officials drove the couple to the far side of the airport away from the main terminal so they would not encounter the crowd.

Harrison was dressed in a bright patterned jacket with blue bell-bottom trousers. He wore mauve moccasins and dark glasses. His wife was clad in a beaded vest over a multicolored minidress and red Roman sandals. Her blonde hair was topped with a silver tiara.

1 August - George Harrison and wife Pattie depart London, bound for LA

2 August - the *Desert Sun* report the arrival of the Harrisons at the airport the previous evening, managing to avoid 200 excited fans who had heard of their visit

3 August 1967 – George and Pattie Harrison and Derek Taylor attend a recording session by The Mamas and The Papas, produced by Lou Adler.

4 August 1967 - George reading that day's edition of the *Los Angeles Free Press*. In the evening, along with Pattie, Neil Aspinall and 'Magic Alex' Mardas, they go to see Ravi Shankar perform at the Hollywood Bowl

11 August 1967 - the *LA Free Press* reports on George visiting Ravi Shankar's music school

1567 Blue Jay Way - Google Maps Image capture May 2019 ©2021 Google

KRLA BEAT

Volume 3, Number 12   August 26, 1967

Mick Freed; Hero Or Not?

LONDON—Is a popular entertainer responsible only to himself, or does he have a duty to his fans as well? That's the question most being asked now that the Rolling Stones have been freed of their previous drug convictions.

Mick Jagger was quick to lecture reporters after his victorious appeals trial: "In private life my only responsibility is only to myself," he said. "Responsibility is on the gentlemen of the press who publish details of a person's private life."

Opinions Differ

His opinion differed greatly from that of Lord Chief Justice Parker, who presided at the appeals trial. The judge told Jagger, "Whether you like it or not you carry great responsibility because you are an idol to a large number of people."

A number of Britain's establishment newspapers have stated that Jagger, because his actions presumably influence millions of kids, was punished severely in order to set an example. Now that he has been freed, however, the papers are beginning to ask whether smoking marijuana and taking pep pills have become more respectable since the Stones' trial.

Originally Jagger had been sentenced to three months in prison for possessing four amphetamine pep pills. His sidekick, Keith Richard, was given a year for allowing guests to smoke hemp in his country home.

On Probation

In the appeals trial, Jagger argued he bought the pills in Italy and brought them legally to England. The judges lifted his sentence but warned Jagger that he would have to serve the sentence if he were convicted of any other crime in the next 12 months.

Richard was freed because, the judge said, the lower court had made a mistake in telling a jury that police had found a naked girl in his house, clad only in a rug. There was no evidence, they said, that the girl had been smoking hemp.

"Lovely," Jagger told his fans after the trial. Richard, whose face was dotted with chicken pox, said "I feel spotty."

The News of the World newspaper gave police the tip which sent them to Richard's house June 29, and teenagers and hippies have since demonstrated against the paper for allegedly persecuting the Stones.

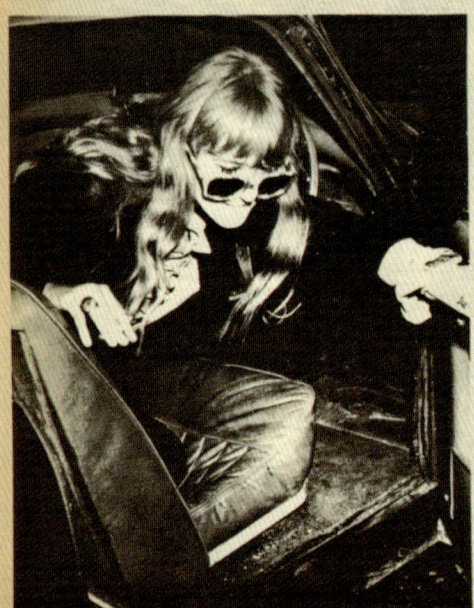

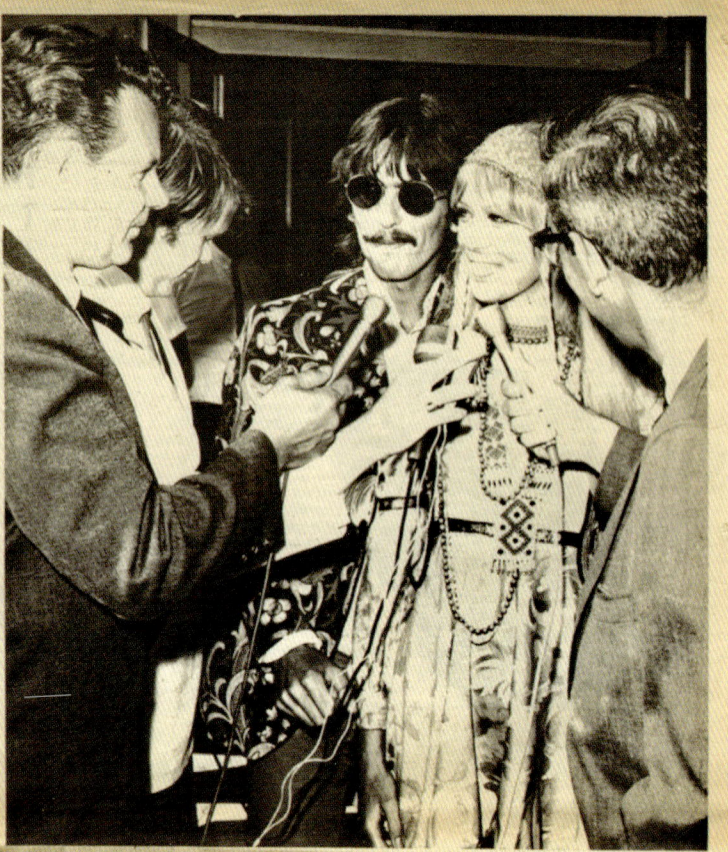

GEORGE HARRISON AND WIFE PATTI step off a Pan American jet at Los Angeles International Airport.

Harrison Arrives Stateside; Explains Controversial Ad

LOS ANGELES — Beatle George Harrison arrived at the Los Angeles International Airport for what he described as a "little bit of business and pleasure." Accompanied by his wife Patti, who was dressed in the Hippie garb reminiscent of the American Indian, the youngest Beatle was greeted by about 300 fans and a battery of the press.

George admitted that he had no plans for an extended stay in Los Angeles. "I expect to be here no longer than about five days. I have no plans, just come and try and get a bit of peace. You know, I'd like to see a few friends and a few people, that's the only thing I'm here for. And just a few things concerning business."

When asked why the Beatles have decided to give up concert tours, George answered, "It would be hard to pinpoint the problem just in a few words. There's so many different things we'd like. You see, we're all growing sort of physically and mentally and we've got to progress, and concert tours are too much in one rut. I think a lot of people realize this. We're more able to experiment with music and just generally do lots more things that we've always wanted to do.

"You know, in order to do something new, you've got to cut something out, and touring was the thing we were getting the least satisfaction from, because it was getting too big. It was too many politics being attached to it, when all we really are was a pop group coming to sing to the fans But it was getting into big political things all related to it, that, you know, added up to the decision to stop it."

One reporter mentioned that there was a rumor that the Beatles were going to produce a new album with the "old Beatle sound." However, George denied the rumor, stating, "the Beatles have always been trying to progress with us. So all I can say is the next Beatle album is, well, we don't know. But whatever we do, we try our best."

Legalized Marijuana

Recently Harrison along with the other three Beatles signed a petition to the English Government urging the legalization of marijuana. The petition was also signed by 61 other British citizens and was addressed to the Home Secretary, Roy Jenkins. The advertisement appeared in a full-page story in the London Times. When asked about his reason for supporting the legalization of marijuana, Harrison said, "I think if somebody can go and buy a crate of Johnny Walker whiskey and drink that and be perfectly within the law then I think somebody, particularly within the privacy of his own home, should be able to smoke a marijuana cigarette. You know, I think marijuana is only as bad as ordinary cigarettes or alcohol or tea or coffee or any of those things.

"They're all drugs, all stimulants you know. The thing is to define between something that is merely a stimulant and something that makes your physical body crave for it. There's no comparison between marijuana and heroin."

Increasing Use

Harrison went on to say, "I think the use of marijuana is increasing everywhere in the world. It's not just America and Britain, but it's everywhere, and it's not just marijuana, you know, marijuana is the thing that society has picked up on, but that's not really the problem. The thing is that the young people want something more out of life than just the physically gained things that they get out of society. They're looking for something more, and it's a natural part of evolution that's taking place."

While staying in Los Angeles, Harrison is expected to attend the Ravi Shankar concert at the Hollywood Bowl.

JAGGER'S GIRLFRIEND, Marianne Faithfull, arriving at court.

> You must have heard about them by now, so come on in and see the..........
> BARTELL FRETLESS GUITARS and FRETLESS BASSES ——
> (George Harrison got the first guitar, maybe if you hurry you can get the second one)
> AL CASEY'S MUSIC ROOM
> 1123 N. Vine, Hollywood
> phone 469 - 3659
> Open 11 A.M. to 8 P.M.

Credit LA Free Press

Late in the evening on 18 June 2020, I was browsing the web for any images I could find of The Beatles with the Bartell fretless guitar in Abbey Road. I don't know what possessed me, but I randomly thought of putting 'Al Casey Bartell fretless' into the search engine, and a few pages in something caught my eye. There in front of me was an advert from the *Los Angeles Free Press* dated 1 to 7 September 1967, and there in black and white, the words leapt out at me:

'BARTELL FRETLESS GUITARS and FRETLESS BASSES

(George Harrison got the FIRST guitar, maybe if you hurry you can get the second one)'

Crikey, really?

This advert for Al Casey's Music Room could only mean that Richard Bennett was spot on and his memory was correct about his conversation with Al about taking the fretless guitar to George.

Richard was hesitant that in his mind it might have been a Hohner fretless. After all, it was a long time ago and sadly both Al and Maxine were no longer around to ask.

This fitted the timeline, Al's wife Maxine taking the Bartell fretless guitar on 1 August to Blue Jay Way, where George Harrison was staying. Just a month later, no doubt jubilant with their delivery, they took out an advertisement in the *Los Angeles Free Press*.

I emailed Richard Bennett, who replied, "This is fantastic. God, I remember the *LA Free Press*, it

Photo credit Alamy Stock Photo

113

was a wild weekly at a wild time in Hollywood. Charles Bukowski used to write a regular column in it. Well done!

"I just heard from a friend in LA that the location of Al and Maxine's store at the address on the advert was destroyed in the recent racial protests over the last 10 days or so.

"They were 'anything goes' times in Hollywood then - hippies, hillbillies, movie stars, record stars, druggies, health foodies, anything and everything went. Everyone got along. It seems like a million years ago now."

Within a week I found a second advert, again from the *LA Free Press* (volume 4, issue 36 (164) 8 to 14 September 1967, page 23).

Al was clearly pushing the marketing on the new Bartell fretless models. He took out the first advert on 18 August, within two weeks of gifting the Bartell to Harrison, followed by three more consecutive weeks in the *LA Free Press*.

John Lennon

On Thursday 6 June 1968, Peter Lewis and Victor Spinetti filmed a TV interview with John Lennon in studio 3 at Abbey Road. They chatted about a stage adaptation of John's book In His Own Write. The filmed interview would air on BBC 2 as part of the arts programme Release.

When the interview concluded in studio 3, while the other Beatles worked on overdubs for Ringo's first composition, 'Don't Pass Me By', John was interviewed by BBC radio disc jockey Kenny Everett.

Kenny Everett in his home studio. Photo credit: Alamy stock photo

The interview was recorded on tape by Kenny's friend Tony Oliverstone, who set up the levels on the recorder as John noodled around on an unusual sounding guitar. The recording was broadcast by BBC Radio One on 9 June. It was a fun interview, involving some classic John Lennon sarcasm, piss-taking and brilliant chemistry with his host, who asked, **'What kind of guitar is that? It's very strange looking,'** with John responding, **'A fretless guitar'.**

The uncut interview appeared on 1986 album *The Golden Beatles*, with Adam Kinn mentioned on the credits for providing the audio for the recording and advised, 'The guy behind that actually cut it up and ruined it!'.

A shorter, edited version was pressed in 1968 as a 7" vinyl disc by Apple for promotional use in Italy, as 'Una Sensazionale Intervista Dei Beatles'.

Beatles recording engineer Geoff Emerick discussed this interview in his book. Apparently, they were arguing like mad before, and changed as soon as Kenny walked in, becoming the loveable Goon-style Beatles again. Then, as soon as the presenter walked out, they went back to hating each other again.

How could we prove John Lennon was playing this actual fretless guitar without a photo from the specific day in question, or confirmation from someone who was there in the studio? We are still searching of course, but I'm sure something will come up, probably from an unexpected source.

On 8 March 2020, Jan Gorski-Mescir messaged me, "The photo I've seen is of John noodling with it in studio 2, looking slightly to his right, towards the camera during the White album recording. It's definitely a (sun)burst, not black (guitar), despite the photo itself being black and white.

"The belief is that Kenny Everett took a camera man along with him – Alan someone - who took the photo, and the famous one of a tired Ringo in headphones looking over a drum baffle. There's another one from the same session showing George talking to George Martin, and the Bartell is visible from about halfway up the neck in the background. But the pic is often cropped so the Bartell neck and that of Macca's RS 1999 Rickenbacker bass are never in the most used version of this".

The fretless is seen at the back right by the curtain, next to George's left arm. And as it turned out, word spread quickly and was soon shared across the music community. Copyright Brian Ari. Used by permission

Conveniently, John's fingerprints were recorded by the Federal Bureau of Investigation on his 1976 application for permanent residence in the USA. I wonder if it's possible to find a fingerprint that matches John from way back in 1968? Clutching at straws of course, but you never know. Perhaps I've been watching too much *CSI*!

John's prints were to be auctioned for $100,000.

His 1970s immigration attorney Leon Wildes told the *New York Times* the fingerprint form was among papers in his possession that were missing after a 1976 television appearance.

There was a lot of hearsay about Bartell giving George Harrison a fretless guitar, but no visible proof. I was determined to track down decades' old images to prove the existence of the sunburst fretless in ownership of The Beatles. It was a relentless search over many months to track down the conclusive proof, but finally ... success, an old image of George at home at Friar Park, Henley-on-Thames with his collection of mainly acoustic guitars finally showed him with the elusive Bartell fretless.

Check, triple check - the headstock, the tuning keys, the truss rod cover, the f-holes, the pickguard, the shading of the sunburst, and the location of the pickups all matched. And most importantly there were no frets. Yes, this was the one.

"My brother swears he saw a magazine cover back in the day of George Harrison surrounded by some guitars, one of which according to him was a Bartell. He doesn't remember the magazine, but he thinks it was Time or Newsweek, something like that. It wasn't a music magazine" - Dave Peckels, June 2019

The *White Album* – an introduction

The Beatles' ninth album in seven years – and their only studio double-album - is considered by many to be among their very best. Recorded between 30 May and 14 October 1968, it was released on 22 November, its working title, *A Doll's House*, dropped after UK progressive rock band Family released the similarly-titled *Music In A Doll's House* earlier that year, the album simply becoming *The Beatles* instead, or as it is more commonly known, the *White Album*. With no graphics or text other than the band's name embossed in grey letters (and, on the early LP, a serial number) on a plain white sleeve, it was the first since the death of Beatles manager, Brian Epstein, and the first released on their own record label, Apple.

Anticipation for the release was huge, as was speculation as to whether the band were going to better their last album, *Sgt. Pepper's Lonely Hearts Club Band*. In many ways they did, the eclectic nature of the resultant double LP's songs showing the four members remained at the top of their game. John Lennon laid down some of his most memorable work, with three of his finest on side one alone – 'Dear Prudence', 'Glass Onion' and 'Happiness Is A Warm Gun'. And then we had Paul's tunes, including the Chuck Berry meets The Beach Boys feel of opener 'Back in the USSR', with McCartney on drums after Ringo quit the group for a couple of weeks. Then there was Paul's ode to his Old English Sheepdog, 'Martha My Dear', and what has become one of his signature tunes, the beautiful 'Blackbird', featuring just his voice and acoustic guitar, plus the warbling of a blackbird.

As for George Harrison's material, when The Beatles recorded overdubs on to his new song 'While My Guitar Gently Weeps', close friend Eric Clapton added the guitar solo, becoming the first outside rock musician to play on a Beatles recording. At first Clapton was reluctant to join them in the studio, saying, 'Nobody ever plays on The Beatles' records', but George convinced him. Eric also loved chocolates, and George wrote 'Savoy Truffle' as a tribute to Eric's sweet addiction – the title and many of the lyrics coming from a box of Mackintosh's Good News chocolates. Completing Harrison's contributions was another fine song, 'Long, Long, Long' and 'Piggies'.

The *White Album* was written and recorded during a period of turmoil for the group, all four members having visited the Maharishi Mahesh Yogi in India in early 1968 and, while abroad, enjoying a particularly productive writing period, many of the tracks penned over the course of that Transcendental Meditation course in Rishikesh. The group returned to the studio for recording from May to October 1968, although conflict and dissent would drive the group members apart, including that Ringo walk-out and resentment over John's new partner, Yoko Ono's constant presence, subverting the band policy of excluding wives and girlfriends from the studio. It wasn't just the playing personnel, producer George Martin taking an unannounced holiday and engineer Geoff Emerick quitting during a session. Many of the songs were 'solo' recordings, or at least by less than the full group, each member beginning to explore their own talent. And as it turned out, those same tensions would continue throughout the following year, ultimately leading to the band's break-up.

Although 'Hey Jude' was not intended to be included on the LP release, it was recorded during the *White Album* sessions and released as a stand-alone single before the release, on 26 August 1968. Its B-side, 'Revolution', was an alternative version of the album's 'Revolution 1'. John Lennon had wanted the original version to be released as a single, but the other three objected on the grounds that it was too slow. A new, faster version, with heavily distorted guitar and a high-energy keyboard solo from Nicky Hopkins was recorded and relegated to the flip side. The resulting release emerged as the first release on The Beatles' new label, going on to become the band's most successful single, with world sales of more than five million by the end of 1968 and 7.5 million by October 1972.

Many fans have long debated what a great 'single' record the *White Album* could have made, and there are some tracks that don't score with everybody. That said, those that upset some people turn out to be the absolute favourites of many others. It would of course top the charts on both sides of the Atlantic, and more than 50 years later, *The Beatles* has clearly stood the test of time, a testament to the sheer quality of many of its classic songs and having proven highly influential.

And for the sake of our story, there were two tracks on that historic double-album that featured a certain fretless guitar gifted to George Harrison and played by both John Lennon and George.

Image artwork Ian T Cossar

Image artwork Ian T Cossar

Top Gear Music

In 1973, The Beatles sent a consignment of George Harrison guitars for servicing to Top Gear Musical Instruments at 5, Denmark Street in Soho, London. Mark Moffatt worked there at the time and recalled in a Facebook post when it was finally identified in 2019 by me to be the Bartell fretless, "It's been almost 45 years since I held that guitar in my hands (back in 1973), but having 'experts' dismiss its very existence ...

"It's funny, working on all those Beatles guitars back then was just an everyday occurrence. The other funny thing

Mark Moffatt at the Top Gear counter

is that Ray (Russell) was a regular up until the place was sold in 1978."

Mark had notified Andy Babiuk as far back as 2002 to consider including the Bartell fretless in his comprehensive book, *Beatles Gear*.

Mark Moffatt - Credit John Scapati

Water

Ray Russell was gifted the rare Bartell fretless guitar in 1985 by George Harrison during the filming of 1985 British comedy film *Water*, directed by Dick Clement and scripted by its director and writing partner Ian La Frenais, starring Michael Caine, Valerie Perrine, Brenda Vaccaro, Leonard Rossiter, and Billy Connolly.

The film was about a small fictional British Caribbean island of Cascara, one so small and peaceful that it had all but been forgotten by the UK Government.

Governed by the laidback Baxter Thwaites, Cascara is not particularly well off, but its pace of life is gentle and happy. Thwaites, therefore, is enraged - both for the peaceful inhabitants, and his own cushy job - when Westminster decides the island is too small to maintain and should be evacuated.

However, everything changes when an American company, having previously explored the island for oil reserves, arrives to film a TV advert at its abandoned well. During production something goes wrong and the well begins spewing forth its plentiful liquid: not black gold, but naturally occurring table water brands.

As London suddenly shows interest in Cascara once more, a race heats up between the motherland, the US conglomerate, and Governor Thwaites - now leading a small band of singing revolutionaries who want to see the nation achieve independence. And then there's the French ...

George Harrison normally did not get too involved in the production of HandMade's films. However, this time he helped out by appearing in a concert at the finale, and got his friends Eric Clapton and Ringo Starr to appear.

The concert scene was shot in a single day at Shepperton Studios, with Clapton, Starr and Harrison paid the musicians' minimum rate for a playback session on set.

Antiques Roadshow

In June 2019, I called Ray Russell, "Hi Ray, the BBC's *Antiques Roadshow* is coming to town, fancy letting them know about your fretless?"

Ray was up for it, so I contacted the BBC in advance, and they were indeed very interested and made prior arrangements.

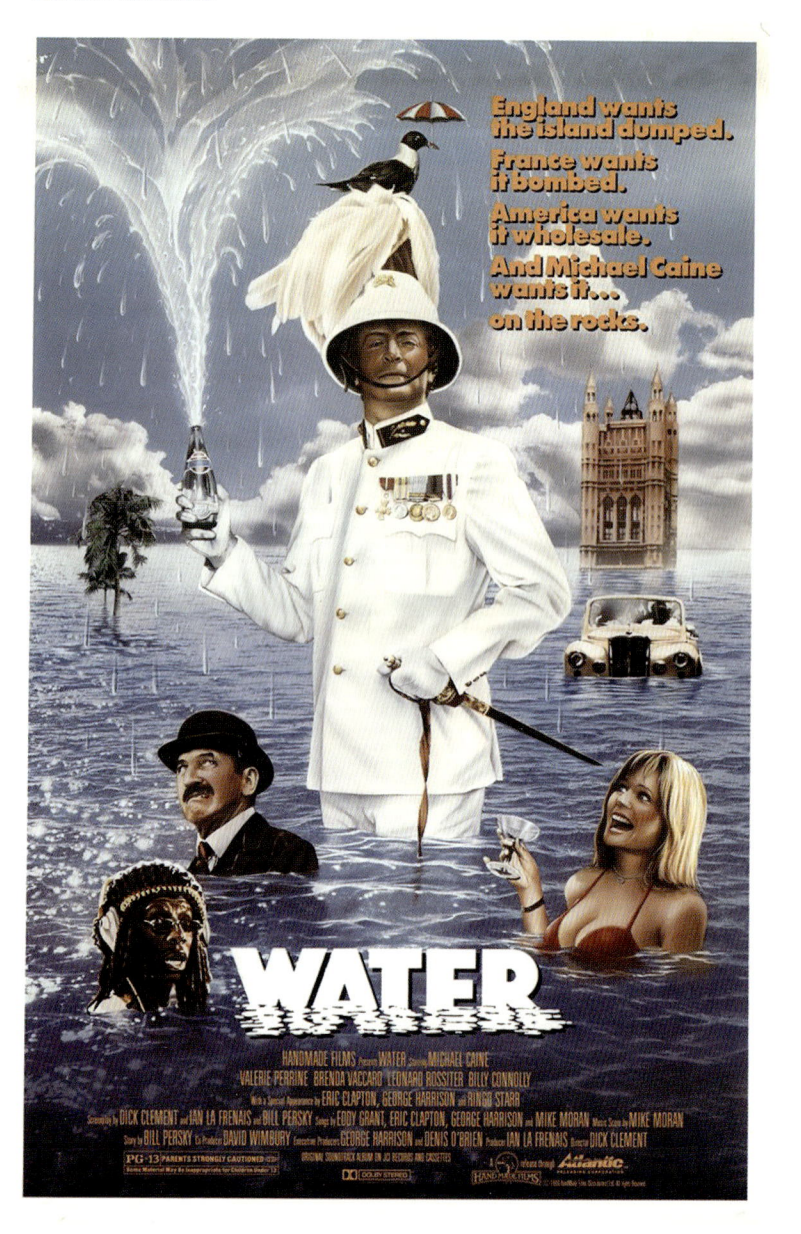

On 9 July 2019, the popular prime time show was visiting the historic town of Battle in East Sussex, where the Battle of Hastings was fought on 14 October 1066, between the Norman-French army of William, the Duke of Normandy, and an English army under Anglo-Saxon King Harold Godwinson, the beginning of the Norman conquest of England.

Antiques Roadshow is an iconic BBC programme that has been running since 1979, journalist and presenter Fiona Bruce and the team bringing together leading authorities on arts and antiques to offer free valuations for family heirlooms or car boot bargains. Local people bring old and interesting items for experts to scrutinise and provide estimate valuations. The Bartell fretless guitar and its strong links with The Beatles, specifically John and George, we hoped would provide a compelling story. What would the experts say?

We were given VIP treatment by a very professional BBC production team, part of a slick and well organised unit, and were introduced in advance to auction house Bonham's highly experienced and respected expert appraiser Jon Baddeley, answering his questions and waiting to see if we would go forward to filming.

Jon Baddeley joined Bonhams as a global director of collectors' sales in 2003, and has since been responsible for many landmark auctions and world record prices. Highlights include British Airways' Concorde auction, the Admiral Nelson bicentenary sale, John Lennon' lyrics for 'Give Peace a Chance', Eric Clapton's guitar collection, and a dress worn by the actress Judy Garland in the role of Dorothy in the film *The Wizard of Oz*.

In 2010, Jon became managing director of Bonhams, Knightsbridge, the busiest of the international auction house's portfolio of salesrooms, where he is responsible for auctions of jewellery, silver, paintings, furniture , works of art, specialist sales of portrait miniatures, arms and armour, sporting guns, coins and medals, science and technology, toys, dolls, and entertainment memorabilia.

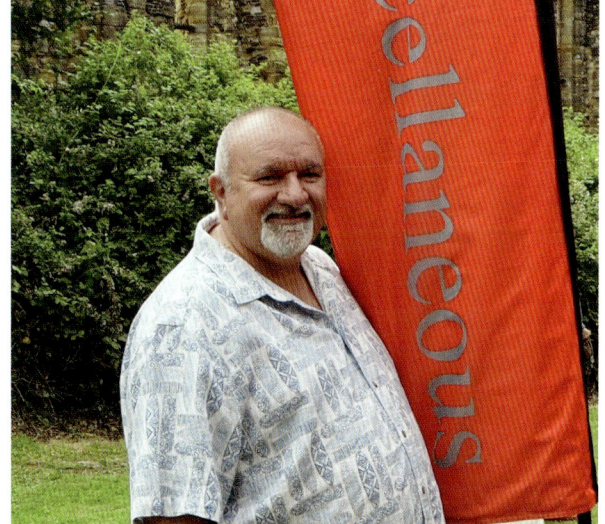

UK guitar legend Ray Russell, proud owner of The Beatles' Bartell fretless guitar since 1985

Paul Brett at Battle Abbey, East Sussex

Antiques Roadshow expert Jon Baddeley, courtesy Bonhams

FINDING FRETLESS

Ray and Jon at Battle Abbey

*Paul and Ray Images
credits BBC*

*The BBC Antiques Roadshow
Battle Abbey July 2019*

Ray in the BBC One Show Green room

Antiques Roadshow photos, Battle Abbey, by Paul Brett

With more than 30 years' experience in both auctioneering and dealing, Jon has a wide general knowledge of decorative arts and is an acknowledged expert in the areas of instruments of science and technology and marine decorative arts. He is the author of the reference work *Nautical Antiques and Collectibles* and is known to millions of people across the world as an *Antiques Roadshow* specialist, having made regular appearances since the show began in 1977.

Ray and I were in great hands, but would we have enough provenance to make the cut? Jon was a veteran of the programme and managing director of a renowned international auctioneer, with such an array of expert experience in the field. I had evidence of the Kenny Everett interview with John Lennon, Ray could recall his time working with George Harrison in the studio recording for the film *Water*, and how George gifted the guitar to him. Crucially I had the critical photo of George with the fretless in his collection of guitars from his Friar Park home.

We were centre stage for the final recording of the day.

The Appraisal

In advance of attending *Antiques Roadshow*, it was all a bit of fun, an interesting, new experience. Did we have any realistic idea of the value? Well, not really. We knew the story was compelling, but initially raising more questions than answers. The fretless guitar had been with both Lennon and Harrison and it was rare, but would that really mean much more than maybe a few thousand pounds and an interesting story? Or was there real undiscovered value in this oddball prototype instrument manufactured by a little known, long forgotten small company.

It was a beautiful day, hot by British standards, thousands turning up with their heirlooms and interesting items. We were surrounded by an inquisitive crowd, a professional BBC production team and technicians buzzing around us, although Ray was used to this after many years in studios and on film sets.

My wife Karen and daughter Kimberley also managed to get there in time, despite parking being a nightmare.

We got the fretless plugged into Ray's small amp, and with the soundcheck done, we were on, cameras rolling …

Jon Baddeley asked me the first question about the guitar, the Bartell company and its roots in California in the 1960s, then moved on to Ray to ask him to explain how it came into his possession.

"In the '70s and '80s I was doing lots of recording sessions on guitar, and one of the things I used to do regularly was sessions for HandMade Films."

Ray went on to explain how HandMade Films was co-funded by George Harrison, who at the end of one of the recording sessions asked Ray to play this 'strange' guitar.

"It's a strange old thing to play, I played a few notes and he said, 'Yeah, you're definitely getting more out of it than I am. It's doing better for you, why don't you have it?'"

Ray played a short piece for effect. While he was talking, I could sense Ray working out in his head and down through his fingers how to play the *Antiques Roadshow* theme tune, mid-interview.

Jon built up the importance of the guitar.

"To a guitar collector, it's initially a very rare guitar. Then to somebody who's a Beatles fan, to own a guitar that was once owned by both John Lennon and George Harrison, can you get a better history? Two of the most important rock stars of the 20th, Century."

He pointed to the photograph of the former Beatle with his guitar collection at his Friar Park home, including the Bartell fretless, right by his left arm.

With the tension and anticipation mounting, Jon added, "What's really important is the provenance, and there it was in the photograph - in George Harrison's collection. Wow, you can't do better than that."

Finally, the dramatic immortal words from the expert.

"I wouldn't be surprised if it made between … 300 and 400 (pause) … thousand pounds"There were gasps from the crowd around us. I rocked back and tapped Ray on the knee, so pleased for him. Ray was stunned, mumbling, 'Amazing'.

There was loud gossiping from the people around us, and I noticed the head of security close by reach for his phone. I could see the excited faces of Karen, my wife and daughter Kimberley as they filmed and photographed as much as they could. Ray played a few bars to wrap things up, to excited applause from the audience.

The filming continued with Ray and Jon for the post-valuation comments.

Ray concluded, "I never really thought about value, George being a mate and all that. I don't know what to say actually. I'm really taken aback by it. I didn't realise it was worth that much money.

"It's lucky I don't keep it in the house!"

Good grief. Really? That much? That's life-changing! Mr Security stepped in quickly and took the guitar.

"Enjoy the rest of your day. This is being locked up. Don't leave without asking for me and my team before you go."

So many people had so many questions. There is so much love for The Beatles of course, and Paul McCartney lived not too far away. Everyone was so excited for us. Time for a cold drink. It was hot!

"Oh shit," Ray gasped, "What are we going to do now?" I felt so happy for him. He's such a genuine fellow, and his lovely wife Sally is going to be *slightly* shocked.

We had a late lunch in the shade of the heat in the abbey grounds, my wife and daughter helping to calm a stunned Ray.

The enormity of the event, the buzz around the grounds, people everywhere pointing, waving, asking questions.

Our extraordinary time at Battle Abbey was soon over. I managed to catch up with the presenter, Fiona Bruce, and she kindly signed some playing cards for my StarCards charity. It had been the most perfect day, now it was time to go home and take it all in.

We went to collect Ray's now priceless possession, Mr Security getting a team of four to carry our gear, providing an escort to the car park. Mr Security said, "That's only the valuation, at auction it could easily go for at least double that!" I gulped.

Ray was given some great advice on home security, insurance, personal protection, and so on, and I could see it really beginning to dawn on him that this was a big deal. I couldn't help but observe our security detachment

FINDING FRETLESS

Ray and Sally "What are we going to do now?"

follow us in the car all the way on to the road, thinking what a professional bunch they were.

We both puffed our cheeks as we took the short drive home, both quite exhausted but excited at the same time. Ray got home safely, I dropped him off and helped him in with his gear, then made sure the door was firmly closed.

I have no idea how that conversation with Ray's wife Sally went, but I think she was stunned and now understandably quite a bit worried. They now both had a wonderful story, a highly valuable asset and a security nightmare. Oh my, I hope I hadn't created an unwanted problem. I hope they will forgive me!

Antiques Roadshow on air

1 March 2020 - Series 42

The long wait from June 2019 for confirmation of when the show would be broadcast was eventually over and confirmed as 1 March. It was agony keeping 'schtum' about the valuation. So many family, friends, work colleagues were as keen as Ray and myself to see the show go out, in prime time Sunday evening viewing. It was revealing how wide the guesses had been, from a few thousand to a highly unrealistic million pounds. Ray was very pragmatic and didn't get over-excited. I couldn't help but secretly be delighted for Ray and his lovely wife Sally and aimed to do as much as I could to help build the story of this rather oddball old prototype from a little known company from the 1960s.

Ray was also busily pre-occupied recording his new album and completing his Doctorate in Philosophy. He's a busy chap.

I pulled together golden nuggets of information that might help the BBC bring to life the story in the hope that they would realise the back story was so compelling, dropping in the links to Jimi Hendrix, Frank Zappa and more. It must have triggered some additional interest as, quoting the BBC, the show included an 'incredibly rare Beatles guitar with an enviable history, which turns out to be one of the most valuable items ever seen on the show'.

Fiona Bruce kindly signed my StarCards, and said, **"Paul has done an amazing bit of detective work. It would put Poirot to shame."**

Bingo, the Beeb know a good story when they see one! Contacting Ray, they asked, "Can you come on *The One*

Show next Tuesday?"

On 24 February 2020, I was Ray's chauffeur for the day, heading to London, where he would be playing a few bars. So we loaded in an amp as well. Ray would be on the show with Jon Bon Jovi too.

Launched in 2006 The One Show is a television magazine and chat show programme. Broadcast live on BBC One on weeknights at 7pm, it features topical stories and studio guests. On this occasion it was co-hosted by regular presenters Alex Jones and Matt Baker. The studio is based in Broadcasting House, the BBC's headquarters in London.

On the show, presenter Matt Baker asked Jon Bon Jovi, "Do you want a little strum on that before we go?" His guest replied, "No - I'm afraid of it." Ray responded, "That makes two of us!"

Over the following couple of days, many of Ray's friends around the world were both surprised and delighted to see him reminiscing about the day George Harrison gifted him the guitar.

It was all set up, everyone was now waiting for the *Antiques Roadshow* appraisal to be broadcast on 1 March.

Fiona Bruce at Battle Abbey, signing Paul's StarCards

Reaction to the *Antiques Roadshow* broadcast?

Flipping heck, that went well!

Lots of family, friends, acquaintances and many more people I didn't know at all were tuning in and commenting on the programme, with lots of shock regarding the valuation but equally much interest in the guitar itself, the story, Ray, and so on.

The social channels went a bit crazy. It even trended on Twitter. The BBC went for it big time, with a full press release picked up by all the national press and the story all over the internet. *The Times*, *The Telegraph*, *The Mirror*, *The Sun*, the music press ... they all picked up on it immediately, and Beatles fans were going crazy for it. There were the usual trolls with negative comments, but strangely I found some of them very amusing.

BBC – 'Beatles guitar valued at £400,000 on *Antiques Roadshow*'

Jon Bon Jovi, Fiona Bruce and Ray. Photo: Paul Brett

'A 'strange' guitar formerly owned by Beatles John Lennon and George Harrison has been valued at up to £400,000 on the BBC's *Antiques Roadshow*.

'The prototype fretless guitar, made in the 1960s, appeared on Sunday's show.

'Its current owner recorded sessions for a film company co-founded by Harrison, who asked him to play the guitar. "I played a few notes and he said, 'Yeah, you're definitely getting more out of it than I am. It's doing better for you, why don't you have it?'"

'*Antiques Roadshow* expert Jon Baddeley said, "What's really important is the provenance, and there it was in the photograph - in George Harrison's collection. Wow, you can't do better than that," valuing the guitar at between £300,000 and £400,000.'

The Times - 'Rare Beatles guitar on *Antiques Roadshow* is worth £400,000'

'It is a guitar that was once given away as a 'strange old thing'" after its owner struggled to play it.'

The Express – '*Antiques Roadshow* tonight no doubt left viewers shocked as a guitar once owned by John Lennon and George Harrison was brought in for valuation and was revealed to be worth a huge sum.'

The Sun – 'Here Comes the Sum'

"Exceptionally rare' guitar owned by The Beatles' George Harrison valued at £400,000 on *Antiques Roadshow*.'

The Mail – 'Guitar once owned by John Lennon and George Harrison is valued at £400,000 by *Antiques Roadshow* expert blown away by 'the most expensive thing I've seen in 25 years.'

Apple News – 'A 'strange' guitar formerly owned by Beatles John Lennon and George Harrison has been valued at up to £400,000 on the BBC's *Antiques Roadshow*.'

NME - Got a bit of spare cash knocking around? The Beatles: 'Antiques Roadshow' value guitar once owned by John Lennon and George Harrison at £400k The current owner said he was given the guitar because he could play it better than Harrison.

Guitar World – 'A rare John Lennon and George Harrison-owned fretless guitar just surfaced - and it's worth over $500,000.'

Lad Bible – 'A man got the shock of his life when he appeared on *Antiques Roadshow* and found out his old guitar, which used to belong to John Lennon and George Harrison, was worth a fortune.'

Liverpool Echo – 'BBC *Antiques Roadshow* guest shocked to learn George Harrison gifted guitar is worth £400,000.'

The first week of March 2020 was a mad week.

Appearances on the BBC's The One Show and Antiques Roadshow were followed by a number of TV interviews, reviews, entertainment programmes and radio interviews. Ray was hot property that week!

For the BBC South East Today regional news programme, broadcast immediately after the national headline news in the UK, the programme's makers filmed at Ray Russell's home in East Sussex.

George Harrison guitar is worth how much? - BBC Breakfast News - Dan Walker and Louise Minchin update the nation on 2 March

The story was even included on Channel 4's Gogglebox, a British television reality series featuring a number of families and groups of friends from different places around the United Kingdom filmed reacting to British television programmes from their own homes.

On Friday 6 March, Ray's episode of *Antiques Roadshow* was reviewed by *Gogglebox* viewers, with hilarious commentary from the featured families and friends.

Then there was BBC Radio 5 Live Drive, a UK-wide programme's round-up of the day's top news and sport, plus interviews with the people at the centre of the stories. Hosted by Tony Livesey and Sarah Brett, the show also interviewed Ray about his incredible Beatles guitar.

Then, on Saturday 7 March, there was ITV's Ant & Dec's Saturday Night Takeaway, a British prime time weekend evening TV variety show, where in the final prizewinning 'make or break' question, the contestant guessed B correctly.

Was the Bartell used on the White Album?

I spoke to freelance sound engineer, musician, luthier, artist and historian Dr Jan Gorski-Mescir to talk about whether the Bartell fretless guitar was played on The Beatles' self-titled 1968 double-album *The Beatles* (aka the *White Album*).

Jan was introduced to George Harrison by Pink Floyd guitarist and co-vocalist David Gilmour, and was a friend of George for more than 30 years.

He has a long career as a top session musician, known mostly as a bass player, backing vocalist, occasional rhythm and slide guitarist (a speciality), finger-picker, percussionist and even an alto sax player.

In late February 2020 he responded to a Twitter post by me, saying, "I know about that guitar quite well. It wasn't a 'George' guitar, it was a 'Beatles' guitar. Given to them in late '67, a fretless guitar, which saw use on the *White Album* the following year, notably on 'Happiness is a Warm Gun' and 'Helter Skelter'. After that, it just hung around."

We carried on the conversation via Twitter direct messages over a number of evenings, and he explained, "John, being the accepted *de facto* leader, got blitzed with all sorts of guitars, pedals, amps, and so on.

"(London-based guitar manufacturer) Burns in particular targeted John, one particularly mad looking guitar given to their 'friend' Alex Mardas. Then came the Bartell, which intrigued him, but he found it difficult to play. They passed it around, but then put it in the studio locker.

"Back in the UK the Bartell Fretless stayed in the studio locker more or less undisturbed for some months. George referred to it as 'the mad guitar'. The Bartell Fretless was used on the *White Album*. During 'Happiness is a Warm Gun' overdubs, neither John nor George were very happy with the bend notes on the 'I need a fix' section, as originally played on George's Les Paul, 'Lucy'. That's when they remembered the fretless in the cupboard.

"Both John and George then played several versions of the very bendy guitar line on the fretless, with compression and a vox distortion pedal. George could not recall whose version was used in the end."

On 15 June 2020, Jan added, "The fuzz pedal used was a Vox Tonebender through a Fender twin reverb. During this period the Beatles were progressively loaded up with Fender freebies.

"I've listened to the original masters of the *White Album* many times, and there is definitely no glass/metal slide sound on 'Happiness is a Warm Gun', or fret 'sparkle' as George would call it. And yes, little 'choked' sustain.

"I'm pretty sure the version on the stereo album is George, and on the mono mix it's John, playing more or less the same notes, but moving notes side-to-side for bends/vibrato like Mike Oldfield, whereas George did the more usual up-and-down vibrato. You can hear the difference.

"It also got Paul's attention and was used on a few short lines in 'Helter Skelter', which once you know, becomes obvious to the ear. George also thought he used it on 'Long, Long, Long' and possibly 'Savoy Truffle', but couldn't recall if it made the final mix.

"Sadly, most of the people involved in those sessions - with the exceptions of Ringo, Paul and engineer Chris Thomas - have since died.

"After the *White Album*, George, who had been learning sitar, felt his lead guitar work was falling behind and a bit old-fashioned, what with Clapton, Beck, Hendrix, and so on, so decided after a chat with Bonnie Bramlett to work on his slide-guitar technique that he would, after 'My Sweet Lord', become famed for. The fretless was therefore set aside.

"To my recollection there was only one fretless six-string guitar, the Bartell, in the possession of The Beatles."

Jan, a mad Liverpool FC fan, currently lives between south west France and Luxembourg, refurbishing his beautiful French country retreat and using his excellent luthier skills on many wonderful guitars.

"In studio no. 2 there is a steep staircase that goes up to the control room. Underneath is a cupboard where they used to keep all kinds of different equipment. There were strange tambourines and Moroccan drums and all kinds of little things.

FINDING FRETLESS

"The studio itself was full of instruments. They used all those different sounds on their records, because they were creative. So when they got to an overdub they would look around the cupboard and see if there was something that would fit, like a fretless for example."

In December 2019, Youtubers Alby House discussed Kenny Everett interviewing The Beatles at Abbey Road in 1968. The interview captured John Lennon playing a fretless guitar, and they pondered the fate of the guitar and whether it was used on any Beatles recordings.

Using an Eastwood version of an Acoustic Black Widow, the team make a serious comparison of various techniques to reproduce the very distinctive sounds of a fretless guitar. They speculated its use on *White Album* tracks, 'Happiness is a Warm Gun', 'Helter Skelter', 'Everybody's Got Something To Hide (Except Me And My Monkey)', 'Revolution (Take 20)' and 'Savoy Truffle'.

After some consideration, they concluded that there was definitely a fretless guitar at Abbey Road and on the *White Album*. Viewer comments included, 'This fretless guitar has such a distinctive sound. As soon I heard it, I thought, 'That's it! That's the *White Album* guitar sound! All those bendings. Sounded so strange to me.'

One viewer concluded, 'That was definitely the fretless guitar. No way it was just a regular guitar. Wow! The Beatles are still the greatest,' and another added, 'I think it's pretty believable on 'Helter Skelter' and 'Happiness' because both solos have really unnatural 'bends' that don't really sound right when played normally'. And then another viewer exclaimed, 'You bastards. Absolutely. You cracked it. I've been wondering about 'Happiness is a Warm Gun' since I became obsessed with it when I was … well, 30 years ago today'.

In February 2020, the *White Album* was analysed by **Kenny Jenkins**, senior lecturer of music performance and production at Leeds Beckett University. Responding to a meeting with Ray Russell, Kenny advised, "I listened carefully to 'Helter Skelter' and 'Happiness is a Warm Gun' from the *White Album*. Having spent a fair amount of time playing a fretless guitar, I can definitely say that's what is being used on both these tracks.

"I've been listening to this

Eastwood version of an Acoustic Black Widow. A modified fretless model was used in their video analysis. Photo copyright: Eastwood Guitars.

Kenny Jenkins

record for over 40 years and I'd never noticed it before, but once I'm listening out for it, it's an unmistakable sound. It's particularly effective on 'Happiness is a Warm Gun', where it's drenched in fuzz - probably a Dallas Fuzz Face pedal.

"There weren't many fretless guitars in the world in 1968, so it seems obvious that it's your Bartell."

Meanwhile, Ian McDonald in *Revolution in the Head* (Fourth Estate, London 1994), a fairly comprehensive account of Beatles recordings, credits both John and George with lead guitar on 'Happiness is a Warm Gun' but only John on lead guitar for 'Helter Skelter'.

Jenkins adds, "So we don't know whether all the fretless guitar is in fact John Lennon. I shall now need to listen to the whole of the *White Album* to see if I can hear any more fretless guitar, which is no hardship at all."

In June 2020, the *White Album* was analysed by London-based guitarist, composer and musicologist **Dr Richard Perks**, a lecturer in music performance at the University of Kent.

Richard, one of Europe's leading exponents of the fretless electric guitar, who delivers masterclasses and lecture recitals promoting the use of the instrument internationally, stressed, "I can say with some degree of certainty that a fretless electric guitar was used during the recording of *The Beatles*.

"On the track 'Happiness is a Warm Gun', the characteristic timbre of a fretless guitar is unmistakable (0:44–0:58). I am also convinced it features at various points throughout 'Helter Skelter' (1:27–1:29; 1:37–1:45; 2:04–2:08). Furthermore, there is sufficient evidence to suggest the use of a fretless guitar on 'Savoy Truffle' (1:27–1:32; 1:35–1:40; 1:43–1:45)."

"In each case, the fretless guitar parts exhibit a 'full' tone, which directly supports the view that the Bartell model – a hollow-body – was used." Dr. Rich Perks (2020).

Richard's research interests include the extended performance possibilities of the fretless electric guitar; guitar-focused musicology/analysis; the combination of composition with improvisation; and intercultural collaboration. In 2019 he was awarded a research grant to explore the fretless guitar scene of West Asia. His latest academic publications have addressed modern-day electric guitar performance.

Dr Rich Perks - Fretless aficionado extraordinaire

The Auction

To Auction or Not … or Not Just Yet

It became clear very quickly that keeping The Beatles' fretless guitar was not realistically going to be an option for Ray. The valuation and subsequent global publicity created a major security headache. The guitar would have to go to a new home and hopefully somewhere it could still be on display and even be played on occasion. Ray is not someone to lavishly cherish a guitar by putting it in a fancy display case, never to be played, or stored in a vault and forgotten in its dark resting place.

Fairly soon, Ray decided to approach the leading auctioneers and find out how to proceed. My only suggestion was to wait until after the *Antiques Roadshow* programme went on air. Then we could benefit from the resulting publicity if there was going to be any. When you go to auction there is no second chance. When it's gone, that's it. So he might as well go for it, big time.

I thought the best way I could support Ray was to help underpin and validate as much of the history of the guitar as possible, and when the time came, in our own way create as much interest as possible using the power of social media. Ray was negotiating with the auction houses, and one stood out. It made sense as Jon Baddeley was the *Antiques Roadshow* expert who gave the valuation and managing director of the international auctioneer, Bonhams of Knightsbridge. A visit was arranged to meet Jon and Stephen Maycock, one of his trusted experts at Ray's home.

The day came and all checked out okay. The guitar was little known but completely authentic. A very rare find with a compelling story, but with Jon keen to advise that his valuation was subject to market conditions and at auction the valuation could be a tad optimistic. Jon advised Ray that after further research the estimate was reduced to £200,000 to £300,000. Timing would be critical, and of course Bonhams would be delighted to be the auctioneers of choice.

It was a deal, Ray was going for it, Bonhams would take the Bartell fretless into their care, and that would at least be a security worry taken care of.

I was now having my own little panic. Ray and I were talking about me writing a book on the back of all my research. I had established contact with a number of people in California who worked at Bartell, including Dave Peckels, son of Ted, and we had ambitions to take a trip over and arrange a reunion of sorts. Dave Peckels had a fretless and Greg Segal was up in Portland, Oregon with one of the three known to exist. What an opportunity to get them all together, maybe for the last time. We were thinking of going toward the end of April 2020. But then … Covid 19 screwed that idea nicely.

The auction was off for now, and the reunion wasn't going to happen anytime soon. Everyone was locked down at home and travel was completely off the cards. Some things are more important in life, global health being one of them. The lockdown months ticked by …

The Auction Approaches

Bonhams started to get the ball rolling, with renowned guitar historian and prolific author Tony Bacon assigned to do due diligence background checks and pull together the catalogue entry for the forthcoming auction.

This was really good news. Tony has a long track record as a researcher, historian and music writer. His numerous books are of the highest quality and he is highly respected.

Tony and Ray spent a couple of hours on the phone, and we made sure all the golden nuggets of information were highlighted. There was so much detail in the story, and although I was confident in my research and sent a comprehensive document detailing everything to Bonhams, it was good to have it picked over, validated and questioned by an expert.

I was contacted by Steve Clarke, who was tasked to take detailed photos and make a technical assessment. Steve has been a guitar tech for more than 30 years and had already undertaken such investigations on the guitars of Pete Townsend, Paul Kossoff, Prince, Angus Young, Keith Richards and even George Harrison, with his work published in his *Famous Frets* publication.

During his time, he has re-fretted, repaired, altered, customised and created relic lookalike guitars. I called Steve, who is really passionate about his work and a proper guitar geek. I felt somewhat inadequate, being neither a proper musician, journalist or guitar expert. However, I do believe in the old adage, 'If a job's worth doing, it's worth doing well', and I was confident in my detailed research.

I gave Steve the high-level story and hinted at some of the hidden details and how there was so much to take in. I sent him links to my @FindingFretless twitter feed and Bartell Pinterest site.

Steve replied after a good rummage around, "Wow! It's really nice to see such information and great pictures - absolutely brill. Thanks for the story, it is amazing, incredible to think that this guitar was at Abbey Road and the tracks it's likely played on. I can't believe the background you have found on the Bartell. The Hendrix story is a gem."

On 11 July 2020, there was an update from Steve, telling me, "I had a great day and have some interesting things to tell. Nice to finally see one of these guitars!".

Here's Steve's tech review of The Beatles' fretless Bartell guitar.

"Some observations after taking the back off: a couple of controls appear to be defective; on the neck pickup, the tone control is not working; the treble control is working in reverse to how it should be; the toggle switch seems to have been replaced at some point, but obviously many years ago.

"The neck is not ebony. It's called phenolic. I've seen it before, they used it on Steinberger guitars. It's interesting stuff, phenolic plastic, going back a long way, used under the trade name Bakelite.

"Polyoxybenzylmethylenglycolanhydride was the first plastic made from synthetic components. It is a thermosetting phenol formaldehyde resin, formed from a condensation reaction of phenol with formaldehyde.

"So we have a sandwich of a phenolic fingerboard (Bakelite) over a rosewood cap fitted to a maple neck. This is unlike other Bartells, where there is a layer of paint on a maple neck that wears thins so you can begin to see the maple. This dates it to an early prototype.

"I also think the rosewood fingerboard under the Bakelite plastic was from a guitar. When using a Blacklight (a very powerful LED light) in certain light conditions if you look carefully you can see lines underneath it. They probably used another rosewood fingerboard from another guitar with the fret slots on it, and used that instead of a new virgin piece of rosewood. That has been glued to a maple neck, hence you have the side-dots already on the rosewood guitar neck, and then it has been milled out on the back to make it thinner.

"I don't think they would have done that on all their guitars, as it's expensive. It's at the prototype stage, where manufacturers do these things to see how the wood performs. It was interesting to see this construction as it is unusual and something you wouldn't see on a production model.

"The fretless neck, rosewood sandwich construction, would have been expensive to produce on this prototype and would probably have been simplified for a production model to be cost effective. It's typical at the prototype stage to be economical and use components they already have for other models as they try new construction ideas. It helps to keep the cost down.

"The control knobs are made by a company called Daca-ware in Chicago. These are radio knobs! Again, made of Bakelite. There are some chips - if you look very closely on the base (skirt) of the knob, that has some tiny little chips. Plastic doesn't do that.

"I took one off, and underneath it was the Daca-ware logo, model Daca-ware 30. Known as fluted dial skirted knobs made by Daca-ware, made to fit a 1/4 inch shaft.

"There is a certain smell about it. If you rub it on the palm of your hand to generate some heat it gives off a smell, because it's formaldehyde! Bakelite is used on amplifiers and tuners, and it all makes sense for that period because it was available at that time."

Steve found the same fluted knob on internet auction site eBay.

"The pots (potentiometers) are made by Mallory - right for the period, famous for making capacitors for all the guitar companies. It's unusual to see Mallory control knobs. These would have been used in a radio. These knobs are 500k, with Centra Lab ceramic caps, which is brilliant (0.5 50Volt CRL). These are very rare to even source today, again dating the guitar to the mid

Steve Clarke - Author of Famous Frets

133

to late-'60s – 1966/67, when these guitars started to appear.

"These are the high-grade components of the time. The later Bartell's with silver caps (like a brushed aluminium inlay on the top), also made by Daca Ware, were tuning knobs for radios.

"There are no stickers, labels, tape or writing on the inside, it's all very clean.

"The tuners are Kluson Deluxe - the strings go through a hole on the shaft, unlike Fender tuners. Leo Fender did a deal with Kluson to produce a Fender only tuner with a slot in the top of the post - to differentiate it from other guitar manufacturers.

"The bridge is an 'aluminium compensating bridge' on a rosewood base. The nut has some packing underneath, which is something they would have done. It all screams, 'Homemade, prototype'.

"This is typical of the big guitar manufacturers of the day - Gibson, Fender and Gretsch, all the big guys, wanting to get their prototypes out to the big names of the day.

"The pickups are single coil with not many windings, the size similar to the neck pickup on a Fender Telecaster. Copper-wire with black tape. Paul Barth or Tom Mitchell probably did this by hand, and it's obviously handmade, not done by machine. The guitar weighs just over 6 1/2 lbs."

Bartell's maple necks were made at Deans Custom Furniture in Riverside, California.

Steve Clarke has been a guitar technician for over thirty years and during this time he has re-fretted, repaired, altered, customised and created relic lookalike guitars. Check out Steve Clarke's book Famous Frets, well worth a read. Credit Steve Clarke

Single coil pickup – hand-wound and 'aluminium compensating bridge' on a rosewood base. Size -80.14mm

Body thickness - 44.18mm, Nut width - 42.40mm, Weight - 6.10lbs, Capacitor centra labs - .05 50v crl. Photo credit, Images Steve Clarke and Paul Brett

Headstock thickness -13.68mm with two different Kluson deluxe tuners. Four safe-T-slot posts and two drill holes through the post. Mismatching indicates a prototype set up using random parts.

Daca-ware 30 - fluted dial skirted knobs. Capping Mallory control knobs (POTs).

A tasty sandwich of phenolic fingerboard (Bakelite) over a rosewood cap, fitted to a maple neck.

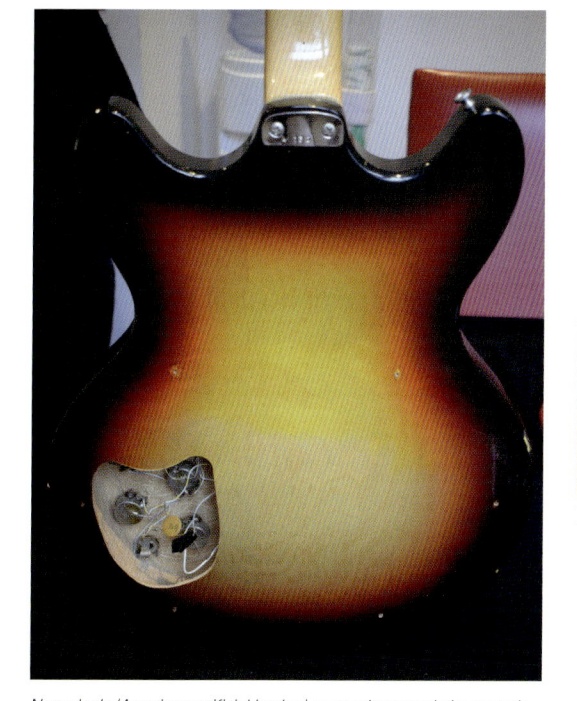

Naugahyde (American artificial leather) rear pad removed, the controls are accessible for servicing.

Tailpiece - Drilled for 12 strings, not six.

Auction Day

The big day finally arrived on 13 October 2020 at Bonhams of Knightsbridge.

Ray, his lovely wife Sally, my eldest daughter Kimberley and I travelled up to London for the big day. Another Covid-affected event with social distancing measures in place added to the bizarre events of the day, a once in a lifetime experience for all of us.

I was hopeful for Ray but concerned about the outcome. There had been a long delay since the story first hit the media, and these were strange and uncertain times. For Ray and Sally, it would be a blessed relief to finally have their day at the auction. Ray was naturally tense, doing well to hide his nerves and philosophical about the original valuation from the *Antiques Roadshow*, which he felt was probably a tad optimistic.

Ray had prior to the auction discussed the likely valuation with Bonhams and agreed to revise the asking price to a more realistic figure. Feedback from the viewing days was that there was much interest, but investors were concerned about playing such a unique instrument, and the lack of frets.

Bonhams did a very professional job with the catalogue, using the information from my research, validated by renowned guitar and Beatles authority Tony Bacon. They also commissioned a video of the headline items in the auction - the Bartell fretless and a Vox Phantom guitar used by Joy Division frontman and lyricist Ian Curtis in the music video for 'Love Will Tear Us Apart'.

The BBC's *Antiques Roadshow* and *South East News* teams asked Ray and I to keep them informed of any developments, and if the Bartell was going to auction.

I let them know how much we had discovered since *Antiques Roadshow*

Joy Division's Vox Phantom V1, as used by Ian Curtis. Photo: Bonhams

had aired, the ever-growing back story and possibility of a reunion of Bartell employees, musicians and families in LA. They were very keen to follow the continuing story and attend the auction.

On 12 August 2020, things were happening, contracts were to be signed, research, background and due diligence checks had been completed by Bonhams, the brochure wording finalised with Ray, including much of the back story I had managed to uncover over the months. The date was a secret for now, Bonhams have a strategy and they are the experts, we had to sit on our hands and wait for the green light before we could contact the BBC and starting our own amateur publicity campaign to ensure we reached the widest possible audience.

Then, on 28 August … well, don't count your chickens. First, the good news - the brochures were ready and the PR campaign was warming up, including videos of the guitar. Things were looking good until …. the dreaded CITES regulations on rosewood for instruments put the auction date in doubt.

Since 2017, CITES (Convention on International Trade In Endangered Species Of Wild Fauna and Flora) restrictions had made transporting guitars containing rosewood internationally far more difficult. CITES originally introduced the restrictions to protect rosewood, bubinga and kosso from overuse by the furniture industry – the effect on the world of musical instruments was not intended. The regulations caused the music instrument industry nothing but headaches, with the possibility of musicians running the risk of losing their guitars (or at least parts of them) to customs officers.

On 28 August 2019, CITES in Geneva, Switzerland voted to exempt finished musical instruments, parts, and accessories from restrictions on all rosewood species, except Brazilian rosewood. The restrictions on Brazilian rosewood, its endangered status and restrictions predating those on other kinds of rosewood, remained in place.

To ensure the auction complied with all current laws and legal aspects, Bonhams had earlier in the year applied for the affected guitars in the planned auction to receive relevant CITES Article 10 certification. Due again to Covid delays, certification had not been received, causing Bonhams to postpone the auction until that was received.

Finally, we got the all-clear though – it was all happening on 13 October, and the BBC's *Antiques Roadshow* - for its 'What Happened Next' edition - and *South East News* confirmed their attendance to film the event.

We couldn't be in the auction hall for the bidding, as buyer confidentiality and privacy is a key element for the major auction houses. We were in a side room, with live bidding shown on a screen, crowded in with cameras and microphones recording our every reaction. It was a long wait, involving several hours of frantic bidding on a whole range of interesting items prior to lot 184, the Bartell fretless.

Finally, cameras rolling, Ray's prized possession was introduced and bidding commenced …

Bidding was brisk to begin with, followed by a stutter, the hammer falling and immediately re-opening as the auctioneer noticed a very risky late bid, the hammer eventually falling at £190,000.

As we were all sat in the room, being filmed, with face marks on, the experience was a real mix of emotions. Ray, I think, was initially relieved that it went for a sensible, if not record-breaking amount, nearer to his expectations, quickly followed by a sense that he would probably never again see his unique, much-loved guitar, as given to him by George Harrison. We all clapped excitedly and congratulated Ray. The press wanted his reaction and comments for the evening news, and we were straight into interviews.

Antiques Roadshow recorded some more and invited us to Pinewood Studios at a later date for more detailed interviews to conclude the story.

Finally, we were done, we headed out into the evening in the Kensington rain, enjoyed an Italian meal in celebration and then headed home.

For now, the story of the Bartell fretless guitar was over. I do believe however, it is holding on to hidden secrets, gems still to be discovered and fresh stories to tell.

Ray's fretless guitar (on the left) sold for £237,563, including the auctioneer's premium

Other highlights of the sale included:

The Vox Phantom used by Ian Curtis on 'Love Will Tear Us Apart' sold for £162,563

Annie Lennox's Steinway grand piano, used at her home, sold for £35,062

The Hasselblad 500c camera Used by Iain Macmillan to photograph the cover image for The Beatles' Abbey Road album in 1969 sold for £35,062.

FINDING FRETLESS

Ray Russell has his day at Bonhams Auctions filming for Antiques Roadshow

140

Paul Brett

Bonhams commissioned a series of stunning publicity shots, pre-auction.

***Antiques Roadshow* – What Happened Next**

For their 2020 end of year review, 'What Happened Next', the BBC's *Antiques Roadshow* included the Bartell fretless guitar story, broadcast on Sunday 29 December.

The BBC invited me to be interviewed by the show's host Fiona Bruce at the iconic Pinewood Studios to catch up on the developments in the story and cover Ray's reaction at the Bonhams auction.

As a result of the *Antiques Roadshow* 2020 review, Adam Olivestone got in touch to tell me he had seen the show and that it was his father, Tony Olivestone, who had recorded Kenny Everett's 6 June 1968 interview with The Beatles, and still had the master-tape.

And Adam told me that Tony was happy to talk. Fantastic! These are Tony's recollections from that night at EMI's Abbey Road Studios.

Tony Olivestone revealed, "By complete chance, I saw the tail end of the BBC's *Antiques Roadshow* 'What Happened Next' show at Christmas 2020, and the item on the fretless guitar caught my attention. When I heard the whole story I thought, 'Oh my goodness, this is the famous guitar I saw over 50 years ago!' And I remember the occasion well.

"I worked for EMI Records at the time, from early 1967 to 1969. At the tender age of 19, I was head of overseas promotions, which seems extraordinary now. I had this idea to do taped interviews with EMI artists who were either going abroad or having an album or single promoted abroad. I was given pretty much free rein to do that.

"One day, the head of the department called me to say, 'We've got a guy coming in from America on behalf of Capitol Records and he wants to interview four DJs'. Capitol Records was part of EMI at the time.

Tony Olivestone - the proud owner of that exclusive tape recorded at Abbey Road, Thursday 6 June 1968. Photos: Tony Olivestone

"I had to find the DJs to interview. One was Jimmy Savile, and I had the unfortunate displeasure of meeting him. Then there was Alan 'Fluff' Freeman and somebody else, I can't remember who. Finally Kenny Everett, who I was a great fan of.

"We arranged to meet at the Hilton in Park Lane, London, where this American guy was staying. We enjoyed a nice lunch, Kenny wasn't as zany as when he was broadcasting, but nonetheless he was good company.

"We went up to the room to record the interviews and Kenny was impressed by my EMI tape recorder. It was very strange, like a bit of Army kit, an old-fashioned reel-to-reel tape recorder.

"Kenny asked, 'Can I borrow that, because I'm doing an interview later this evening and it would help me greatly'. I said of course and showed Kenny how to use it. He said, 'Oh, it's a bit fiddly, would you mind coming with me?' I said, 'Well, who is it?'. When he said The Beatles, well, I couldn't believe it, and agreed immediately.

"Kenny told me to be at EMI Studios at Abbey Road by 8pm. When I got there, Kenny hadn't arrived, but I flashed my EMI card to show them I wasn't an imposter, and I was in!

"I was greeted by the sight of all four Beatles in different parts of the studio, doing this, that and the other. It was quite mind-boggling. Like most people at that age I was a massive, massive fan. I just couldn't believe what I was seeing! I'd already met a lot of famous people, including some big names from Motown, but there was something about The Beatles that was quite unreal.

"I wandered around for a few minutes waiting for Kenny. Nobody spoke to me. When Kenny arrived, we both went across to where John Lennon was sitting, cross-legged on the floor, with this strange apparition in white laying on the floor next to him, which turned out to be Yoko Ono.

"I turned on the tape recorder straight away to pick up what I could. From there on, I was holding the microphone throughout.

"It was a great big barn of a studio. I think it was studio 2. I wouldn't have known that at the time, but I believe that's where they did most of their recording from what I have read.

"Paul McCartney was standing at the far end. John, If I remember right, was sitting cross-legged on the floor. I could be wrong, but in my mind's eye I can picture him sitting on the floor playing the guitar, although on the tape John is saying he is sat on an amplifier, 'strumbling' the guitar. That's when Kenny asked what kind of guitar it was, and John said it was a fretless.

"Then Kenny said, 'Can you get Paul over to do something. That's where you can hear me and Kenny calling him from the far end of the studio, and McCartney came over. Eventually, George and Ringo joined the party. At one point, Kenny asked John, 'Can you sing a jazz version of 'Strawberry Fields Forever', and he started doing this funny scat thing.

"They were all standing around me. I don't think I appreciated at the time what an historical moment that was! A lot of people have met them, but to actually be in the studio with them, it was absolutely forbidden. Even Brian Epstein wasn't allowed in the studio with them. And there I was sitting there with Kenny Everett, with all of The Beatles around us. It became really zany.

"Although Yoko was there, I didn't know who she was at the time. She wasn't publicly known yet. She was strangely lying on the floor, dressed in white, motionless, silent throughout the whole thing. John went public with her about six months later.

"Then I did a bit at 13.45 where I say, 'This is Tony Olivestone...'

"I was standing at the far end of the studio where I had done the interview with Kenny, trying to eke out as much time as I could in the studio, and I added that little bit in to give myself a namecheck, and that is how I saw things, as I said them.

"John Lennon was right next to me, banging on a drum, Paul McCartney was playing lead guitar, and Ringo was pensively walking around thinking up new ideas. The whole scene was quite incredible!

"I don't remember the fretless going out of the area where we were sitting, so I can't be sure if McCartney was playing it at the end. But it was 53 years ago, and that is a detail I wouldn't remember.

"The track they were recording that day was, 'Don't Pass Me By', for the *White Album*, Ringo's song. I don't remember anyone else being there at the time, (other than) maybe Mel Evens, their roadie. At the end, I asked if I could stay a little bit to watch some more, and they said, 'We'd rather you didn't!'. I didn't want to push my luck, so on I went.

"If I hadn't have seen the Bartell fretless on *Antiques Roadshow* and told what is was, it might not have struck a chord … pardon the pun. I could see it was a fretless guitar, and John said it was a fretless guitar during the recording.

"I often wondered why the tape was out in the public domain, because I recorded it and kept the original recording. I ran it off back in my office at Manchester Square, then ran it round to Kenny at the BBC. He then edited most of it out and played it on his Radio One Sunday morning show, but most of it had been edited out and I assumed had been destroyed as it was never used. I confirmed with the BBC my entitlement to copyright ownership. I still have the letter authenticating that.

"I have never played it in that form since I first got it. I had it put on to a cassette several years later, then on to CD. I have one, and both my sons have a copy.

Final Observations

The rediscovery of the Bartell fretless guitar in late 2019 and the evolving story of its creation, journey to England and history with The Beatles has been seen as quite contentious in some circles, and expert opinions are split. There is reluctance by some to accept its history as claimed, but these are my findings to date.

Why was it not known about before? It was claimed by the family and workers of the Bartell company that a fretless prototype was given to a Beatle. This has now been proven conclusively. It was gifted to George Harrison between 1 and 4 August 1967.

John Lennon was playing the fretless on 6 June 68 during a long interview with Kenny Everett that was recorded by Tony Olivestone, who still has the master tape. Paul McCartney was possibly messing about on the fretless at the end of the same interview, while John banged away on the drums.

It seems that opportunities to note, investigate and research the Bartell fretless since that recording at Abbey Road - where John clearly states 'It's a fretless guitar' - had been over-looked and inadvertently missed by numerous Beatles experts, and therefore it didn't make the history books … until now. To be fair, there was little knowledge of the Bartell fretless guitar before 2019.

Top Gear in London did raise the question of the fretless a number of years ago, when they serviced The Beatles' guitars in the 1970s. This was again overlooked.

Ray was gifted it in 1985 by George. Ray is a hard-working, modest, professional guitarist who regarded it more as a tool of the trade than a high-value collectible. He played it occasionally and liked it. It was played on his 2006 album Goodbye Svengali.

Why are there no photos of the fretless at Abbey Road? It is true that at the time of writing we have not yet discovered any images at Abbey Road, despite many months of searching.

However, Jan Gorski-Mescir has seen images in the past. He said, "The photo I've seen is of John noodling with it in Studio 2, looking slightly to his right toward the camera during the *White Album* recording.

"There's another one from the same session showing George talking to George Martin, with the Bartell visible from about halfway up the neck in the background. But the pic is usually cropped so the Bartell neck, and that of Macca's RS 1999 Rickenbacker bass are never in the most used version."

The current non-existence of a photo does not disprove its residence at Abbey Road or its use in any particular recording. But finding photographs would really help!

And why didn't we ask the Apple Corps, EMI Archives, Paul McCartney, Abbey Road, Giles Martin, the George Harrison estate, and so on? Well, we tried.

To the counter-argument that it could have been any other guitar or effect used on the *White Album*, and assertions that the available evidence isn't strong enough to warrant noting the guitars used on the *White Album* sessions, well …

There are no other fretless six-string electric guitars known or claimed to have been in the possession of The Beatles at any time. In fact, there weren't many electric fretless guitars in the world in 1968.

Respected Beatles scholars who are acknowledged fretless aficionados consider the fretless was used on the album, not least Dr Kenny Jenkins and Dr Richard Perks.

Furthermore, we have listened to the personal accounts of Dr Jan Gorski-Mescir, a friend of George Harrison for 30 years, with inside knowledge and recollection of personal conversations with George, specifically on the fretless.

Identifying a fretless guitar requires a skilled musician with a trained ear that can tell the difference in bends, slides and sustain that are different to any other type of guitar.

The only other known Bartell fretless guitar in regular use is owned and played by Greg Segal, and he is also convinced that the Bartell can clearly be heard on the *White Album*.

Master tapes and liner notes did not always refer to specific guitars. There are no known specific notes on the use of a fretless, or indeed other instruments they used occasionally.

Youtubers Alby House, using a fretless Eastwood version of an Acoustic Black Widow (a very different instrument to the semi-hollow Bartell) concluded that a fretless guitar was used on the *White Album*.

John Lennon mentions the fretless guitar on the January 1969 Nagra reels – a renowned set of audio tapes from the filming of the 'Get Back' / *Let It Be* rehearsal and recording sessions.

Doug Sulpy informed me that on page 25 of *Drugs, Divorce and a Slipping Image: The Complete, Unauthorised Story of The Beatles' 'Get Back' Sessions*, John mentions that he'd like to emulate the peculiar guitar sound George achieved in his song 'Long, Long, Long', which appeared on *The Beatles*. John wasn't present for the 'Long, Long, Long' recording session and assumes that George had used a fretless guitar. George informs John that he used his Gibson on that number, but that really doesn't matter – it isn't the specific kind of guitar that interests John, but the tone that it produced.

The question is, was the Bartell fretless used on any other recordings between 1967 and 1985?

John was particularly intrigued by the fretless. However, George became the custodian, keeping at his Friar Park home. Could it have been used by George on debut solo album, *Wonderwall Music*, the soundtrack to the 1968 film, *Wonderwall*, or his 1969 follow-up album, *Electronic Sound*, or indeed any of his solo material up until 1985? Well, at present we simply don't know, but it is possible!

Why did Harrison take it to Mike Moran's studio for the recording of Water in 1985 if he didn't think it was a valuable tool that might add something to the session?

It would seem the sensible course of action would be to establish the historical facts, with all sides of the argument collectively considered by all the experts. Besides, The Beatles continue to be able to surprise us.

Dave Peckels' Bartell fretless

Serial Number: A163. A very early Bartell-branded, acoustic fretless guitar, from around 1966/68, as owned by Bartell company president Ted Peckels' son Dave.

"A couple of years ago, I managed to buy a fretless acoustic guitar from a guy on eBay who said he bought it at a swap-meet. I don't really know what to make of it. I don't know if it's a one-off, a prototype." - Dave Peckels, 21 July 2019

On 26 February 2020, Dave updated me, saying, "It seems crazy that the seller got it at a swap-meet, but that's what he told me. I actually didn't buy it from him. I traded him a Bartell double-neck - also fairly rare, but I had two of them so I reluctantly let go of one."

From eBay, 3 July 2014, a long and rambling listing read, 'A lot of guitars on eBay get labelled rare, but this one truly is! This could have been owned by a famous rocker. No way to say it was or was not.

"Serial Number: A163. A very early Bartell made in the USA, acoustic Black Widow fretless guitar. Bartell was the original and first maker of acoustic guitars. Based in California, the company was founded by Paul Barth - a designer for Rickenbacker and Magnatone - and Ted Peckels.

'Bartell was approached by Acoustic Control Corporation to make its guitar and bass line. Bartell made very few before production was moved to Japan, the reasons being Bartell could not make enough and they could be made cheaper in Japan. The vast majority found today are the Japanese-made normally fretted guitars. Supposedly, Mosrite made the last 200, before production stopped in 1974.

'Collectors of these say fewer than 1,000 were made, and that was the normal fretted version. How many fretless? Who knows. Jimi Hendrix owned a prototype Black Widow, photographed in October 1968 in studio with it. He also owned a fretless version he used for slide, but it was stolen, and Jimi requested another. As it was being made, Jimi died.

'That is confirmed By Ted Peckels' son Dave, on Unfretted.com. He says his Dad often told the story of making a couple Of fretless guitars For Jimi. Dave often wondered what happened to No.2 and speculated that it may have been the one (Frank) Zappa purchased years later.

'On 6 June 1968, John Lennon along with The Beatles appears on The Kenny Everett Radio Show, recorded at Abbey Road Studios. Kenny asks, 'What kind of guitar is that? It's very strange looking.' John replies, 'It's a fretless guitar.

Dave Peckels' Acoustic fretless guitar

'According to Mark Moffett of Top Gear Guitars in London in 1973, Apple Studios sent a shipment of guitars to be cleaned and set up - Rocky, Lennon's Epiphone; the rosewood Tele; Rick 12-String ... I can confirm there was a Black Widow fretless guitar that came from Apple to be worked on, in an email from Unfretted.com on 11 December 2011.

'Frank Zappa purchased a fretless Black Widow in 1973 from Guitar Center. According to Zappa.com, that guitar

FINDING FRETLESS

was stolen. Zappa also had a fretted version, pictured on Zappa Gear.com, taken at UMRK in 2012.

'All the fretless guitars here were obviously made by 1968. This guitar dates to the same time or earlier. I have never seen one with Kluson tuners, and no other tuners have ever been on it, no binding on body or headstock, it has f-holes (like Jimi's). Production guitars did not have f-holes. Walnut color is original as this predates the black ones, neck is burst color, one pot is stiff to turn but works. Opportunity to own a very rare special specimen, like three of rock's legends owned and played.'

I asked Tom Mitchell on 6 May 2020 about Ted Peckels' son Dave's brown walnut-coloured fretless guitar, and how much he remembered about that.

He replied, "Not too much. It was a rough one to do because it was a natural colour and it was hard to get a finished colour on it to be standard. As we went along, we had to have a close standard set for guitars because Ted wouldn't let them go out the door unless they were right up to power."

What journey had this rare Bartell fretless taken since the late '60s? If you know anything of its history, I'd love to hear it.

It seems that the eBay seller that traded the Bartell fretless with a Bartell double-neck from Dave Peckels was James Mayfield, from Warrior, Alabama. Dave has confirmed this.

I found this listing on *Reverb*, with the following description:

'Rare Bartell double-neck guitar. Designed by Paul Barth of Rickenbacker and Magnatone fame. He and Ted Peckels Started the Bartell guitar company in Riverside, California.

'I obtained this guitar from the Peckels family. Rare and only one with maple fingerboard in excellent condition. Might trade for Martin or Gibson acoustic guitar.'

It would be lovely to be in contact with James Mayfield in Alabama to find out more about how he acquired this branded, acoustic, walnut-coloured fretless guitar.

Where and when was this swap-meet, who was the previous owner and how long did they have it? There is more to discover on this model, for sure.

Dave Peckels has a passion for guitars made by his father's company, Bartell, and has acquired a neat collection of the company's fine products from the 1960s, including a

Bartell Spyder Serial #F-155 A solid body model built from 1965

Bartell Apache. A solid body model built from 1965, The bridge and pickup mounting differ from the Spyder

148

Bartell Spyder, serial no. F-155, a solid-body model built from the year 1965; and a Bartell Apache, its bridge and pickup mounting differing from the Spyder, and with added confederate flag sticker.

Dave Peckels said, "The photo here is of my Dad Ted, playing my yellow double-neck. About 10 years ago, I was searching on eBay, and one of the posted photos for the guitar was this one. I almost fainted when I saw it, and quickly made a deal with the seller.

"The seller said that the photo was in the guitar case when he bought it. The location of the photo is inside the Cooper's Music store."

Another rare Bartell double-neck oddity. Could this be the one on which Les Paul was working on the design with Paul Barth?

Paul's grandson, Steven Sagar remembers Les Paul of the Gibson company coming to dinner on more than one occasion, and Paul's daughter said he was making a double-neck for him.

Dave Peckels' Bartell double-neck, found on eBay. Photo: Dave Peckels

FINDING FRETLESS

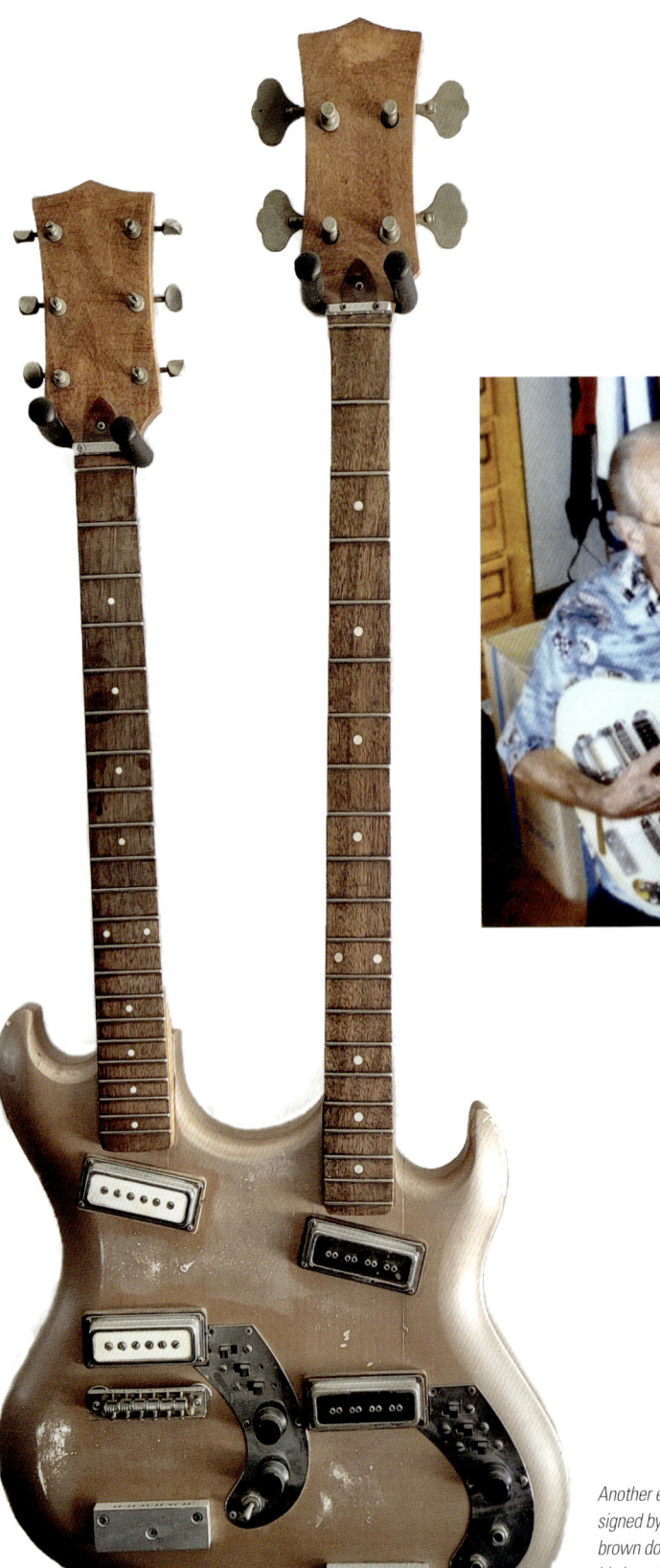

Ted Peckels inside Coopers Music with a cream Bartell double-neck

Another eBay find for Dave Peckels, signed by the band BobaFlex. A unique brown double-neck Bartell he's doing his best to restore

Greg Segal's Black Widow fretless

Serial No. A130: an acoustic, branded, Black Widow fretless guitar, circa 1966/68, belonging to Greg Segal, a talented musician and artist who plays multiple instruments, and records and produces for the Phantom Airship Records label, based in Portland Oregon (for more detail, try www.gregsegal.com).

Greg has been involved in progressive music since the late '70s, improvising, writing and recording his own music independently. He discovered and bought his black acoustic fretless guitar on 13 April 1985 from a now-defunct music store in Reseda, California, formerly owned by Michael O Paganelli, called Harmony Music (around the corner from what was the Reseda walk-in theatre, next to Sherman Way and across from the Country Club).

He said, "The acoustic fretless showed up there in 1982 and they wanted $1,400 for it, and I couldn't ever imagine even having that kind of money. But even at that price, I figured it would be gone inside a week.

"Instead, it sat there for three years. Every time I came in, I'd look for it - it was love at first sight - figuring it would soon be gone. The price kept dropping. I asked the owner of the shop why he thought it wasn't selling. He said people would come in and try it, but it ended up being too weird for them. I was dumbfounded. The fretless took years to sell."

Greg recalls all sorts of people playing it but deciding against buying it.

"I was told Gary Moore was one of them, but I don't know. I also know Rory Gallagher and David Lindley shopped there. Finally, in April '85, I had saved my tax return to go into the studio, and if memory serves I had gone in there to sell them back a neck I couldn't use, and had bought from them previously. The fretless was still there, and the price had dropped to $175, if I recall correctly. I still have the receipt somewhere. So instead of getting the cash on my exchange, which was supposed to allow me to buy more studio time, I put it toward the fretless and took from my studio money to pay for it. I have never regretted that decision."

Harmony Music, 7227 Canby, Reseda, California. The company was registered on 10 May 1979 by Michael O Paganelli. Most people knew him as Mike.

Greg Segal added, "Mike was gold. If I was interested in a used effect, he'd tell me to take it out on a gig, and if I liked it, come back and buy it. And I always did! But how cool is that? I have a lot of gear from there still.

"Mike who owned and ran the place would let me take effects to gigs, and buy them after if I liked them. Who does that? I bought my fretless guitar there too. It is one in a million. I was not a happy guy when Harmony closed. Best guitar store in LA."

Regarding thoughts that this could have been the acoustic, branded fretless once owned by Frank Zappa, later believed stolen, Greg speculates, "I would think with Zappa and family being very local, they lived at most 10 minutes from the shop. If it was his, it would have been spotted. I asked the guy that owned the shop where it came from, and he said some guy had just come in and sold it to them. I never could get any more out of him than that.

"He lived close enough to me that this could easily have been the case. Encino and Reseda are right next to each other, and most musicians in the valley hit all the shops. I did. So maybe the Zappa connection is solid.

"The story about him taking off the acoustic logo might not be true. I don't think Zappa actually took the logo off. He said that had been requested by the maker, who told him it was a prototype. But Zappa also said it was stolen, and Dweezil said otherwise."

I had an update in April 2020 from Greg, who added, "I have just reconnected today with a good friend. He's been totally out of touch, so he knows nothing about the fretless Bartell group. This was in his email today:

"He said, 'A few years ago my wife and I went to a Zappa Plays Zappa show. Afterwards, we got to meet Dweezil. I mentioned in passing, 'I have a friend who may own one of your Dad's guitars.' He said, 'What one?'. I told him you had an acoustic, branded fretless that you bought in the mid-'80s. Dweezil asked, 'Where did he get it?'. 'Reseda'.

'Dweezil laughed and told me that in '81 Frank sold off a bunch of stuff that was collecting mothballs, so he could purchase a Synclavier.

Greg Segal

He said the fretless was definitely in that lot, and the fact that Reseda is only 10 minutes away from the Woodland Hills Zappa house. This probably means you own Frank's guitar.'

"The fretless showed up at Harmony Music, Reseda in '81 or '82. The Barcus Berry modification that Zappa spoke about could easily have been taken off with no trace if it wasn't hard-installed (via suction cup, a wire under the bridge, etc)'.

"I recalled there being a gummy circular mark near the bridge from a suction cup Barcus Berry on it before I owned it. Not only had the physical traces been there when I bought it, but it was offered to me to have it put back on, but I couldn't afford it. It took me a lot of hard work and a few different kinds of furniture polish to get the round sticky mark off it! It was so difficult to get off. I actually left it there for a couple of years. According to Dweezil, the fretless was among instruments sold around the same time the fretless arrived at the music store."

So, is there a link from Greg Segal's fretless to Frank Zappa who lost or sold an acoustic Black Widow in the same area that Greg lived? We'll look at that later.

We all know it's a small world, of only 7.7 billion people, but unknown to two musicians living either side of the Atlantic - Greg Segal in Portland, Oregon, USA, and Ray Russell in Hailsham, East Sussex, UK – and yet aware of each other's work and connected on Facebook, they were the owners of two of only four Bartell acoustic fretless guitars known to exist at the time.

In Greg showing appreciation of the release of Ray's 2017 album *Now, More Than Ever* in 2019, I linked the two together, and they became 'fretless buddies'.

Greg added, "I started trying to make a list of tracks I used the fretless on, and to my surprise it kept growing. Most of the time I used it with an e-bow. It's just a good combination for the instrument. But there are some picked recordings as well.

"With my solo stuff, I just record things with whatever sound I think it needs, and then promptly forget all but the most obvious instruments. Plus, as I go through all the old Paper Bag recordings, more things keep turning up. The fretless pretty much always came to the studio with me for those sessions, and I think something I recently put out has a fretless track on it. Again, once it's out, I forgot and will have to revisit the album and check."

Greg finally took time out to sit down and rediscover his recordings using his prized fretless, and it turns out he was being very productive with it. (Greg's recordings are listed in the Discogrophy).

"The Bartell acoustic fretless has a really distinct sound. It sounds hollow and live. You can tell it's not a solid body. But more than that, if you've heard one, or played one, you recognise it right away. It just does not sound like any other guitar I've ever heard. The first time I heard Zappa's 'Down In De Dew', bang, there it was. I saw Ray Russell on TV with one, and there was the sound.

"If I'd just come into the room and hadn't looked at the screen, I would have known. It's that distinct. People discuss differences in sound between Gibson and Fender, but this is way more distinct than that. The pickups are not loud. And because it's a hollow body, if you crank the volume, it feeds back, and not in a good way. I raised the bridge pickup hoping to elevate the volume, but it didn't do much. The best way to do that live would be to put it through an amp with its usual low volume, without trying to push it, mic that and then run it to the PA. Recording, it doesn't matter.

As you might expect, barre chords are about the only kind you can play, at least without many years' practise. If you wanted to become exclusively a fretless guitarist, you'd have a long road to become really good. You can't just pick it up and sail with it, no matter how good a guitarist you are. Open tunings work well with it and offer a lot more possibilities than standard tuning.

On a fretted instrument, you have a sort of idiot-proofed pitch guide, where, if the intonation is set up right and you press your finger between the frets, you'll hit the note. Fretless instruments are microtonal - or continuously tonal - and it's difficult to get proper pitch. It's a major reason why a fretless guitar looks like a guitar, rather than *is* a guitar. It shares a shape and a tuning setup and many design similarities, but it really is its own instrument".

"The Bartell/Acoustic fretless has a really distinct sound. It sounds hollow and live. It's absolutely unique, like a voice." – Greg Segal

"Playing slide is different from fretless in a couple of ways. With slide guitar you have that continuous/microtonal freedom. You use the frets as pitch markers (directly over the fret is your pitch, not between frets).

"Slide is glide - you're rubbing one object against another and it's a completely different feel. With a fretless, you feel the strings, you feel the drag of your finger directly on them, and to an extent you have to dig in. There's not much resistance at all, unlike a fretted instrument. And unlike a slide, your finger isn't perfectly straight, so you have to work to keep it that way as much as possible if you're playing more than one string.

"If you're playing slide on a fretted instrument and your action isn't high, you have to be careful not to press down with the slide or you'll hit the frets. It's very noticeable. You hear the clunk, it stops your note and your sustain. Slide on a fretless might seem redundant, but actually has its own sound. No frets to hit, for a start.

"But the change in timbre from low to high string is still there and easily heard. Slide on a standard guitar is more glossy, and it has the advantage of being able to make notes well above the fretboard. But even played with a slide above the board, the fretless has its own sound. It may just be this make, the pickups may colour the sound in such a way as to make the difference obvious. I've honestly never played another fretless, so I don't know.

"I think guitarists who are familiar with classical stringed instruments, especially cello, would have the most affinity with it. Not only is having experience with a fretless board a great advantage, but the sound of the plucked strings is very much like on a cello. The lower strings have a round, full tone and more sustain. The higher strings sound increasingly like pizzicato cello, the higher you go. The tone and sustain dampen really noticeably.

"If you finger pick, you get that pizzicato sound, but if you're using a pick it's kind of odd. It has that defined strike sound of a pick but it's weaker, the decay is very quick, and the sound is not nearly as bright as pick stroke. That has its uses too, it's just different than what you'd be used to.

"On most of the recordings I made with it, I played the fretless with an e-bow. The e-bow generates an electromagnetic field which vibrates the string, producing infinite sustain. Playing with one on a fretted instrument, you get breaks and interruptions of the sustain when you hit a fret, and you have to go over them pretty fast if you want to lessen that. On a fretless, that's not a problem, you just glide, as long as you want.

"It can be mistaken for a synthesiser, both with the e-bow and without, but especially if you add some effects. On the track 'Wednesday Night, 10 pm', I added some delay and octave divider, played with a pick right up by the bridge, and the result sounded very much like a sequencer off an old Tangerine Dream record.

There's one other big advantage of playing it with an e-bow, and that's that it boosts the volume. You have to find the 'hot spot', the place where the field drives directly into the pickup, and your volume jumps dramatically. This was one of the few ways I was able to take it out live, but even that eventually didn't merit the risk of potential damage to the instrument, lugging it around clubs. But with all that, I think the charm of this particular guitar is still very much in its original sound. It's absolutely unique, like a voice".

George was seen as the d'Artagnan of the group, a devil-may-care rogue who was actually a kickass fencer. In fact, he nearly killed Bruce Dickinson, of Iron Maiden fame. They were sparring and George's epee broke, leaving a very sharp point on the end. George didn't know this until he was thrusting forward at Bruce's heart. Protective gear or no, that point would have gone straight through. Thankfully George caught it in time and stopped short.

Paper Bag promo shots, March 1987, with Greg Segal on the left. Credit Naomi Peterson

… FINDING FRETLESS

FRETLESS – MISSING IN ACTION

The fretless models that are known to be out there somewhere.

Mike Deasy's Bartell-branded sunburst fretless (serial number unknown)

In late June 2020, I found a Facebook post from six months earlier involving an obscure story about a further LA session player that had a chance meeting with George Harrison, the writer posting on 11 December 2019 about the December 1967 release of the album, *The Voice Of Scott McKenzie* on Ode Records, which included major hit 'San Francisco (Be Sure to Wear Flowers In Your Hair)'.

The writer explained, "In August 1967, (John) Phillips assembled a proper series of recording sessions to record more songs for the release of an album by McKenzie. During one of those sessions at United Western Recorders, Studio B, an entourage of people invaded the studio, led by a long-haired man in a white robe. The man stepped out of the booth into the studio and sat down in front of the guitarist, and they talked and jammed for about 30 minutes before he left with his followers.

"The guitarist was Mike (Deasy), who had to turn and ask another musician who the guy was. The man was Beatle George Harrison, who apparently had a lot of fun playing Mike's fretless guitar."

Apparently, the 3 August 1967 session was recorded, and could well be with Lou Adler, Bones Howe or the record company archives now. And according to Mike Deasy himself, "It was recorded. Wherever the Scott McKenzie masters are, our jam will be there … I would love to hear it also!".

Looking back further, I found a post from 26 February 2019 concerning a 2006 interview by author Dawn Eden Goldsteing with Mike Deasy, who told her about a 1967 recording session by The Mamas & The Papas. It read, "I had this guitar that didn't have any frets, and it could make some really interesting sliding sounds. This guy was interested, so I handed it to him, and he was a good guitar player. We played guitars for about 30 minutes. It turned out he was George Harrison! I had no idea."

Mike added, "George came into the studio and we sat down and played together for around a half-hour. I gave him the fretless to play. It enabled you to do things no other guitar was capable of. It was a relaxed, fun jam time. When he left, I asked Lou Adler, 'Who was that guy?'"

Larry Knechtel, a keyboard player, was also at the session. He more or less said the same, adding, "The session stopped as an entourage entered the control room. Harrison was wearing a long, white meditation shirt or gown and stepped down into the playing area of the studio and went right over to Mike and sat down in front of him.

"The two talked and played guitar for 20 to 30 minutes and George was especially interested in the fretless guitar Mike had. Then he got up and went back into the control room and the entourage left. Mike asked, 'Who was that?'. He didn't know it was a Beatle."

United Western Recorders was a two-building recording studio complex in Hollywood, one of the most successful independent recording studios of the 1960s. In 1984, Bill Putnam sold the studio complex to Allen Sides, who renamed the buildings Ocean Way Recording, as they would be known until 1999. Today the studios are known as United Recording Studios. Studio B was completed by Bill Putnam in 1958. It is one of the most celebrated rooms in the recording world. From Nancy Sinatra's 'These Boots Are Made for Walking' to Radiohead's *Hail to the Thief*, and from Green Day's *American Idiot* to Beck's Grammy-winning *Morning Phase*, Studio B is a favourite of some of the world's biggest artists, producers and engineers.

In January 2021 I contacted the owners of United Recording Studios, and studio historian Victor Janacua advised me, "Unfortunately all the records/studio logs from the '60s left with the previous owner many years ago." I then found another contact, Gary Boatner, who worked there in the '70s, and he told me, "All the tapes were thrown out, unless someone claimed them". So it does looks like a lost cause, but never say never!

George Harrison was to return again on 16 October 1968. Harrison flew to Los Angeles for a third recording session, to produce songs for Jackie Lomax's debut album, *Is This What You Want?* On the album were Harrison on rhythm guitar playing a three pickup Gibson Es-5, Joe Osborne on bass guitar, Larry Knechtel on piano, electric piano and organ, and Hal Blaine on drums.

Incredibly, George had received his Bartell fretless guitar – that first prototype - a day or two earlier from Al Casey, his wife Maxine taking it up to Blue Jay Way where George was staying. Richard Bennett (Neil Diamond, Mark Knopfler) who worked for and was mentored by Al, remembered this, with this recollection of events also confirmed by Mort Marker.

And whilst peeling back the story of how George Harrison became the owner of the first of the prototype fretless models, I discovered the link between Al Casey, George and Mike Deasy.

Al and Mike were both Wrecking Crew members and two of the best first-call session players in LA. They both played on the *Elvis '68 Comeback Special* and many other sessions. So when I discovered Mike had a Bartell fretless, the obvious connotation was that Al had also sold one to Mike.

Mike Deasy was a very interesting character, and I carried on the conversation with him via Facebook, first picking up on the possibility that – with George in California that first week of August 1967 - Al Casey gave him a Bartell fretless and also got one to George.

He replied, "All probability."

Accordingly, I sent Mike an image of the three surviving fretless guitars we knew about, to see if he recognised any of them. He responded, "The one on my album cover *Letters To My Head* may be the one George had."

I searched frantically for the album cover. Could there possibly be another Bartell out there? And there it was, on Mike's 1973 album - a Bartell sunburst fretless by his right shoulder, and an acoustic Black Widow on the floor by a National Resonator.

I chuckled, thinking about how all three guitars were incredibly linked through Paul Barth.

I asked Mike if both guitars were from Al. George Harrison got his in 1967, and it was back in London by 1968. Did Mike still have those guitars? He replied, "I don't have the guitars. I may have bought them from Al. After I moved to Washington and commuted to LA, I gave all the guitars I wasn't playing to a church in Sacramento, California that had their instruments ripped off, and that included the Black Widow and the Bartell fretless".

That was a generous thing to do, I suggested, and no doubt very much appreciated. The fretless model didn't make it into full production, so there are just a very small number of them about, but they have an incredible history – including links with Jimi Hendrix, The Beatles and Frank Zappa. And now it turns out that he had one too! Not bad for a handful of guitars.

After chatting with Mike, it was clear that thosee dates in the first week of August were critical in understanding exactly when and how both George and Mike received their fretless guitars from Al Casey.

From the *Beatles Bible* website, I learned that on 3 August 1967 - on the third day of their US trip - George Harrison, Neil Aspinall and Alexis 'Magic Alex' Mardas returned to Ravi Shankar's music school in Los Angeles. George and Ravi held a press conference at the Kinnara School of Music to promote Shankar's Hollywood Bowl concert, which was taking place the following day. Pattie Harrison was not present - her sister, Jenny Boyd had flown over, and the pair went sightseeing in Los Angeles. That evening, the Harrisons and Derek Taylor attended a recording session for The Mamas & The Papas.

The session was arranged by the band's leader, John Phillips, and produced by Lou Adler. It was at that recording that George chatted and jammed with Mike Deasy, liking his new Bartell fretless guitar.

Mike Deasy and Tommy Tedesco were interviewed in September 1972 by *Guitar Player* magazine, and during the interview Mike mentioned the fretless he took as part of his musical armoury when on tour. The article was about what it was like and what it took to be a successful studio guitarist.

Mike said, "I have a cartage company take all my equipment on the dates. I bring a six-string Martin, a 12-string Martin, a Gibson Heritage 12-string which is tuned an octave up, an old National Dobro, a 1928 Vega banjo, a

FINDING FRETLESS

Above is Mike Deasy with a unique 1951 Fender Broadcaster - carved by Doug Raul "The body is a scene of Christ's tomb. The stone has been rolled away and Christ is ascending to heaven surrounded by a dozen angels. Mary stands in front of the open tomb. The pick guard is black on black . . . engraved in it is the text of "John 3:16." On the headstock, the original decal was copied in bas relief, preserving the word 'Broadcaster.' Credit Mike Deasy

Mike's 1959 Fender Stratocaster carved with Jesus the shepherd and a surrealistic Jesus on the pick guard - Mike said 'it was stolen while I was in California doing a TV show 30 years ago. I put a photo on the internet and got a call from California from the Deacon of a church saying he had the guitar, his brother had bought it from a drug dealer, he was in an AA group with. They shipped it back to me. A miracle everyone who touched it got saved!

(Opposite page)
Original image of the Album cover 'Letters To My Head'
The Bartell fretless at the back by Mike's right arm and on the
floor an Acoustic Black Widow (same as Hendrix and Zappa)
next to a National Resonator designed by the Dopyera's.
(Photo by Michael Ochs Archives/Getty Images)

Washburn mandolin, a Stratocaster, a Telecaster, a Broadcaster, and a fretless guitar".

I told Mike it was interesting him saying George didn't have his Bartell fretless before that 3 August 1967 session, having been told Maxine Casey took Al's first prototype up to George on Blue Jay Way the day he arrived on 1 August. Did he think Al delivered it after George had shown an interest in his fretless, then claimed George had the first one (having taken out that advertising in the *LA Free Press* saying George got the first fretless)? Mike replied, "Al would get no mileage out of me having the first one, but George had neither heard of or seen one before the August 3 session."

Whatever the sequence of events, either Al Casey had delivered a Bartell fretless before the 3 August session and George didn't know about it, or - maybe more likely - it was delivered a day or two after Mike showed George his fretless, but Al claimed in his advert to maximise the impact that George got his first. Either way, that first week of August 1967 was a big week for Bartell.

Mike added that the church in Sacramento he donated his fretless and acoustic Black Widow guitars to was called The Warehouse. And that made me wonder if the church was still standing and if there was any possibility the guitars were still in their possession. I was really clutching at straws by now, but felt it was worth asking.

The Warehouse Christian Ministries were formed by Pastor Louis Neely, who had returned to Sacramento after missions throughout Africa, India, the Middle East, and Brazil, preaching the Gospel. Their church officially opened its doors on 28 April 1974, putting on Saturday night concerts. The pastor's wife, Mary and a couple of others started a radio show to present an alternate point of view on modern culture. It grew into a programme called Rock Scope, which was heard on more than 200 radio stations across the United States.

On 15 February 2021 I heard back from the Warehouse. They were intrigued by the story. Julissa Neely and Michael Roe picked up the search and asked around their members, and I received an update on 1 April.

Jan Volz told me, "I clearly remember when Mike Deasy brought those guitars to the Warehouse when he was playing with the Sanctified Boogie Band with Ronnie Tutt, but only recall the Hagstrom and the Jaguar guitars. I have no recollection of seeing that guitar or any inkling of who it ended up with or if it even existed."

But Tom Goodlunas said, "I remember the six-string fretless pretty well!"

It seems that dozens of extremely talented and gifted musicians and songwriters visited the Warehouse. In the early days, the Saturday night concerts and Sunday worship services provided a great environment for those musicians to develop their gifts and skills. It became apparent, however, that the unique music of the church should be shared beyond the borders of Sacramento.

As they put it, "The Lord expanded the vision again, this time to include a recording studio and record label that would enable Warehouse to distribute their musical message to the world. The first records were designed to appeal to young alternative and college music fans. These records were widely accepted all over the country. As things have progressed, the music has spanned everything from country music to rap."

Mike Deasy was born 4 February 1941 in Los Angeles, California. From an early age he had an aptitude for the guitar, and at high school he played in backing bands for visiting musicians such as Ricky Nelson, and played in Ritchie Valens' touring band. Graduating in 1959, Mike joined Eddie Cochran's band, the Kelly Four, and also played with Duane Eddy.

Mike very soon became a popular session player. In the words of Richard Bennett, "Mike was a unique player and would get the rock session calls. He was definitely different from the other session guys - real long hair and hippie vibe, but everyone liked him."

Today, Mike Deasy is called the most recorded rock guitarist alive today. Starting in the 1950s, he helped shape and create rock'n'roll.

Mike went on to work with a prolific and impressive list of A-list stars, from the afore-mentioned Eddie Cochran to The Monkees, Randy Newman, Fats Domino, The Byrds, Michael Jackson, and Frank Zappa.

He also played guitar on film soundtracks, with 69 musician credits in Hollywood, including for movies such as *The Graduate*, *Dirty Harry*, *Forrest Gump*, *The Rock*, and *Boogie Nights*.

In 1968, Mike played guitar with Tommy Tedesco and Al Casey on Elvis Presley's 1968 *TV Comeback Special*.

Elvis borrowed a 1968 Red Hagstrom Viking II for several sections of the show, including his stand-up performance in front of a live audience. The guitar through the years has been mistaken as his, and is often referred to as the 'Elvis guitar'. In fact, it belonged to Al Casey.

Al said, "The producer, Bones Howe, came to the studio players asking if anyone had something flashy Elvis could use. He thought it would make a better shot if he was playing something. I had the Hagstrom in my instrument trunk, and offered it.

"Once Elvis had a guitar to play, he needed an amp to play it through, and the Benson is what I had with me."

The guitar was exhibited in the Rock and Roll Hall of Fame and auctioned by GWS Auctions on 27 March 2021 for $500,000.

After Al moved back to Phoenix, he sold his Benson 200 amplifier to one of his students, Doug Miers.

Elvis played my guitar and used my amp - Al Casey

That wasn't the end of that story though. Al Casey's amp, as used by Elvis Presley, ended up with Richard Bennett.

In June 2020, Richard emailed, telling me, "Doug Miers got in touch with me 10 or 12 years ago and wanted me to have it as a gift. The Vox speaker is not original, but something Al put in years ago. The amp needed some work, but I had it restored to its original specs, and it sounds fantastic. I kept the Vox speaker because the amp sounds so good just like it is.

"I contacted Ron Benson, who built the amp. He told me the original would have been a 12" Jensen. I may put one in there someday, but like I say it sounds great like it is. I've been using it on a new album I'm making for myself.

"The Benson 200s were never commercially produced for sale like the 300 and 400. Ron made them custom for the session guys who wanted one. They are scarcely larger than a briefcase and put out so much sound. A great recording amp due to its clarity and focus. Its size was a plus as well. Prior to musicians having cartage, which began to happen in the late '60s, guitar players had to pack as much stuff as they could into the trunks of their cars, so a small amp was the order of the day. One of the reasons they all drove Cadillacs was the size of the trunk".

I have one more astonishing story about Mike Deasy.

In 1969, record producer Terry Melcher, who had made stars of The Byrds and was the son of one of old Hollywood's most wholesome, stars, Doris Day, innocently invited Mike to work with a group of hippies and a newly-discovered singer-songwriter, Charles Manson. Mike was sent up to the Spahn Ranch, an old film- and-television set in the western San Fernando Valley, to record Manson, who was desperate for stardom.

Mike is quoted as saying, "I had a trailer with a four-track unit that I was

Benson amp. Photo: Nick Bennett

going to use to record the Hopi Indians. Manson and the Family lived like a bunch of Indians, so Terry said, 'Why don't you go check it out?'. So a friend of mine and I went up there to record their songs."

Deasy left Manson's hippie commune after three days, calling it a descent into hell. Overwhelmed by LSD, Mike did everything he could to conquer his demons and resurrect his career.

Manson, the infamous cult leader and criminal whose obsessive followers, known as the Manson Family, just two months later entered the home of Hollywood actress Sharon Tate and murdered her, her unborn child and four others. It seems Mike was lucky to leave when he did.

"I left cult leader Manson's home after three days, in a state of drug-fuelled paranoia." - Mike Deasy

The Los Angeles district attorney said Manson was obsessed with The Beatles, particularly their 1968 self-titled album, the *White Album*. Manson claimed to be guided by his interpretation of The Beatles' lyrics, adopting the term 'Helter Skelter' to describe an impending apocalyptic race war. Manson twisted the lyrics in The Beatles' songs to fit his own warped view of what he wanted to happen, teaching his followers that the music was filled with subliminal messages and symbols, and that they all pointed to one goal - the uprising and Helter Skelter.

In Manson's mind, songs like 'Blackbird', 'Piggies' and most prominently 'Helter Skelter', foretold a bloody, apocalyptic race war. But when the battle never began, he decided to kick-start it with the murders. At the trial, the prosecution submitted that Manson and his followers believed that the murders would help precipitate that violent race war.

Mike Deasy saw that tragic at Spahn Ranch as his call to deliver a message of hope and salvation, finding his faith at a Billy Graham crusade in 1969.

"I heard the gospel of Jesus Christ. I ran to Jesus to set me free from all the terror of drugs." – Mike Deasy

From then on, Mike concentrated on producing, writing and performing contemporary Christian music, often supported by his wife Kathie. His skills as a musician were influential in many Christian recordings, with acts like Keith Green, Larry Norman and Barry McGuire. He's toured around the world many times, keen to spread the message, performing in schools with his 'Yes to Life' positive anti-drug mantra.

In 2021, Mike celebrated his 80th birthday, and has many amazing stories to tell.

The Wrecking Crew, part two

It is no surprise that Mike Deasy and Al Casey, two of the top LA session players, were mates, with a history of playing together, part of the collective group of the very best Californian session musicians in the '60s and '70s nicknamed The Wrecking Crew. These unsung instrumentalists - at least for many years to come - were the 'go to' backing band on hit records by The Beach Boys, Phil Spector, Frank Sinatra, Nancy Sinatra, Sonny & Cher, Elvis, The Monkees, and many more.

They are now considered one of the most prolific and successful session recording groups in music history. The entire Wrecking Crew was inducted into the Musicians' Hall of Fame and Museum in Nashville, Tennessee in 2007. And in 2008 they were the subject of the excellent documentary film, *The Wrecking Crew*, directed by Denny Tedesco, son of Wrecking Crew guitarist Tommy Tedesco.

The Wrecking Crew worked on more projects with George Harrison than any other members of The Beatles in their solo careers. In 1968 Harrison produced Jackie Lomax's album, *Is This What You Want?* The sessions took place at Sound Recorders Studio from 20 October to 11 November. Seven songs were recorded at this time, six of which were used for the album: 'Is This What You Want?'; 'Speak to Me'; 'Take My Word'; 'Baby You're a Lover'; 'How Can You Say Goodbye?'; and 'Little Yellow Pills'.

Lomax was supported at these sessions by George Harrison on guitar, Larry Knechtel (keyboards), Joe Osborn (bass) and Hal Blaine (drums). The remainder of the album was recorded in England.

In 1971, members of The Wrecking Crew played in the band for *The Concert For Bangladesh*, namely Leon Russell (piano/music director/performer), Jim Keltner (drums), Carl Radle-bass (during Leon's solo set only), Jim Horn (saxophones, horn arrangements), Chuck Findley (trumpet), Jackie Kelso (saxophones), Lou McCreary (trombone), and Ollie Mitchell (trumpet).

And in 1974, George Harrison recorded parts of his album, *Dark Horse* at A&M Studios in Hollywood, his band including Jim Horn and Chuck Findley (flutes), Emil Richards (percussion), Max Bennett (bass), and John Guerin (drums).

Frank Zappa's fretless Acoustic Black Widow

Frank Zappa purchased a branded, acoustic, fretless Black Widow

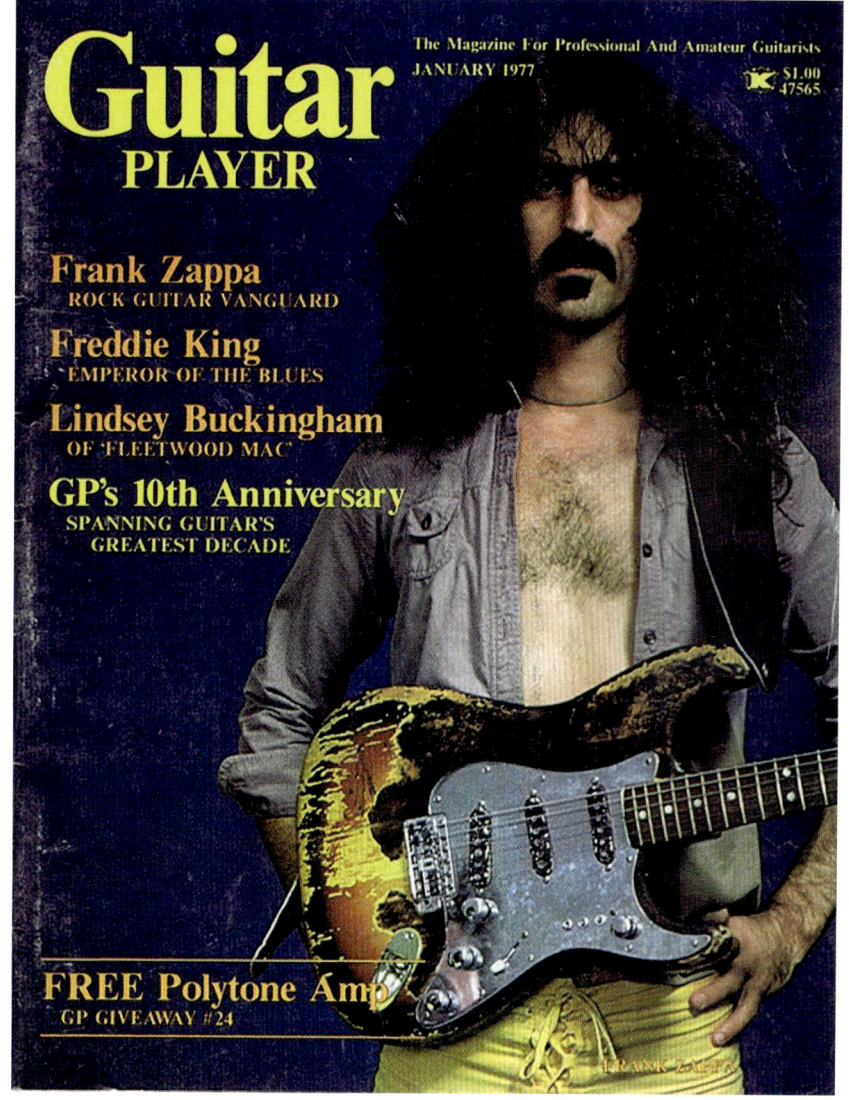

Copyright Guitar Player magazine, 1977. Used by permission

guitar in 1973 from Guitar Center. In a January 1977 interview published in *Guitar Player* magazine (Vol. 11, No.1), Steve Rosen started by asking if he ever plays slide guitar, to which Frank responded, "No, but I do have a fretless guitar, and I'm pretty good on that.

"At one time, Acoustic manufactured a fretless guitar, they made a prototype and tried to interest people in it, but nobody wanted it. So the prototype ended up at Guitar Center. I walked in there one day, asked if they had anything new, and they said, 'Have we got one for you!' They brought out this thing, and it was really neat, so I bought it for $75.

"The only restriction was they had to take a chisel and some black paint and scratch off the word Acoustic on the headpiece, because Acoustic didn't want anybody to know they had made such a grievous error as to make a fretless guitar. I've put a Barcus-Berry on that, too, and I send the magnetic pickup to the left and the Barcus on the right.

"The thing that sounds like a slide guitar on 'The Torture Never Stops' is actually a fretless. It's also on 'San Ber'dino' and 'Can't Afford No Shoes' (both from *One Size Fits All*). It's different from a regular guitar; you don't push the strings to bend them, you move them back and forth like violin-type vibrato, which is a funny movement to get used to. But you can play barre chords on it - it's fun."

The Guitar World According to Frank Zappa is a 1987 compilation album featuring guitar solos by Frank Zappa. It was issued as a cassette from *Guitar World* magazine.

Side 1 – 'Friendly Little Finger'

Recorded in a dressing room at Hofstra University in 1975 and over-dubbed at the Record Plant, Los Angeles, California. Guitars featured: Gibson acoustic-electric; Custom fretless; Hofner bass.

Side 2 – 'Down in de Dew'

Recorded at Paramount Studios, Hollywood, California in 1975. This selection was an out-take from the *Apostrophe* album. Guitars featured: Gibson acoustic-electric; Custom fretless; Hofner bass.

Another example of Frank Zappa's fretless guitar soloing can be heard on the song 'San Ber'dino' for the *One Size Fits All* album.

Greg Segal, reviewing Down In de Dew, wrote, "This is the track I was thinking of. There's fretless throughout, but there's a very upfront solo in the middle. It sure sounds like a Bartell acoustic to me in that. Not only does that particular hollow body have a unique resonance, but the pickups are unique too.

"This sounds to me just like the bridge/lead position. And the combination of these with the way the guitar sounds in low, mid, and high registers is, again totally unique. In fact, when I first played it, it was the first thing I noticed. The tone thins and sustain is harder to produce the higher you go. In what would normally be the high lead range, it plays like a pizzicato viola, not much like a guitar at all. Whatever it is, Zappa sure got the best out of it."

One Size Fits All by Frank Zappa and the Mothers of Invention (1975) was reviewed by fretless guitar expert Jeff Berg, who said of 'Can't Afford No Shoes', 'First off you think the solo from 1.07 was done using a slide. But on second listen, yes its fretless.' And as for 'San Ber'dino', he wrote, 'Not as obvious as the first track, in fact you have to listen real hard to spot the fretless. Both tracks are really curiosities, for enthusiasts only.'

In the liner notes for *The Guitar World According to Frank Zappa*, we read that 'Down in de Dew', said to be 'previously unreleased - will be included in the next guitar boxset', was engineered by Kerry McNabb, originally on 24-track analog tape, featuring Frank Zappa (Gibson acoustic-electric, Custom fretless, Hofner bass) and Jim Gordon (drums).

The notes read, "This piece began as a recorded jam session at Electric Lady Studios, New York City. The only thing that remains from the original recording is the drums. Everything else was layered on in overdubs at subsequent sessions in Los Angeles. This selection was an out-take from the *Apostrophe* (') album. Another example of fretless guitar soloing can be heard on 'San Ber'dino' on the *One Size Fits All* album. Unfortunately, the fretless guitar was stolen several years ago.

The Zappa.com website also maintains that the Acoustic fretless guitar was stolen, shortly after the recording of *One Size Fits All*. However, in the *Guitar Player* interview of January 1977, Frank said he still had it, when talking in the interview specifically about the Acoustic fretless guitar.

So did Frank in fact sell it in 1981 to pay for his Synclavier? And is there a link from his fretless to Greg Segal, who got an Acoustic Black Widow in the same area Zappa lived, as previously discussed?

FRANK ZAPPA - ACOUSTIC BLACK WIDOW

American artist Bob Coronato, of whom we'll hear more of soon, said, "Frank Zappa had an Acoustic-brand electric Black Widow guitar he purchased in 1969. He used it on two tracks to record 'Shut Up 'n Play Yer Guitar', plus there are photos of him with it in 1969 in Laurel Canyon, as well as Lowell George playing it on stage in the early Mothers era. Frank kept it his whole life. He talks about it in several interviews. He had a fretted and a fretless Black Widow made by Acoustic."

"I've got a bouzouki and a sitar, and two Acoustic Black Widows made by the Acoustic Control Corporation, one of which has a special pickup shaped like loops for the strings to go under, similar to what they use on the Condor." – Frank Zappa (from Zappa by Tony Bacon, International Musician and Recording World, March 1977).

'Shut Up 'N Play Yer Guitar' (series of live albums, released in 1981)
'While You Were Out' - Guitar used: Acoustic Black Widow with EMG pickups direct into recording console
'Stucco Homes' - Guitar used: Acoustic Black Widow with EMG pick-ups direct into recording console
Both tracks were recorded at the Utility Muffin Research Kitchen (UMRK), Frank's home studio in the Hollywood Hills, Autumn 1979.

In November 1979, Dan Forte interviewed Frank Zappa for *M.I.* magazine, for a feature titled 'Pop Music's Central Scrutinizer' and asked him about the guitars he was set to use on tour. Frank replied, "It's probably going to be a toss-up between the Les Paul and maybe an Acoustic Black Widow that I had souped up. It's got a 24-fret rosewood neck, and I had two EMG pickups put in it, and new fretwork by Carruthers."

On 5 November 2016, Julian's Auctions in Los Angeles, put up for sale property from the Estate of Frank and Gail Zappa, where the auction catalogue revealed, 'There are some pretty tasty guitars in the offing - including an Acoustic Control Corporation Black Widow, a very rare guitar that made news about a year ago when Jimi Hendrix's was the object of a lawsuit."

Lot 489 of 944 was Frank Zappa's Acoustic Black Widow guitar, with a guide value of $1,000 to $2,000. It sold for $12,500.

An Acoustic Black Widow solid-body guitar used by Frank Zappa in the studio. Image Julians Auctions/Summer Evans

Bob Coronato is the very proud owner of Frank Zappa's Acoustic Black Widow guitar.

Bob posted on the Zappateers internet forum on 18 November 2016, "I went to that auction. I drove a couple of thousand miles to attend. For me it was more of a rescue mission. I only went for one item - the Acoustic Black Widow guitar. That guitar has a heartbeat and a soul.

"Yes, I own every album, every boot, every book and every re-release of the boots. I gave more than a few pay checks to save the vault. I've been a diehard since 15 years old, saw him play, registered to vote at his concert,

Photo Bob Coronato with the Black Widow. Photo credits Bob Coronato

played his music until my ears bled.

"Frank's music of all variety has played in my studio for decades and never a day has gone by without it. It's the fuel that fires my soul and only the diehards can relate. Frank's madness, his dedication, artistic honesty and all the layers of all the experimentation of his music ... He was and is the inspiration that led to my personal success.

"The Acoustic Control Corporation Black Widow electric guitar by Bartell of California, designed by Paul Barth, was bought by Frank in 1969, give or take, went through the killer Mothers of Invention era ... Lowell George played it for a few months on the road in '69. It was not going to end up suffocating in a plexy-box!

"So I sat in the auction seats, waited for seven hours and never raised my hand until it came up.

"Mission accomplished."

I spoke to Bob about his search for information on Frank and his subsequent, prized auction buy. He replied, "I have worn my fingers down to the bone trying to find pics of Zappa playing the Black Widow. I have only found a picture by Tony Franks of him holding it (the fretted) and Lowell George on stage in 1969 playing it.

"There is little else I've been able to find historically about either of them. It's a like a mystery! I also see very few mentions of what tracks Frank used it on.

"After all the millions of hours I spent researching, it seems Frank used these as tools to lay down pieces and parts on recordings over the late '60s and '70s but made few notes as to what ones. I would love to know, but so far have not found anyone that can tell me much. The one I have that came from his house has several alterations - the pickups have been changed several times and tuner knobs are Schaller.

"I talked to Dweezil about it. He said it laid at the bottom of the stairs next to the Hendrix Strat in pieces, where all the guitars go to die. And he did not bother to get it restored.

"Dweezil did not have much to say about this guitar, because it was not a Gibson. He said he paid no attention to it and kind of suggested Frank did not care much for it. However, Dweezil would have been a year old when Frank had this, and Frank could have played on it for a decade and Dweezil would not remember that.

"My Zappa guitar shows many modifications, numerous pickup changes, and several holes where pickups have been moved. The tuner keys were changed to Schaller, unless Bartell did use those, but I've seen Frank's other guitars and several had Schaller tuner keys. I assumed they were added.

"Someone played the heck out of it, the pickup is nearly cut in two from use! It's had numerous modifications and - get this - in the light you can see that the tuner key closest to the last fret on the top is covered in tobacco patina from a cigarette sitting just where Frank always had it. So to me, he played it in the studio on a lot of stuff, since it takes a long time to get that kind of tobacco patina. And it's only on one key, right where he always had his Newport!

"It would not surprise me if many of the tracks from the '69 to '77 era had numerous tweaks and overlays using both the fretless and the fretted, like a tool, for making a specific sound.

"FZ kept it around for a reason!"

On 9 November 2020 I spoke to respected *Zappa Gear* author Mick Ekers. He was very generous with his time as we compared our research, swapped notes and discussed stories we had heard. We were broadly in agreement and Mick kindly sent me photographs taken in 2012 of the Black Widow he found in the basement workshop under Zappa's UMRK studio. The same guitar that ended up with Julian's Auctions. Mick said, "The conditions were far from ideal and my equipment was limited. It's not possible to see the logo on the picture of the headstock, but it was definitely present, as is the cleaned-up guitar that was finally sold."

Photo Credits - Mick Ekers

Bob Coronato is also an amazing 'Western Artist' located in Hulett Wyoming. He moved to Wyoming in the early 1990's, and cowboy'd all over Northeast Wyoming and Southeast Montana.

Bob has been painting, drawing and printing for over 20 years aspects of the contemporary Cowboy and American Indian life.

His antique American Indian, Western artwork, American artefacts, beadwork and weapons can be seen at his brilliant Rouges Gallery Museum. Check it out, you will be amazed!

Jimi Hendrix's Bartell fretless

What do we know about Jimi Hendrix and his Bartell fretless guitar?

Dave Peckels, in a piece sourced through the unfretted. com website, relates, "In the late 1960s, my Dad - Ted Peckels - manufactured electric guitars in Riverside, California. He produced some of the Black Widows for Acoustic there, and also made guitars with the St. George and Hohner names. It was mostly fretless basses for Hohner. He died several years back, but a story he often told was about a fretless guitar that was built especially for Jimi Hendrix.

"According to the story, Hendrix really liked the guitar. It was probably an Acoustic or my Dad's own brand, Bartell. At some point, it was stolen, and Hendrix ordered another one. It was in the process of being built when Hendrix died. I always wondered what happened to that second one, but maybe it was the one that ended up in the Guitar Center with the name scratched off.

A comment on the site adds, "I was in Ace Music in Santa Monica in the late '60s when I saw an Acoustic Black Widow fretless guitar. I think they were made in Japan back then. As I recall, it had a 'mother of bowling ball' fretboard. It was designed by Harvey Gerst, I think.

"Ace was a store on Santa Monica Boulevard, just up from Ocean Avenue, owned by brothers Hank and Jack. Ken Daniels and Paul Flynn worked there until the store closed, and they set up TruTone Music in 1998."

On 21 July 2019 I had an email conversation with Dave Peckels, who told me, "I don't know a whole lot about the history around the fretless guitars … only what my Dad told me when he was alive.

"I know that one was made for Jimi Hendrix. It was a left-handed model. He apparently really liked it, but at some point that guitar was stolen. He asked that another one be built for him. Unfortunately for us all, he died before it was finished.

Bob Coronato's Rouges Gallery in Wyoming. Credits Bob Coronato

"I've always wondered what happened to that one... as well as the stolen one. I read a story about Frank Zappa buying a fretless guitar at the Hollywood Guitar Center store. He said the name had been removed from the headstock, which makes sense as the fretless model was custom and not a part of Acoustic's regular line. At some point, that guitar was also stolen.

On 6 May 2020, Tom Mitchell, a former Bartell employee, confirmed that two fretless guitars were made for Jimi Hendrix and both were left-handed. But he had a slightly different account as to what happened to Jimi's two six-string fretless guitars.

Tom recalled, "Well, Jimi got the guitar and lit it on fire. And then he wanted another one, so we sent him another guitar and told him, 'This time, don't light it on fire, or we will just set it on fire for you if you want!'. Anyway, he didn't light it on fire this time. He saved it. But Jimi was really a crazy one. I visited him in the Hollywood hills one time and he was a trip. He was really a trip to talk to and to be around."

I bet. So, he had the first fretless he set that on fire. Is that what you're saying?

"Yeah, he had a fretless and it was pretty rough to change around the strings so everything was right as he was left-handed and he had to have it left handed, upside down. So it was really rough with Jimi on getting it right."

Do you remember if you branded them? Some were branded for Bartell but also for Acoustic and other companies as well. Do you remember was it branded Bartell or Acoustic for Jimi?

"Well, it was a Bartell at first. That's who we started with, you know, and then we finished up with Ted Peckels. Not Ted's name on it - he had a different name on the guitar. But I can't remember back that far."

What happened to the second one you gave to Jimi? Do you know what happened to that?

"He kept it and packed it away. I don't know what happened to it but he packed it away. He kept it."

We heard from other people that Jimi had one, then it was stolen, so you made another one for him. But what you are saying is that the first one wasn't stolen - he actually burnt it and asked for another one.

"Yeah."

So there you have it - we have two fretless guitars confirmed as being made by Tom Mitchell for Jimi Hendrix. The details we know are that it was:

Manufactured around late 1967

Coloured black

Branded Bartell on the headstock (assuming Tom is right - it could be branded Acoustic)

Left-handed, and bespoke for Jimi Hendrix

One was possibly burnt or stolen

I sent a number of emails to the Hendrix LLC organisation, and received a reply on 25 February 2021 that read, "You are

Greg Segal's right handed fretless, would Jimi's left hander look like this?

correct in that Jimi Hendrix was provided a couple of guitars from Bartell; however, neither of those guitars were the fretless models you are in search of. These guitars have frets and are not the fretless models. Best of luck in your future research."

So it would appear that if the company legend and the memory of the fretless maker is correct, one or both fretless guitars are out there somewhere, to be discovered, with the full story still to be revealed.

There are no known images of the two Bartell-made fretless guitars made for Jimi Hendrix.

This isn't the end of Jimi Hendrix's association with Bartell guitars though. As confirmed by Hendrix LLC, Jimi had two fretted Bartell guitars, commonly known as Black Widow guitars.

Acoustic Control Corporation was a manufacturer of instrument amplifiers used by artists such as guitar legend Jimi Hendrix.

Founded by Steve Marks, with the help of his father in the late 1960s, Acoustic was based in Van Nuys, California. Its original location was a shack on Sunset Boulevard, Los Angeles. The company address was 7949 Woodley Avenue, Van Nuys, CA 91406.

Best known for its powerful Acoustic 361 bass stack, Acoustic became the go-to bass amp in the '70s and '80s as larger venues demanded amps with more power and stadium-filling tone. During this time, players such as Larry Graham (Sly and the Family Stone), Robbie Krieger (The Doors), John Paul Jones (Led Zeppelin), John McVie (Fleetwood Mac), and Jaco Pastorius were avid users of Acoustic amplifiers, helping them to develop their trademark sounds.

Acoustic decided to diversify into guitars supplied by manufacturer Bartell, who produced the prototype Black Widow electric guitar around the end of 1968 into 1969. Their guitars and basses were based on designs by Paul Barth for his Bartell guitars and basses and first featured in Acoustic's 1969 catalogue.

Barth's company, Bartell made the first instruments in the line. The small number of original Bartell-made models are the rarest and most collectible, although the Matsumoku build quality was good.

Acoustic's Harvey Gerst took Barth's original design and revamped it, with deeper cutaways and an increased fret count. Barth eventually couldn't keep up with production demands, leading to Acoustic taking production to Matsumoto Moko in Japan. Acoustic in 1975 brought production back to the USA, Semie Moseley (of Mosrite fame) claiming to have built the last 200 guitars.

Harvey Gerst was born in Chicago, moving to California when he was 10. Performing with The Byrds, he co-wrote two of their early hits. He was sponsored by Acoustic Control Corporation and owned the very first Black Widow six-string fretted guitar.

Harvey was working at JBL then, learning all about speakers and amplifiers. He said. "A friend of mine says, 'I'm sales manager of this amplifier company, Acoustic Control. Come check it out.' I go play the amp and say, 'This is the worst I've ever played!'. A week later my friend quit, because he couldn't sell them. I went back to the owner of the company and said, 'I don't think I impressed upon you how bad these amps really are.' He said, 'Well, what would you do?'. I told him, and the next thing I know, I've been there for eight years, designing Acoustic amps."

The 1974 catalogue featured the Mosrite version of the Black Widow. The guitar had narrow pickups with two rows of polepieces, although some have full-sized Mosrite humbuckers, with at least one unit having what appear to be original Maxon humbuckers. The guitar has 24 frets.

The bass features a narrow pickup, like the guitar, with two rows of polepieces as well. The fretboard of the bass features 20 frets, with a large blank area of fretboard past the 20th fret.

Jimi Hendrix's Black Widow

Jimi Hendrix had taken delivery of four Acoustic Control amplifiers and could not get his head around them. Harvey Gerst was asked by Steve Marks, President of Acoustic to go along to TGG Studios in Hollywood and show Jimi how to work them. Harvey could not get on with Hendrix's Strats, so he decided to show him using his own left-handed Black Widow. Hendrix loved the sound, and when it was time to go Harvey asked for his guitar back, to which Jimi replied, "What guitar? This is my guitar, but you can have any of my others."

Harvey Gerst took one of Hendrix's Strats, but could not get on with it and told Acoustic that Hendrix had his Black Widow, to which he was told, 'Don't worry, we'll give you another'. Which they did.

Harvey recalled, "I ran into Jimi at the airport in Oakland, and asked, 'How are you liking the Black Widow?' He said, 'I love it! It's my studio guitar'.

"I said, 'Well, I finally got my new Black Widow in, so here's your Strat back.' He stared at me for a second, then said, 'Huh?'. I said, 'Here's your Strat. I don't need it anymore.' 'Oh, okay'.

"It wasn't till a few years later telling this story that it hit me. He wasn't *expecting* me to give the Strat back. He was *giving* it to me! And I, like an idiot, gave it back to him - one of the first four Strats he owned. What's it worth today?"

TGG Studios was established by Amnon 'Ami' Hadani and Tom Hidley on 8 June 1965. The studio was one of the first to be equipped with a 16-track Ampex tape recorder, at a time when four-track recording was still the norm. Due to its high decibel level threshold, the studio became popular with the up-and-coming rock musicians of that time. Jimi Hendrix, who was introduced by Eric Burdon to the studio, raved about the studio's sound.

It was located on the corner of Highland and Sunset, just a couple of blocks away from the Dolby Theatre, Grauman's Chinese Theatre, Hollywood Bowl, Pantages Theatre, and the Hollywood Walk of Fame.

The same control knobs are on the Hendrix Guitar and the acoustic amp, likely due to the modifications made by Harvey Gerst. The Black Widow bass (but not Hendrix's) has the same.

In February 2021, the Hendrix LLC organisation confirmed to me that Jimi Hendrix was provided a couple of guitars from Bartell. It is believed that Jimi was given these guitars in the late summer or fall of 1968. Jimi used at least one of the guitars in the studio, on at least one occasion in October 1968. Believed to be limited to an estimated three, these guitars were somewhat similar left-handed instruments, two of which were owned by Jimi.

The other Jimi Hendrix Black Widow, this one branded Acoustic, can be found in the Collection of Experience Hendrix at the Rock and Roll Hall of Fame in Cleveland, Ohio.

In a conversation with me on 1 July 2019, Harvey Gerst and his wife Karen confirmed, "Jimi took my left-handed Black Widow and ordered another one. At the same time, I ordered a new one to replace mine, so there were three left-handed Black Widows, and he may have found a Bartell".

Harvey had a third left-handed Black Widow made for himself to replace the one Jimi took. So there were known to be three left-handed Black Widows produced.

Harvey Gerst at his Indian Trail Recording Studio. Photo credit - Harvey Gerst

Jimi Hendrix gifted a guitar each to two of his bandmates, twins Tunde Ra Aleem, who died in 2014, and Taharqa Aleem, also known as the 'Ghetto Fighters', just before his death in 1970.

"Jimi Hendrix's Estate takes guitar shop owner to court in $1 million lawsuit over possession of musician's acoustic guitar.

"There was a Mosrite double-neck and an Acoustic-branded Black Widow electric guitar that Jimi used in his recording of 'Mojo Man', which was released on posthumous 2013 album *People, Hell, and Angels*. The Aleem twins were vocalists on the track.

"When Jimi died, the Hendrix Estate purchased the guitars back from the bandmates for $30,000. But in 2016, the Aleem twins sued Experience Hendrix LLC, Rainbow Guitars Inc., Harvey Moltz, and the Rock & Roll Hall of Fame & Music in a bid to get back two guitars that Jimi gave them. The brothers claimed there was an oral promise that they could buy back the guitars at any time, as long as they gave notice and paid back the $30,000.

"The Estate denied making such a promise, and argued that there was no written record of the transaction. The twins were unsuccessful in their initial attempt and appealed the decision, but in 2019, US district judge Edgardo Ramos determined the twins had no ownership rights to the guitars, also deciding that Experience Hendrix was not the sole and exclusive owner."

At the Rock & Roll Hall of Fame, some of the rarest recording instruments used by Jimi Hendrix are displayed, including a white, double-neck Mosrite electric and a black Acoustic Black Widow, that Hendrix used and later gave to the Allen twins (aka the Ghetto Fighters). The displays also include one of Jimi's Fender amps, which he used in 1969.

Comparisons with Greg Segal's Acoustic fretless and the Jimi Hendrix Black Widow can be seen in a number of areas. Note the neck pickup, the semi-hollow body indicated by the f-hole, the German carved-top body and the tailpiece, showing the same design ideas and matching components.

They also have the same hand-wound single-coil pickup, the same string tailpiece, 12 slots in total, and the top screws inset from bottom screws.

Mort Marker – the Guitar Man

Mort Marker was born on 3 August 1937, in Dover, Delaware. He taught himself to play guitar from the age of 12 and played in country bands as early as 13. His first guitar hero was Chet Atkins. When Elvis Presley and rockabilly came in, he heard Scotty Moore and was converted.

In 1958 Don Robey called and set up a session at Bradley Studios in Nashville, Tennessee. The record was released in November 1958. Two television shows kicked the record off - The Buddy Deane Show in Baltimore and The Milt Grant Show in Washington, DC. It made the top-40 playlists in three states. Mort had a successful career before eventually making his move to Los Angeles in 1964.

It was in 1965 that Mort and Al Casey first met, becoming good friends. Al got Mort involved in the session scene. At that time in Hollywood it was a gold mine for recording studios. They were everywhere.

Mort's first big session was with Gary Puckett and The Union Gap. More work came flooding in, including live TV for shows with Sonny and Cher, the Hudson Brothers, the Smothers Brothers, John Davidson, and a few others.

In 1968, Al Casey asked Mort to do some work on Elvis' *'68 Comeback Special* at NBC TV's studio in Burbank, California. Mort was thrilled to be in the same room as Elvis and Scotty Moore. The session was a warm-up to go through some songs and loosen up a bit, playing mostly '50s hits like 'Blue Suede Shoes'. Mort played his Gibson L5 that he bought in 1959, just like Scotty Moore's.

Don Randi, the band leader, told Mort that Elvis really liked his playing. While performing 'Heartbreak Hotel', Elvis turned and said to Mort, 'That's it, that's it!'. He seemed really excited with Mort's Scotty Moore licks.

Later, Mort got a call from producer Billy Strange for a soundtrack session at United Artists Recorders on Sunset Boulevard. It was another Elvis Presley session. Elvis was in a great mood, joking with the crew. During a break, Elvis went over and chatted with the session players. Inviting them to help themselves to food from a catering truck located at the back of the studio.

Mort Marker

Mort Marker's Bartell-branded red fretless (serial number unknown)

During my investigations, I found a number of Facebook groups very helpful as sources of information and to network with. Two particularly stood out as helpful and interested in my research – 'We Grew Up in Riverside in the '60s & '70s, and 'Inland Empire Music Hall of Fame (IEMHOF)'

On the latter's pages, I shared information on Richard Bennett and his Bartell fretted guitar, one of his first guitars. And Ed Greenwald replied, "I'm a very close friend of Mort Marker from the Buckhorn in Mt. Baldy. I played bass for him for eight years and drums for the last year until late 2018. Richard was a guitar student of Mort's many years ago at Al Casey's studio in Hollywood, down where Eddie Van Halen used to hang out. Tell Richard that Mort says Hi."

Richard was amazed to hear from Mort, and I subsequently gave Richard a call on 3 July 2020 to catch up and see what Mort remembered about Al Casey and Bartell guitars.

Richard told me, "I just got off the phone with Mort Marker. He *did* remember the Bartell fretless going to George Harrison via Al and Maxine, but like me doesn't have any further clarity or detail about it. However, Mort said he bought two Bartells from Al and Max - one being a fretless and the other a double-neck. He said he thinks he's got a photo of the double-neck, which was red. He ended up selling both Bartells when funds ran low.

"The fact that he owned two Bartells blew me away. I hadn't known that before. He's a fine guitar player, did some session work, played with John Davidson for many years, and did lots of club work. He was originally from Delaware and started out as a Rockabilly guy. He's been inducted into the Delaware Music Hall of Fame but has lived on the LA area since 1964."

Consequently, I emailed Mort, in his 80s now. It's a lot to ask of memories from 50-plus years ago, but it's funny what sticks sometimes. I appreciate it was a long time ago, but sometimes it's harder remembering why you opened the fridge door, right?

On 19 July 2020, I had a conversation with Mort, starting out by asking about how he knew Richard Bennett?

"There was lots going on at Casey's Music store in California and I moved from Delaware and started doing work almost immediately. I met Al through Maxine, she hired me at the music store to do some teaching. Al said, 'I've been listening to you teaching and I think I could get you some session work if you are interested.' Which was exactly what I wanted to hear! He set me up right away, and I met Richard there".

You bought some Bartell guitars from Al's store?

"Well, I had a band and was living in the area, and I met the guy who was selling Bartell guitars. Al asked if we wanted to buy one or two of the instruments. The Bartell rep had just finished up making what was called a fretless guitar.

"I got two guitars from him, a double-neck which had six strings, and another small neck like a mandolin size that was tuned an octave higher than the regular neck.

"I also bought what they called the fretless guitar, and my bass player Bill Carter bought a fretless bass. I have a photo of him holding the fretless bass."

What colour was your fretless guitar?

"The fretless? It was red."

Was it red or sunburst red?

"No, it was red, fully red. All the instruments I brought were bright red."

How were the Bartells to play?

"They were really nice. My instruments played okay, you know. What I was impressed with was the finish and the colour, most of the stuff they made back then was bright red."

What was Al doing with the Bartell guitars?

"I know Al Casey's store became a dealer for the company (Bartell). They sold a lot of guitars to a lot of studio people, most of them guys I was doing some studio work with. Just about everybody I ran into all had Bartell

Guitars. I don't know if you could even find one today! I said to Richard I almost completely forgot about it.

"At that time the fretless was a new thing. My bass player played it well and I was playing my double-neck a lot as well. I remember we went into the studio and everybody loved the look of these guitars. They went crazy over them.

"At that time, they were up to date with the design, the instrument played well. Most of the new people that were playing were looking for that rock'n'roll guitar. But I never did see another one! I was talking to Richard about it and he had one too."

What do you remember about the fretless, and how long did you have it?

"Six to eight months, close to a year maybe. My instrument as a rule, well I had two instruments, I had a Fender Telecaster, but my baby was a 1960 brand new one that I brought in Delaware, where I'm from. I brought a Gibson L5 and that was my main guitar. I put a different pickup in the bridge so I could get the rock'n'roll sound."

Did you let the double-neck go, sell it?

"I had it on a stand at one of the clubs I was playing at, and a guy came up to me and wanted to know about it. I said I just brought it a few months ago and I've been playing it, I kinda like it. He said, 'I would like to buy it'. He offered my like $150 I think. It didn't cost that much when it came out."

Do you know anything about George Harrison getting the first Bartell fretless?

"I heard about that, I was not there, but I was invited to go, many times I thought about it and I should'a went, but I was working a six-nighter in a club and I had to go to work. But Maxine Casey was telling me they were having a big party at this big place in Hollywood, I don't know where, I think it was a big house of somebody, I heard it was a *really big* party. I remember even the news carried a big thing on it."

What we know is that George arrived in Hollywood on 1 August 1967, when Maxine took the fretless up to Blue Jay Way …

"You know, that sounds about right … exactly right."

George went down to a recording session for The Mamas and the Papas. Mike Deasy was playing. Mike and George got talking about Mike's Bartell fretless guitar, and George was liking it.

"Yeah, I remember some of that stuff, because Al came back the next day. They came back with a lot of different stories."

Tell me about some of your session work.

"One of my big items I was lucky to get on was The Union Gap. Gary Puckett was the lead singer. I did an album for them in '68. I still get some residuals from that. They were popular in Europe. I went to work for John Davidson right after that.

"There was a guy I worked for in 1956 called Jimmy Staton. He did a lot of stuff and was known as one of the early rockers. I played lead guitar for him. We heard Elvis, Scotty Moore and all them way early, and we started copying that style."

Didn't you work with Elvis?

"I did the movie, *The Trouble with Girls*, but before that I did the *'68 Comeback Special*, which was a biggie. I heard Scotty Moore and I wanted to play some of that. I'd been waiting for this for years - this was the guy I wanted to sound like. Before that it was all Chet Atkins, you know."

Al Casey was on that as well.

"Yeah, Al was on that, and the guitar that Elvis used was Al's guitar. That was a Hagstrom, that had that same red colour as we were talking about on the Bartells. I had a Hagstrom too for a while. I still have a 12-string Hagstrom, which is great. It's like a big Gibson J200 with an electric pickup in it.

"I also met Mike Deasy at that gig. I did a few sessions with him. He did so much work at that time."

Do you remember selling the fretless guitar?

"It was a long time ago, 50 years or so. I think it was a little town somewhere 30 miles east of Hollywood at a club that isn't there anymore, about 10 miles from where I live now in Glendora.

"We were setting our stuff up and a guy walked in. I hadn't seen him before - a complete stranger. He said, 'What's the story on the Bartell guitar? I've never heard of them before.' Nobody had at that time.

"I don't remember his name or anything. He wasn't a great player, just he liked the guitar, liked the look of it. I didn't make any modifications to it, and only played it occasionally. I used to put it on a stand on the stage. It used to get a lot of attention. He gave me a good price.

"In those days we never thought of holding on to anything, I let go of a few things. Sometimes you have to."

Bartell's fretless bass

I could write a whole new book just on the Barth-designed fretless bass, which went on to be the most popular model and was widely rebranded for Hohner, Acoustic Black Widow, Lancer, Contessa, and St. George.

Today, fretless bass guitars are readily available, with most major guitar manufacturers producing fretless models. It is often thought that the first use of fretless bass guitars dates back to Bill Wyman in the early 1960s. Bill de-fretted his bass while he was playing, pre-Rolling Stones, with The Cliftons.

In fact, Bill talks about this in his autobiography, *Stone Alone: The Story of a Rock'n'Roll Band*, (Viking, London, 1990), written with the help of Ray Coleman, revealing why he chose to play bass and create his own custom-made fretless bass guitar.

Bill wrote, "One of the biggest turning points in my life came at the beginning of August 1961 when Diane (*Bill's first wife*) and I went to Aylesbury to visit to my sister Anne and her husband David. We went to a dance in an old converted cinema. On stage were the Barron Knights, who later became popular by brilliantly mimicking other people's hits. The sound of their bass guitar hit me straight in the balls. Staggered by its impact and the foundation it gave to the sound, I realised immediately what was missing in The Cliftons. From that moment. I wanted to play the bass.

"It suited my personality. At 24, I didn't see myself as an 'up front' musician, singing or playing at the head of a band. I was always more attuned to the overall sound, the need for internal dynamics and *precision*. I'm an orderly person; bass playing suits my outlook. I bought a set of bass strings and tried unsuccessfully to fit them on to my six-string instrument. Back in Beckenham, I told our new drummer, Tony Chapman, that The Cliftons needed a bassist and I intended to find an instrument. He found me a second-hand bass guitar for £8, which I couldn't really afford, but somehow I scraped the cash together.

"I got to work on it immediately, re-shaping it with the help of a neighbour's fretwork machine. I took all the frets out, intending to replace them with new ones, but it sounded so good that I kept it like that, making it the first fretless bass in England."

All credit to Eben Cole at the Cole Music company for the background on this charming Bartell Bass. In a post from 28 November 2019, he writes, "My friend Derrick is a glutton for odd guitars. He came in one day with an unbranded hollow-body bass he had bought off *Craigslist*, claiming it was the first fretless bass guitar ever produced for the mass market. Since I am a self-proclaimed expert on vintage guitars, I informed him that Ampeg made the first fretless bass. Duh! But Derrick had already done his research and had placed it as some sort of relative of the famed Acoustic Black Widow bass even before he bought it off the original owner. What he was most surprised to find was that it may be the first of the first fretless bass guitars!"

Ampeg is often credited with the first production electric fretless bass guitar in 1966, but Paul Barth actually beat them to the market in 1965 with his Bartell-branded fretless bass. Was this the first commercially-produced fretless bass? Quite possibly, Barth and Bartell did it again!

Key observations:

There is no branding and no logos, possibly indicating early prototype production before Bartell and Hohner branding.

Doug Donaghue (former Bartell employee) stated, "I don't remember where the serial numbers on any of those guitars began, but it might well have been at 91190, or even 91191". This bass in question is 91164.

Donaghue also stated that he handled the majority of the assembly, with the exception of the first few. The early pieces had masking tape on the wiring harnesses, then switched to electrical tape. This example has masking tape.

On all other examples the four control knobs descend towards the bridge. On this example they ascend - like a Les Paul.

From what I have seen in pictures of other Bartell Basses, the fret-markers seem to be much more erratic in length on this one. As if they still hadn't figured how to consistently saw the fret-markers.

Hohners were made in Germany after the Bartell factory closed. The pickups are completely different from Bartell models, with both pickups featuring three-point adjustment while the bridge pickup has offset pole-pieces, looking more like a P-bass pickup under a humbucker-sized cover. The knobs are black skirted knobs with numbers. You can also see that the bridge pickup has moved closer to the bridge and is now below the neck adjustment screw.

Dave Peckels' Hohner fretless bass. Photo: Dave Peckels

Hohner advertisement featuring the Bartell-designed fretless bass model they adopted, modified and built in Germany, branded as their own in 1970. Credit: bartell.vintageusaguitars.com

IRCA 1965 Bartell fretless bass

A beautiful rear with a naugahyde derriere. Photographer: Erick Doxey

FAMOUS BARTELL, BARTH AND ACOUSTIC PLAYERS

John Frusciante (born 1970) - St George XK12

American musician, singer-songwriter and producer John Frusciante is best known as lead guitarist of the rock band Red Hot Chili Peppers. His XK12 features two single-coil pickups, a non-adjustable aluminium bridge, individual switches for the pickups, a phase switch, and control knobs for volume and tone.

The Bartell-made 12-string, branded St George, is one of his least known guitars, and John said, "That thing is a pain in the ass to tune! I'd play it more if I could get it in tune".

A little history on St. George. Paul George owned the music store in Hollywood 1963 to 1967, and his father Tony owned up to five stores in New York. Mostly the guitars were Fender-type designs, produced in Japan and imported to the States. Tony George and 'Uncle Herb' kept the ones in New York running through the mid-1970s. The company emblem, stamped on the headstocks, were designed by Paul. Bartell-built guitars had the emblem applied and St George by Bartell of California inscribed on the headstock.

Paul George Jr. recalls what happened shortly after the 1965 Watts riot that led to the store front and warehouse being set ablaze. He said, "We took off on a sailboat and set sail for Hawaii. We sailed around the Pacific for a few years until we sank the sailboat after 88 days at sea and 22 days without food!"

Jim Stedt worked for Glenn Duncan at Duncan Music in San Bernardino in the mid-1960s. He said, "I worked for him from '65 to '69 and repaired guitars and amps. Some of those St George guitars played better than CBS-owned Fender Guitars!

"I took new St George guitars, smoothed the frets, aligned the necks and put new Fender strings on them, and had people trading in their Gibsons and Fenders for St George guitars!"

John Frusciante had his 1959 Fender Stratocaster modified some time in mid to late-2006, deciding to modify the guitar and replace the original neck with a fretless one. This was done by Ned Evett, and was arranged by his guitar tech, Dave Lee. Ned used a vintage Warmouth replacement neck and fitted it with

John Frusciante's St George XK12

John Paul Jones (born 1945) Hohner fretless bass

Former Bartell employee Chris Ellington always said he thought John Paul Jones of Led Zeppelin had a Bartell fretless bass. After much research, two images showed up on Jeff Strawman's website of Jones, sat down, playing a 'Hohner' fretless bass at the Led Zeppelin 1972 gig at Sydney showground in Australia. Although it appears to be branded Hohner, it depends when it was made at the Bartell factory - after 1969, Hohner took over production. Strawman commented that Jones used the Hohner XK-250 fretless bass on their 1972 Australian tour and some dates on a Summer 1972 US tour for Bron-Y-Aur Stomp. The specs are described as: double-cutaway semi-acoustic, cut-out F-holes. Finish jet black, neck maple bolt-on, 34" scale. Fingerboard ebony, side dot markers. No frets or pick-guard. Painted Logo, Gotoh tuners, pickups, single-coil at the bridge and humbucker at the neck. Controls two- volume, two-tone and a three-way selector switch. I contacted luthier Hugh Manson, known for his association with Jones, but received the reply, "I spoke to John about this, and he has no memory of it." Well, no surprise, it was a long time ago and he's probably had more guitars than I've had chip butties.

Walter Becker (1950-2017) - Bartell Spyder F-155

Owned by Walter Becker of Steely Dan fame. Provenance from the Estate of Walter Becker.

Walter Becker amassed an impressive collection of 645 pedals, 628 guitars and 375 amps/cabs that went under the hammer.

You will recognise this one from Bartell owner Ted Peckels' son Dave Peckels' guitar collection. Dave purchased this lovely candy apple red Bartell Spyder at Julian's Auction House as part of the Becker's estate auction on 18 October 2019. It was lot number 3244, with the winning bid $2,240.

Becker also owned a Magnatone Typhoon solid-body electric guitar which carried the serial number 200315, manufactured in 1965.

This was included as it's probable that Paul Barth was involved in the Starstream design. It clearly shows the same design elements and DNA to guitars he made under the Bartell name.

Like the Bartell, this top of the range X-20 Typhoon model was a well-made, light, and good-sounding guitar. Like a Stratocaster, it has a similar contoured body, while the bridge, vibrato, and electronics are similar to the Jazzmaster/Jaguar models.

The maple neck is combined with a rosewood fingerboard; the quality of work is to a higher standard than many 1965 guitars. "American made, by American craftsmen" was a selling point.

St George SK12 badge

FINDING FRETLESS

Walter Becker - Steely Dan
Red Bartell Spyder F-155
guitar

Walter Becker Bartell

182

*Walter Becker
Magnatone Head*

*Walter Becker - Steely
Dan Magnatone Typhoon
X-20 P*

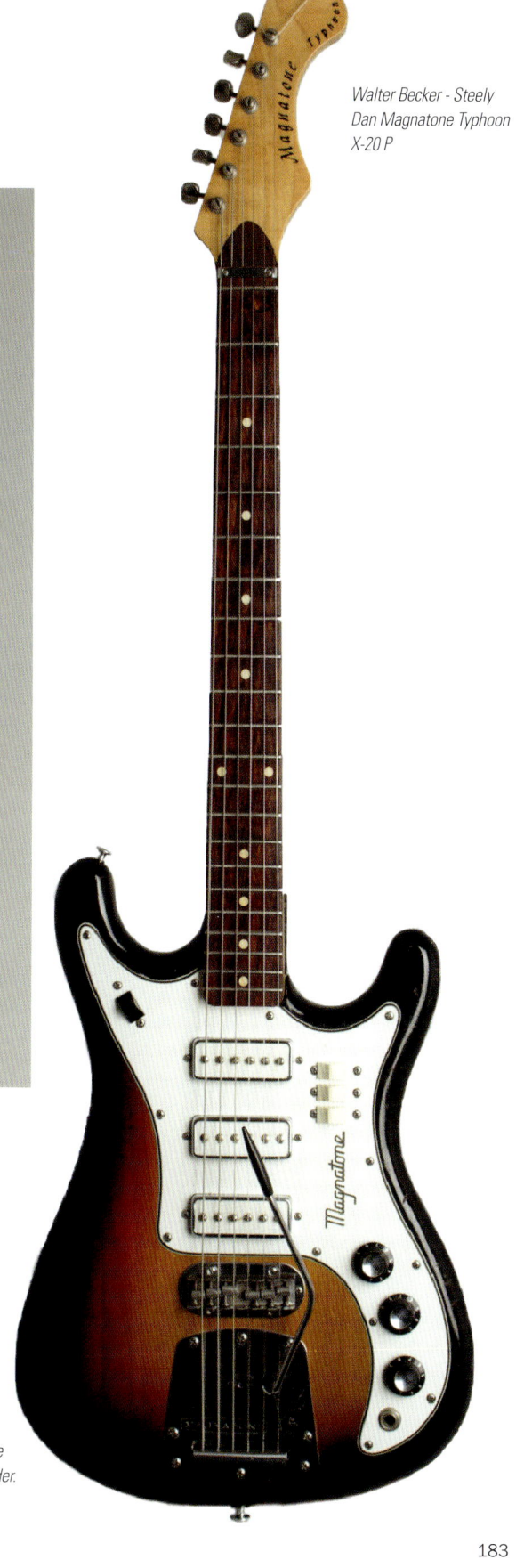

*Credit - Retrofret Vintage
Guitars/ George Aslaender.*

183

Chuck Berry (1926-2017) – Acoustic Black Widow

Chuck Berry's Black Widow guitar, at the Missouri History Museum for the St Louis Sound exhibition

The founding father of rock'n'roll got his start in the clubs of St Louis and East St Louis in the early 1950s, when he began playing guitar with the Johnnie Johnson Trio. Audiences responded to his showmanship and the hillbilly riffs he incorporated into blues ballads.

When Chess Records released 'Maybellene', Chuck Berry's cover of the country song 'Ida Red', in 1955, American music changed forever. That No.1 hit sold over a million copies, and by 1959 he had 17 chart singles, including top-10 hits 'School Days', 'Rock & Roll Music', 'Sweet Little Sixteen', and 'Johnny B. Goode'.

Chuck was among the first inductees at the Rock and Roll Hall of Fame's 1986 opening. In 2004, he ranked fifth

The home at 3137 Whittier Street, where Chuck Berry lived from 1950 to 1958, still stands today and is listed on the National Register of Historic Places - Google Maps Image capture Aug 2018 ©2021 Google

on *Rolling Stone* magazine's 100 Greatest Artists of All Time. He is also one of 50 people featured in the Missouri History Museum's 250 in 250 exhibition.

Larry Coryell (1943-2017) - Acoustic Black Widow

American jazz guitarist seen as the Godfather of Fusion. Born in Galveston, Texas, Larry learned piano from age four before switching to guitar. In his teenage years he moved to Richland, Washington. Larry was into pop and blues but attempted jazz when he was 18. Hearing jazz guitarist Wes Montgomery changed his life. Larry moved to Seattle, attending the University of Washington, and in 1965 went to study art at the Mannes School of Music in New York City. Larry was highly regarded as a fusion and jazz master. He died in a New York City hotel room at the age of 73.

In 1974, towards the end of the Acoustic Black Widow run, the guitar got an endorsement from this jazz fusion great, the only big-name player in that field to align himself with these guitars.

Larry's son Julian doesn't recall this particular guitar though, saying, "Dad was given every guitar under the sun for decades. He fell in and out of love with all those free guitars often … I could write a chapter on it!"

Rick Sowden on Facebook said of Larry's Black Widow, "He never played it much. It's the only picture I ever saw of him playing with it. Larry wasn't a collector but had many guitars, mostly given to him by guitar companies. The only ones I know of that he chose or bought were his Gibson Super 400 (which may have been given to him by Gibson to replace a stolen one) and a Spanish-made Ramerez nylon-string classical guitar he used on some recordings."

Larry Coryell. Credit - John Pierce Jr

Sheriff John Show, Wagon Camp, Knott's Berry Farm, circa 1963 - band playing Barth guitars. Photo courtesy Orange County Archives

The Wagonmasters

Close to going to print, Mike Butler found this wonderful image of a band supporting The Sheriff John Show at a band camp at Knott's Berry Farm, Anaheim in 1963. The Wagonmasters were the house band for the covered wagon circle at the farm, and they're all playing Paul Barth guitars!

Sheriff John (Rovick) was an American children's television host who appeared on two series for KTTV in Los Angeles from July 1952 to July 1970 - Sheriff John's Lunch Brigade and Sheriff John's Cartoon Time.

The Wagonmasters was originally a group of performers who played under the supervision of Dick Goodman. Formed in 1957, the band featured Billy and Bobby Beeman, Eldon Eklund, Harvey Walker, Jim Eisenberg, Don Richardson, Dick Goodman, Vern Jackson, David Bourne and Rachel Cadwalader. In 2012, John Rovick died in his sleep, aged 93, at a nursing facility in Boise, Idaho.

Rory Gallagher (1948-1995) - Barth guitar

From the earlier chapter on Frank Zappa, it was thought that Rory Gallagher frequented Harmony Music in Reseda, California, where Greg Segal finally got his hands on the Paul Barth-designed Bartell-branded Acoustic fretless.

What we do know is that Rory did at some stage acquire this Barth-made guitar, sold via Natural Music Guild. Made in the late-'50s as Barth, after working at Rickenbacker and before working at Magnatone, was contracted to the Natural Music Guild in Santa Ana, California to distribute his guitars. The current owner, by the name of Vincent, thinks Rory probably found this guitar touring in the States in the '70s whilst visiting music and pawnshops during tours. Who knows, maybe he found it at Harmony.

Rickenbacker fans will recognise the resemblance to the 325 Capri, used by John Lennon and designed by Barth. It is all original except that someone has moved the chrome bridge cover back behind the bridge.

The Zero fret was one of Barth's designs.

In 2007, during the Born to Rock exhibition at Harrods of London, more than 40 of Rory Gallagher's guitars were on display, including the Barth guitar.

Examining the scratch-plate of the Barth guitar, it seems that the pot code dates this guitar to 1958.

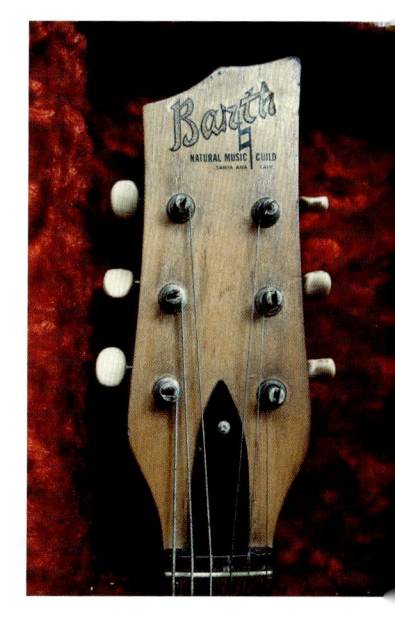

Photo Credits - Vincent Wolting

C C Deville - Barth guitar

The following is a Reverb listing from 2019 by Tom Sprafke of Tom's Vintage Gear Emporium in Santa Barbara, CA.

"A vintage Paul Barth '1961' guitar, said to be once owned by guitarist CC Deville of Poison, it has been in the vault for 18 years, unplayed. Featherweight semi-hollow body. Three prototypes were made in the development phase, Serial Numbers B100, B101 and B102. This is the second. From this design, the Rickenbacker 330 was launched. Dale Fortune knew Paul Barth personally, and said about this guitar, "Barth built most of these guitars after he left the Rickenbacker factory. His shop was in Riverside, where he built this guitar and then gave rights to the Magnatone company to build this same guitar with their logo. The pickups are made by DeArmond of Ohio, the same pickups Rickenbacker used before they made the toaster pickups. These are great guitars that have a very similar shape to the 325 and 330 guitars, with a 24.75-inch fret scale."

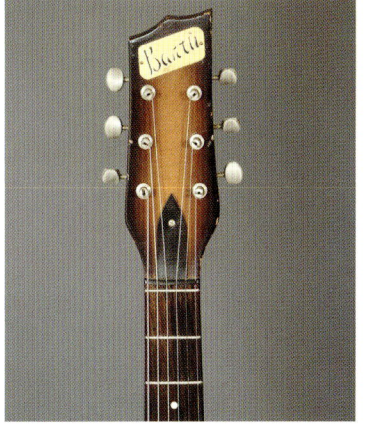

Tom Sprafke of Tom's Vintage Gear Emporium in Santa Barbara CA.

THE BARTELL REUNION

Oh, come on, we have to, don't we?

I mean, there has been so much interest and so many memories from all those folk who either worked, played, jammed or just plain enjoyed the music in Riverside and the wider California region during that formative period when popular music was infecting the lives of people around the world. The tales that are to be told of the connections, from The Beatles to Hendrix, Zappa and more, from just a handful of unusual guitars made by a small company that was only in existence for five brief years. I really didn't make it up, honest!

To the Peckels family, what on earth do they think about all this? Did they ever imagine that a random stranger from England would ever want to write a book about their Dad? Thank you for so much your support, I am so grateful. To the Barth family, Paul's rich history is barely documented, his story almost unknown, and it is not fully understood how entwined Paul is with the development of the electric guitar.

I finally managed to locate his family, who fully deserve their history to be recorded. To his daughter Sharon, I am honoured to start that process. Your Dad helped change the world with his guitar innovations.

To the employees and co-workers, I can only apologise for being that crazy Brit who had the audacity to pick up the phone, email, message on social media, and beg for instant recall on 50-year-old memories. Who the hell does this guy think he is? I thank you all for putting up with me and for shining a light on the dimming memories of a time passing us all by.

To The Beatles fans, I thank you for your detailed knowledge, your fascination for the obscure and enduring love for a band that really do still live with us today. They still surprise us, new and old things are out there, and oh, the stories they can tell! Happiness is a Warm Fretless!

To my fretless friends, the owners - Ray, Greg, and Dave - I hope it's been worth dusting down that vintage guitar and looking at it again with fresh enthusiasm. That the life story of that special guitar, the one with the missing frets, goes forward with it, whenever and wherever they go next. Just let me know, okay?

If it hadn't been for the global Covid-19 pandemic, we would have all been in a bar by now, reliving those stories somewhere, uncovering more gems and hopefully making some music. After all, that's what it's all about.

Now, where are those missing fretless guitars?

I will forever be Finding Fretless. I'll get my hat … and my face mask and hand sanitiser!

BARTELL DISCOGRAPHY

BARTELL (Acoustic) Fretless Recording Discography

THE BEATLES	Suggested and confirmed recordings		
ALBUM	**TRACK**		Confirmed/Unconfirmed
The Beatles (White Album)	Happiness Is A Warm Gun	Helter Skelter	Unconfirmed
The Beatles (White Album)	Savoy Truffle	Long Long Long	Unconfirmed
The Beatles (White Album)	Everybody's got something to hide	Sexy Sadie	Unconfirmed
Anthology 3 & The Beatles (White Album) 50th anniversary box set	Not Guilty		Unconfirmed

FRANK ZAPPA			
ALBUM	**TRACK**		Confirmed/Unconfirmed
Zoot Allures	The Torture Never Stops		Confirmed
One Size Fits All	Can't Afford No Shoes	San Ber'dino	Confirmed
The Guitar World According to Frank Zappa	Friendly Little Finger	Down In The Dew	Confirmed

RAY RUSSELL			
ALBUM	**TRACK**		Confirmed/Unconfirmed
BBC Antiques Roadshow	TV live broadcast		Confirmed
BBC The One Show	TV live broadcast		Confirmed
Water - By Handmade Films	Film		Confirmed
Time bandits - By Handmade Films	Film		Confirmed
Forensic Detectives	TV Series		Confirmed
Goodbye Svengali - slide solo on title track	Goodbye Svengali		Confirmed

GREG SEGAL			
ALBUM	**TRACK**		Confirmed/Unconfirmed
A Man Who Was Here	King Of Illusion		Confirmed
Darkland Express part two	L.A. River Rafting		Confirmed
in Search of the Fantastic	Wednesday 10 p.m.		Confirmed
Asleep or Somewhere else (with Eric Wallack)	Zap 'n' the Cap'n	Faro Inspects the Border	Confirmed
An Awareness of Frameworks	The Place of Three Roads	Dream Catcher	Confirmed
Standard	Neal Smith's Invisible Trike pt. 2		Confirmed
Bret Hart/Greg Segal /Duets 1	Sting it	Free Row	Confirmed
A Play of Light and Shadow	Revolving Doors		Confirmed
The Old Familiar Place	Processes Unknown		Confirmed

Electric guitarists around the world will forever be grateful to the creative minds of the inventors and designers of the world's most popular instrument. George Beauchamp and Paul Barth were great friends. Little did they know just how much they would influence music globally with their great idea for decades to come.

Paul left the world some amazing artefacts, including his personal collection of vintage Rickenbacker Electro guitars. What stories they could tell!

I am extremely grateful to the Barth family for sharing their history. I am sure that Paul's daughter Sharon, seen here with his Frying Pan, is so very proud of her Dad!

Sharon Sagar with Paul Barth's personal Rickenbacker Frying Pan. Credit Simon Purll - VHF Media

ACKNOWLEDGEMENTS

To my wonderful wife, Karen, and my two very special daughters, Kimberley and Rachel. Thank you for your steadfast support, love, encouragement and perseverance!

- Ray Russell - for frets' sake, it's all your fault!
- Richard Bennett – for such a great memory, and those wonderful stories you shared so kindly.
- The Peckels and Barth families – for such amazing family histories, and being such nice people.
- Simon Purll at VHF Media - for the fantastic photography featuring those vintage Barth guitars.
- Greg Segal - for the inside story and the connection to Frank Zappa of that black fretless beauty.
- Jeff Berg – for being on the case long before me, and his fantastic knowledge and unfretted.com site.
- Harvey and Karen Gerst - for taking time to recall your memories of the fretless and Jimi Hendrix.
- Ron Neely - for the excellent Bartell vintage guitars and Acoustic Black Widow fan pages.
- Jan Gorski-Mescir – for incredible insights from a 30-year personal friendship with George Harrison.
- Bob Coronato – for a valued American artist, cowboy and Zappa Black Widow owner.
- Dr Richard Perks at the University of Kent - for analysing those relevant *White Album* song tracks.
- Kenny Jenkins at Leeds Beckett University – for further analysis of those *White Album* tracks.
- Eben Cole, Cole Music Company - for details on the first Bartell fretless bass.
- Mike Stax - for the excellent *Ugly Things* article from edition 24 (Summer 2006).
- The Inland Empire Music Hall of Fame Facebook pages and the lovely informative people on there.
- We Grew Up in Riverside in the '60s and '70s Facebook pages and all the info there, friends!
- The Rock and Roll Hall of Fame, Ohio - for information on Jimi Hendrix's Black Widow guitar.
- *KMENtertainer* magazine – for those vintage advertisements that told us more.
- Steve Clarke – for great technical expertise and being a font of all knowledge on some famous frets.
- Bonhams of Knightsbridge - what an experience this has been!
- Dave Auld and Fusion Guitars – for the Fusion iPhone guitar with integrated amp and speakers pics.
- Mick Eckers – for access to his *Zappa Gear* publication.
- Tony Olivestone - thank goodness he made *that* recording of John Lennon with the fretless.
- Vincent Volting - for the information on and images of Rory Gallagher and his Barth guitar.
- Mark Makin - for technical, historical and photographic advice on Dobro, National and the Dopyeras.

Photo and image credits: Page 21 Newspaper cuttings: e San Bernardino County Sun. Images on pages: 45, 46 Google Maps - Image capture Mar 2019 ©2021 Google. Page 58: Images by Elderly Instruments. page D.L. MacLaughlan Dumes - http://krlabeat.sakionline.net/ Page 31, 150 and 182, image credit - Dave Peckels, Page 112 image credit krlabeat.sakionline.net webmaster D.L. MacLaughlan Dumes. Page 140 Photo credits Paul Brett.

ABOUT THE AUTHOR

Paul Brett, born 4 March 1964 in Carshalton, Surrey, England, grew up in the nearby town of Morden and went to school at Morden Farm Junior and Middle School before going to Raynes Park High.

In 1979 in his final year at school, aged 15, Paul wrote to music papers and magazines seeking an interview as part of his sociology paper on 'Pop Music and its Impact Today', using Paul McCartney's 'Pop music is the classical music of now' quote as part of his studies. That led to an interview with *Record Mirror* editor Alf Martin and young journalist Paula Yates, who had a column called 'Natural Blonde', joining shortly after posing for *Penthouse* magazine. Slightly intimidating for a fresh-faced teenager, especially when Paula invited Paul out that evening to a Gary Numan gig marking the release of Gary's first solo chart-topping album, *The Pleasure Principle*.

Paul served as a Royal Navy radio operator, joining up in 1980 and serving on a number of ships, notably Leander class anti-submarine frigate HMS Naiad during the Falkland Islands conflict. While he didn't see active service

Paul Brett - with that 'mad' guitar

during the conflict as the ship was sent to the Mediterranean on NATO duties, he subsequently spent six months down in the South Atlantic shortly after liberation. He also spent a number of years bouncing around the wild North sea with the fishery protection squadron on HMS Alderney, protecting Britain's coastal waters and offshore installations, taking home freshly-filleted fish that paid for his beer on leave.

Paul and future wife Karen were engaged on HMS Alderney in the shadow of Tower Bridge and married shortly after in 1987 when Paul left the Royal Navy from the Admiralty Communications headquarters tucked away by the side of Admiralty Arch at the end of The Mall. Moving to the sunny South Coast town of Eastbourne, they raised two beautiful daughters, Kimberley and Rachel.

From 1987 until the summer of 2019 Paul continued his career in communications with British Telecom. Notably during this time, a mile from Paul's home in the early hours of 30 July 1990, a bomb was planted by the

IRA under British MP Ian Gow's car, killing him instantly. Paul and his colleagues rushed in the multiple comms services required by Sussex Police and security services in advance of a speedy visit by Prime Minister Margaret Thatcher.

Paul had a chance meeting with the subject of his school project when Sir Paul McCartney came to ICC Studios in Eastbourne, interviewed over a satellite link his namesake provided to the USA for a radio phone-in with students. The Pauls had a brief chat before Macca left for a pint at a pub called 'The Bitter End'.

In 2012 Paul, a seasoned project manager, was recognised by BT Chairman, Sir Michael Rake for his fundraising concept, 'StarCards', in aid of London's iconic Great Ormond Street Hospital charity.

Almost two decades of fundraising followed, supported by seven Prime Ministers, former US President Gerald Ford and hundreds of musicians, including Mark Knopfler, David Gilmour, Jimmy Page, Brian May, Madonna, Phil Collins, Bob Geldof, George Benson and Kylie Minogue), plus sports legends, film stars and celebrities from around the world, helping Paul raise more than £300,000 for the charity, with a few glitzy fundraising parties at the BT Tower and with Richard Branson at Kensington Roof Gardens along the way.

And then, in 2019, Paul and his friend Ray Russell started a new adventure, and some intensive research led to Paul's first publication ... *Finding Fretless*.